PRAISE FOR
PARTICIPATION MARKETING

'Employees are the most valuable asset of any company. If you know how to unlock their passion, you can build an army of powerful advocates for your brand. It's not about training your employees to parrot your company's message. It's about building passion around your company's brand and its purpose – and shaping your company's culture such that it empowers your employees to advocate. Brito, a leader in the industry, helps you do just that, beginning with the fundamentals and then sharing practical tips on how to weave employee storytelling into the fabric of your organization.' **Maria Poveromo, Vice President, Communications, Adobe**

'It's widely known that employees are viewed as trusted and credible sources when others are seeking information about a company or brand. Brito delivers a very structured plan that guides large and small companies on how to truly activate employees to be storytellers and drive brand relevance.' **Jascha Kaykas-Wolff, Chief Marketing Officer, Mozilla**

'If you're wondering how to inspire and mobilize your employees to be brand storytellers, ask Michael Brito. His book is an exceptionally thoughtful and actionable "how to" guide and a journey through the learnings of courageous companies creating true engagement and informed, digitally connected brand advocates.' **Jerilan Greene, Chief Communications Officer, Yum! Brands**

'The key to successful digital transformation is building a culture of trust and transparency, starting with the employee experience. Brito does a fantastic job of bridging the gap between internal employee engagement and external customer relationships. The result is a powerful community of brand storytellers who are constantly engaged and adding value with customers, prospects and partners.' **Elisa Steele, former CEO, Jive Software**

'Your business is already filled with promoters and every marketer needs to figure out how to unlock the power of employee advocacy. Brito shows you how to do this and then integrate that trusted employee-driven content into larger brand marketing initiatives.' **Lauren Vaccarello, Vice President, Marketing, Box**

'Trust and authenticity are critical factors for marketers today. And there's nothing more trustworthy than employee voices. Brito builds a strong case for employee advocacy and shows marketers how to integrate trusted employee-driven content into broader marketing initiatives.' **Jackson Jeyanayagam, Chief Marketing Officer, Boxed**

'*Participation Marketing* unequivocally puts the transformation back into digital transformation by focusing on the single most underplayed element of successfully reimagining markets – our people. Brito offers a practical blueprint for how to put your employees at the tip of the spear of your transformation goals by first making them your biggest fans and then, your most genuine and loudest advocates.' **Sameer Patel, CEO, Kahuna**

'Brito does a brilliant job connecting the challenges of today's workforce with the promise of turning employees into advocates. It's a practical, step-by-step guide for how to launch great employee programmes and how to earn the reward of making them succeed.' **Katy Kiem, CEO, LQ Digital**

'Storytelling is a visceral part of human nature. I have observed that brands who tap into the employee voice to surround sound their customers with relevant, and trusted, content, build longstanding and highly profitable customer relationships. Once again, Brito has written a book that delivers; this time it is one that provides an actionable playbook for companies of all sizes to launch and operationalize employee advocacy programmes.' **Lisa Joy Rosner, Chief Marketing Officer, Otonomo**

'With *Participation Marketing*, Brito has delivered the field manual for engaging today's workforce in telling your company's story. He has masterfully connected the nuts and bolts of orchestrating technology with advice for engaging employees at an authentic, human level. Mastering both of these areas is critical to driving value from employee advocacy programmes – and Brito has delivered the road map.' **Jim Rudden, Chief Marketing Officer, Spredfast**

Participation Marketing

Unleashing employees to participate
and become brand storytellers

Michael Brito

KoganPage

First published in Great Britain and the United States in 2018 by Kogan Page Limited

2nd Floor, 45 Gee Street	c/o Martin P Hill Consulting	4737/23 Ansari Road
London	122 W 27th, 10th Floor	Daryaganj
EC1V 3RS	New York, NY 10001	New Delhi 110002
United Kingdom	USA	India

www.koganpage.com

© Michael Brito, 2018

ISBN   978 0 7494 8210 7
E-ISBN   978 0 7494 8211 4

British Library Cataloguing-in-Publication Data

A CIP record for this book is available from the British Library.

Library of Congress Cataloging-in-Publication Data

Names: Brito, Michael, author.
Title: Participation marketing : unleashing employees to participate and
   become brand storytellers / Michael Brito.
Description: London ; New York : Kogan Page, 2018. | Includes index.
Identifiers: LCCN 2017044895 (print) | LCCN 2017035778 (ebook) | ISBN
   9780749482114 (ebook) | ISBN 9780749482107 (pbk.)
Subjects: LCSH: Branding (Marketing) | Marketing–Management. |
   Management–Employee participation. | Corporate culture. | Employee
   motivation.
Classification: LCC HF5415.1255 (print) | LCC HF5415.1255 .B749 2018 (ebook)
   | DDC 658.8/27–dc23
LC record available at https://lccn.loc.gov/2017035778

Typeset by Integra Software Services, Pondicherry
Print production managed by Jellyfish
Printed and bound by CPI Group (UK) Ltd, Croydon, CR0 4YY

In memory of my mom, Sarah Luna (1954–2017)

Thank you, for being my best friend.

Thank you, for being my mom and dad.

*Thank you, for making every Christmas feel
special, even when we didn't have a lot.*

*Thank you for buying me a GI Joe and Plain
M&Ms every Friday when I was a boy.*

*Thank you, for attending every one of my soccer games
and cheering me on from the sideline.*

*Thank you, for writing me letters every day when
I was away and in trouble.*

*Thank you, for writing me letters every day when
I was away in the military.*

*Thank you, for the 'can I give you a piece of advice' conversations
even when I didn't want to hear it.*

Thank you for my sisters, Alex and Vanessa.

Thank you, for loving my wife as your daughter.

Thank you, for loving Milan and Savannah.

I'm going to miss you, mombre.

*But I promise that I'll see you soon and I'll be sure
to bring you some M&Ms too.*

CONTENTS

PART THREE Blueprint: launching your employee advocacy programme 107

ABOUT THE AUTHOR

Michael Brito is a digital strategist, published author, TEDx speaker, adjunct professor with over 20 years of experience helping brands break through the clutter and reach their audiences with game-changing content.

In all his experience working, teaching and writing about digital marketing and social media, he has learnt that consumers are real people with real passions, not just target markets or segments. In order to turn friends, fans and followers into true connections, he believes that brands need to listen more than they talk, and social media provides an easy and powerful way to connect with them, personally.

He also believes in the power of data to tell stories. For someone who struggled with algebra in high school and college, he has learnt to appreciate how social data can help brands tell passionate and relevant stories in a human, authentic way.

As an Executive Vice President for Zeno Group, he is responsible for helping his clients reach their target audience with precision – the right content, at the right time, in the right channel and to the right customer. This requires a combination of audience insights, narrative development, targeted media relations, influencer engagement, creative content and laser-focused paid media.

Previously, he was the Head of the US Digital Practice for LEWIS Global Communications where he oversaw an office of over 60 team members and was responsible for business growth, culture, team development and the management of a multimillion-dollar profit and loss (P&L).

He also held roles as the Head of Social Marketing at W2O Group, and Senior Vice President of Social Strategy at Edelman, where he consulted for Fortune 500 companies implementing integrated content and digital marketing programmes, globally. This included integrating with PR teams to pitch and win new business and launching employee advocacy programmes for large technology clients.

Michael was born and raised in Silicon Valley and he has been fortunate enough to work at innovative brands such as Hewlett Packard, Yahoo and

Intel, building online communities before social media was even a thing. He has a business degree from Saint Mary's College of California (Go Gaels) and a master's degree from Golden Gate University. He also teaches strategic business communications and social media at San Jose State University and Golden Gate University.

He has written two other books: *Smart Business, Social Business: A playbook for social media in your organization* (2011) and *Your Brand, the Next Media Company: How a social business strategy enables better content, smarter marketing, and deeper customer relationships* (2013).

Myers-Briggs: ENFJ
StrengthsFinder: Woo

FOREWORD

Digital transformation is a hot topic, but if you haven't heard the term before, it doesn't mean you are not experiencing its profound impact on our lives. While there are countless definitions of digital transformation, I like to make it as simple as possible by breaking it into the two words and then piecing it back together:

> *Digital*, meaning technology and the powerful new ways that technology is changing the way we work, the way we live and the way we communicate.

> *Transformation*, meaning the evolution of people, and how we as a society are adapting and changing in order to deal with the impacts of the aforementioned technological change.

When you put the two words back together, what we are really talking about when we say 'digital transformation' is change management in an era where rapid technology change and disruption are the rule rather than the exception. In short, digital transformation is about building a company that can thrive under the pressures of rapid change. This means businesses need to be more astute than ever at adapting, adopting and embracing change while even becoming more accepting of failure as time and planning become secondary in many ways to efficiency and innovation. To become good at this, you must build a culture within the company that is passionate about change and how it can create a healthier business and happier customers. Change starts and ends with your people, or is perhaps better summed up as:

Employee advocacy is the heart of digital transformation

We will come back to digital transformation shortly, but let's put all the terminology aside and just read on for a minute. Take off your 'marketer' or 'entrepreneur' hat and think like a consumer. Think about the ride that technology has put you on. Consider the new ways that you buy things, or talk to people – and how much that has changed in just a few years. After spending the last decade working side by side with the world's greatest technology brands to explore digital transformation, I can tell you a couple of things for sure: 1) the change will only get faster and more significant; 2) people are the core of every business and this will not change for the foreseeable future.

A foreword to the foreword? Perhaps, but it's okay – in a time where we are drowning in content, a little context can make all the difference. So here goes...

I don't wake up in the morning and think, 'I wonder what Disney is going to share on their social media channels today', or 'I really hope to have a really great conversation with Amazon before lunch.' It simply doesn't happen this way because I don't aspire to talk to logos. I want to connect with people, real people... people like me, with similar interests.

This is the reason I roll out of bed every morning, reach for my iPhone, log into LinkedIn or Facebook and see what my network is talking about. This is my chance to reconnect with the world, family and friends, and get acquainted with new products, services and experiences. I connect every day to be inspired, educated and engage with people on the internet.

This is the world we live in. And for marketers, this means that there are new rules for how we engage our customers. Sure, there are still traditional media vehicles, but at the heart of every brand is their community; those who are genuinely connected to a brand so much that they advocate for them even when no one is looking, or without the brand even asking.

For marketing, this is the holy grail – creating mobs of superfans around the world who are pasting their logos on their cars or taking pictures while drinking their beverages. Apple is one brand that has achieved this. They have a user community that is so deeply committed to their brand that they would never even consider using a competitive product, no matter how superior it may be in its product specs. Starbucks has a similar dedication from its consumers – their customers walk around town drinking the slightly overpriced frappuccinos and wearing their logo like a badge of honour.

We call them 'love brands', my co-author Olivier Blanchard and I in our book *Building Dragons: Digital transformation in the experience economy*. By love brands we were reflecting on a rare magic that a few select brands have been able to achieve, an almost unexplainable power they have over their consumers that can only be achieved by building experiences that go far beyond what any product or service can ever deliver on its own. So what makes these companies so unique and so seemingly untouchable that they get bestowed upon them the glorious label of 'love brand?' While there are many factors that can be equated with building a successful company, there are a few strikingly unique characteristics about the brands that truly are able to achieve the unachievable. In summation, there are three:

- They understand that the experience is the foundation of building a strong brand.

- They have an almost unshakable commitment to creating happy customers.

- They see their employees as their most important customers and they create a culture that embodies the people who represent the brand.

While each of these three items may appear to be unique in both their importance and their execution, it is imperative to realize that they are not mutually exclusive and, in fact, there is a strong interdependence between an employee-focused organization and a company that is able to evolve and deal with the rapidly increasing rate of change that technology and society are imposing on our organizations.

Above I referenced the passionate customer who advocates endlessly for their brand. While somewhat unique outside of an organization, every company on the planet has a subset of customers who are eager to serve as superfans of your brand. These people are entrenched in the business and they are intimate in the knowledge of the company's vision, mission and values that set them apart in the marketplace. The problem is that many companies do not see the potential in this subset of customers because they choose to see them as a sunk cost, a financial liability or perhaps less overtly as something other than a customer. Don't be mistaken however, this group is a powerful cog in your brand's wheel and if you choose to unleash their potential they can have an exponential impact that leads to more business, greater profits and a stronger culture that yields a cycle of growth and innovation, so long as they are nurtured.

Who are these people? It's simple, they are your employees; the dedicated workforce that can either wear your brand like a badge of honour, or, if you ignore their potential, they may wear it like a ball and chain.

However, it is your choice, and if you make your employees part of the process, share the passion and the trials that come with growing a business, they will excitedly share, create and document their contributions and they will desire to participate in sparking the growth of the company. They will become your employee advocates, and this is more than just a catchphrase, this is the foundation of building one of the most powerful cultures in business – a company with an army of employees telling its story in a way that cannot help but be contagious for anyone within earshot, or, better yet today, within their web of social relationships.

In this book, Michael Brito will teach you and inspire you to embrace the power of employee advocacy. You will see through the stories he shares, the examples he provides and the empirical data that he presents that building a tribe of employee advocates who participate in telling the company story is more than table stakes, it's a bet that the great companies have made and it's a strategy that the majority have simply ignored or failed to implement. Your employees are a powerful force and if you nurture their passion for your business they will reward you by becoming a catalyst for your word-of-mouth marketing. Furthermore, you will also realize that Michael doesn't try to wrap a 'one size fits all' bow around what employee advocacy means. This has been one of the fatal flaws in employee advocacy reaching its full potential. For some brands, employee advocacy may mean participation in a social campaign, but for others it may be documenting experiences, blogging or participating in the community.

The beauty is that in many cases, once the employee feels connected and realizes that their participation is valued, they will seek to take on more, share more and push their love of the company onward to others in a way that cannot be mistaken for anything other than genuine love for the brand. I've seen this work first hand with companies like HP, IBM, Microsoft, Dell, SAP, SAS and Adobe. These are just a few of the companies that I have worked with that have deployed employee advocacy to help their employees connect more deeply with their employer. More importantly, the results have been outstanding with almost all companies citing improved employee engagement as a result of these programmes.

Each day as we rise from our slumber we will continue to be part of a seismic shift that is changing the way we live. Our almost eternal connectedness serves as a reminder of a changing landscape for marketers and brands, and for those looking to build 'love brands' the greatest opportunity may lie in summoning the help of our most important customers, our employees. We may not wake up each day wondering what one brand or another has to say, but we do look forward to reading the updates from our friends, neighbours and loved ones, a group of people who work and have the opportunity every day to subtly influence our perceptions about those companies that they work for.

Employee advocacy is not an 'idea du jour', it is a foundation for building a business that can take on anything that the market can throw at it. When your employees are passionate advocates for your business, they are also ripe to participate in change and to help your company get from wherever it is to wherever it needs to go. This is the most important ingredient for digital transformation, so let it start with your people because, if you let them, they will take you exactly where you want to go.

Michael, I'll let you take it from here.

Daniel Newman
Principal Analyst at Futurum Research and CEO of Broadsuite Media Group, and bestselling author, *Forbes* contributor and global digital transformation thought leader

Introduction

Your people are your brand

The idea of getting one's employees, fans, customers and advocates to say nice things about your business is as old as time. Advocacy is the original form of marketing. The best advertisement that a business can hope for – from hundreds of years ago to today – is positive word-of-mouth marketing. Once societies began trading, when people gathered in town marketplaces or bazaars, word-of-mouth marketing was how news of the best black-smiths, butchers and bakers spread.

Despite today's rapid advancements in technology, not much has changed. Nielsen research from 2015 shows that 84 per cent of consumers trust recommendations from friends and family more than any other form of advertising (Nielsen, 2015). Even though new channels of communication and advertising are constantly being created, nothing compares to the recommendation of a friend, family member or neighbour. Word-of-mouth continues to be the most powerful form of advertising a brand can get.

However, many companies have lost track of how to inspire and sustain this form of brand advocacy. As advertising has grown and evolved into a multibillion-dollar industry, brands have gradually shifted away from word-of-mouth marketing. We see billions spent every year on TV commercials, billboards, print and online ads. But these are all one-way conversations. After spending over 10 years in advertising, I witnessed multiple brands struggle with creating strong connections with consumers this way. Brands can track data on how consumers are interacting with their ads online and they can estimate the impact of commercials and billboards, but too often they get lost in the noise, hype and buzz that is the competitive online ad space.

But with the rise of social media, all of this changed

Marketers have long wanted to find a way to track and scale word-of-mouth marketing. Social media has created ample opportunities for marketers to leverage the power of influencers, customers and employees to advocate for their brand. Channels such as Facebook, Twitter, Pinterest and others have created a way for brands and consumers to finally have a dialogue. Social media has completely changed how people find and share information worldwide. Marketers can finally track and measure word-of-mouth marketing, social influence and consumer engagement with their content. Even more, they can empower their employees to advocate for the brand, creating thousands of new marketing channels, driving leads, sales and brand awareness.

Employee advocacy creates authentic, human connections

When Michael Brito first approached me about his idea for this book, I was excited about his vision to create a playbook that would help brands get started with employee advocacy. Marketers today are inundated with information on *why* employee advocacy is important. But most marketers already understand why employee advocacy is important. According to Altimeter research, interest in employee advocacy has grown 191 per cent since 2013, with 45 per cent of marketers naming it a top objective. What marketing leaders really want to know is *how* to get started (Altimeter, 2015).

Employee advocacy is still a new and evolving category. There are not many marketers who could consider themselves 'experts' in this field. Michael is definitely an exception. With almost 20 years of experience working with brand and marketing leaders, Michael has seen multiple evolutions of advocate marketing programmes in the enterprise. He was an early believer in employee advocacy after seeing how a successful programme can create authentic, personal connections with consumers. This book will help you to give everyone, from the chief executive officer (CEO) to the newest hire, the ability to advocate on social media on behalf of the brand.

Employees are already using social media

When I launched Dynamic Signal in 2010, employee advocacy did not even exist as a software category. It was a completely new but fairly simple idea – give employees a way to safely and effectively advocate for your brand on social media and they will drive brand awareness and revenue.

But as the category has grown, it has become much more than that. While employee advocacy is proven to increase revenue and awareness, the act of engaging employees with content also increases productivity. Research from McKinsey and Company shows that employee use of social software can improve productivity by up to 25 per cent (McKinsey, 2012).

Unlike other marketing channels, with employee advocacy brands can start to see success from day one. At Dynamic Signal we have seen that once an employee advocacy programme is live, it stays live.

Employee advocacy builds an entire workforce of brand advocates

Marketing and communications teams are under a lot of pressure to come up with new ideas to capture more leads, engage their audience and build brand awareness. Some spend millions of dollars a week on content distribution alone. But they could be getting even more engagement and interactions with consumers by empowering the hundreds to thousands of employees they work with to distribute company content.

Employees are a powerful marketing channel and are more likely to be considered an expert on your brand than anyone else. Almost half of employees – 44 per cent – who participate in an advocacy programme become recognized as thought leaders in their industry (Hinge Marketing, 2015). Additionally, for employees, it is incredibly motivating to be given the opportunity to drive business outcomes for their brand.

> With new algorithms and advertising options on each platform, it is becoming increasingly more difficult for a brand to tell its story without paying for an audience. A social media advocacy programme allows the people behind the brand to organically tell their team's story.
>
> Alexandra Shockey, Social Media Advisor at FedEx
> (Employee Brand Storytelling, 2016)

To effectively and appropriately represent their brand, employees need a formal programme. While passionate employees who take to social media to share their brand pride mean well, they may not have the most up-to-date information or clearly understand what is approved for public consumption. Any time an employee at your company engages with a customer, prospect, friend or family member, they are representing your business.

Companies need engaged and communicative employees who can knowledgeably inform others about the brand you have worked so hard to build.

This is also how the employee advocacy movement creates an advocacy-driven culture within a company. Employee advocacy is unlike any other marketing channel because it touches every part of the organization. It is truly horizontal and can be utilized by every department, in any industry. From social selling that drives revenue, to social recruiting that attracts top talent, employee advocacy is the only marketing channel that can drive company-wide return on investment (ROI). This gives marketing the opportunity to collaborate with every external and internal department in the company.

Employee advocacy puts marketing at the core of company culture and communications

Marketing departments have traditionally only focused on external-facing communications. But the requirements for marketers have changed drastically over the past few years. Internal pressures now push companies to innovate much more quickly and stay a step ahead of the competition. As the brand voice and communication branch, marketing is increasingly involved with influencing recruiting, company culture and customer service – as well as all of the channels that marketing traditionally manages.

Additionally, consumers are putting new external pressure on brands. Millennials want to see brands that are more human, authentic and transparent. They expect to engage with real employees on social media for customer service and even general inquiries. As more and more services are automated, consumers increasingly want authentic, human experiences with brands.

Participation marketing is critical in addressing internal and external business challenges

At Dynamic Signal we speak with hundreds of marketing, communications and human resource (HR) professionals every day who are looking to engage employees in advocating for the company. Many of these initial conversations were the inspiration for this book. Both Michael and I have seen what makes or breaks an employee advocacy programme and where marketers need the most help with launching and scaling a programme.

In this book, Michael answers the 'how' questions for marketers who are either already running an employee advocacy programme within their organization or are considering starting one. By reading, you will find answers to common questions we hear every day, such as:

- What motivates employees to participate?
- What are the benchmarks of a successful programme?
- How is a content strategy built specifically for employees?
- What are the best ways to train employees to advocate?
- How can brands launch and activate their own programme?
- How can employees build influence and become brand storytellers?

Every brand and every industry has different requirements for an employee advocacy programme. The guidelines and case studies we chose for this book will showcase best practices from successful programmes, answer common questions and help solve typical roadblocks.

What motivates employees to advocate?

Perhaps the most common question we hear is, 'What's in it for employees?' Most marketers and company leaders understand that simply asking employees to share on social media is not enough. The effectiveness of an employee advocacy programme is contingent on how it is received by employees. Within large organizations change can be difficult. There is a culture shift that occurs when an employee advocacy programme is launched. While employees have always shared about their company, online and offline, doing so in a brand-approved way is new and different.

To address this change, when IBM launched their programme they looked to their company culture to develop a programme that would inspire employees. IBM leaders are proud to be able to attract some of the best and brightest talent in the technology industry. With employee advocacy, they saw an opportunity to spotlight their employees' knowledge and position them as thought leaders with social media. This strategy worked out well for them. Employees now run 45 different blogs, hold online training sessions and help maintain massive social media followings.

While marketers have a lot to gain by empowering employees to become thought leaders, employees have a lot to gain as well. They are able to grow their social following, make new industry connections, and gain recognition for their ideas and work. Employees will see a thought leadership programme as the company making a long-term investment in their personal brand. This will also inspire loyalty, making it less likely that an employee will look for work elsewhere. By supporting thought leadership, you can show how your company is open to new ideas, which will result in increased productivity and a stronger sense of teamwork.

What does a healthy, successful employee advocacy programme look like?

Just like IBM, other brands have achieved a wide range of business results after launching their employee advocacy programme. Take Salesforce, for example, who started out focused on using employees to drive registrations for their annual event, Dreamforce. Their programme not only helped them drive registrations but has since expanded into driving leads, conversions and brand awareness. To date, they have over 5,000 employees involved who have driven almost 1 million clicks through social sharing. They have achieved a few of the top benchmarks we look at when rating the health of a programme:

- an active and engaged community of employee advocates;
- strong audience engagement with social content;
- increased share-of-voice for the brand.

In this book, Michael breaks down how to track and measure success in more detail (skip ahead to Chapter 8 if you're ready to read more now). Benchmarks can vary widely based on the goals of the brand, but we have found that high employee interaction with content is often a vital sign of a healthy programme. Employee enthusiasm is contagious and often results in both employee retention and increased audience engagement with content.

How can marketers train employees to represent the brand?

Social media training is the starting point for most successful employee advocacy programmes like we have seen with Salesforce and IBM. Before a programme can really take off, employees need to feel confident to share on social media on behalf of the company. The best training programmes provide employees with the guidance, safety and tools necessary to start sharing. Brands also have to keep in mind regulations, such as the Federal Trade Commission (FTC) guidelines and industry-specific limitations, which govern how and what is appropriate for employees to share publicly. While this may sound complicated, it is actually a fairly simple – but crucial – step that protects both your brand and employees on social media.

A great example of how to do this is from Autodesk, a leading software and design company with over 2,000 employees. Their marketing team created a video to train employees on social sharing. The training video explains the benefits of the advocacy programme and simple guidelines for sharing on behalf of the brand. In just a few minutes, employees who are new to the programme can get a full understanding of what the programme is and why they should get involved.

Other brands prefer to do in-person training. Capital One, for example, holds regular training sessions every other week. Says Rich Pesce, Senior Manager, Social Media Communications and Digital Media at Capital One: 'We have 1,000 employee advocates and want to keep growing that number. We are constantly recruiting to get more employees involved.'

Every company is different and so there is not one way to train employees. In Chapter 10, Michael discusses different ways that brands have found success with training and how you can apply their best practices to developing your own training programme.

What technology solutions are available?

It is hard to recommend launching an employee advocacy programme without also advising brands to partner with a technology solution provider. I've seen many brands launch their own programmes with DIY solutions, such as sending out mass e-mails asking employees to share, but which don't give them a way to sustain and scale a programme. At Dynamic Signal we are laser-focused on providing brands with a world-class platform that makes it easy for marketers to manage their programme and track results. But even more importantly, we make it easy (and fun) for employees to find and share content.

In this book, Michael will walk you through the features you need from a technology solution to provide employees with a great user experience that will keep them coming back, as well as a platform that will help you collect data to test, iterate and grow. The key is to find the right solution for your company's needs.

Marketers have to think beyond the campaigns

Consumers today are inundated online and on social platforms with articles, clickbait, GIFs and ads. Commercial placements and banner ads are not enough to make a meaningful and memorable impression on today's consumer. The people who have built your brand and work hard to evolve it every day are the absolute best marketers you could have. This is what participation marketing and employee advocacy is all about.

Participation Marketing is not your typical business or marketing book. Instead of belabouring the benefits of employee advocacy, this book will show you how to start and sustain an employee advocacy programme. Think of this book like a playbook or a choose-your-own-adventure guide – you can read it cover to cover or skip ahead to the sections most relevant to you.

You will find everything that you need in this book, from tried and true best practices and industry research to advice from marketing leaders across a variety of industries. You'll get the full download on creating a plan of action, launching a programme, training employees, creating goals and measuring success. This is just the beginning of what will be an extremely exciting journey and initiative for your company.

Russ Fradin
CEO of Dynamic Signal

PART ONE
Setting the groundwork

Employee advocacy

Making a believer out of you

There's a secret I want to let you in on. And the fact that you bought, borrowed or downloaded this book means it's a secret you probably already know. Some subconscious, intuitive space in your brain is already privy to what others will soon learn: *employee advocacy is a company's biggest opportunity for growth*.

It is a concept that causes many naysayers and sceptics to roll their eyes, and that is understandable. As people who are immersed in business culture, especially that of Silicon Valley, we are absolutely spoiled on ideas. Strategies and best practices seem all too fleeting, and there is always some buzzword making the rounds, promising the world and more. Sometimes it pans out, sometimes it doesn't. But you have to admit, there are worse things than a surplus of seemingly smart business blueprints (say that three times fast), but many of us lack the time and energy to test them.

Employee advocacy is not just another flash in the pan. The very nature of it is steadfast because, simply put, as long as there are companies, there will always be employees, and as long as there are employees, there will always be an opportunity to mobilize them to be storytellers. In other words: employee advocacy has always been an area worth investing in, but as the combination of constant connectedness and conversation becomes standard in our everyday lives, so too grows the importance of leveraging it. Marketers? This means you.

Rewind: the whole social business thing

I know what you're thinking: more social media? Haven't we had enough already? It has been a topic of conversation for over a decade. And it's true – social has been a hot topic in the professional space for a number of years now, but I firmly believe we have not even come close to seeing what it is capable of, especially as companies are now embracing digital transformation.

In the recent past, marketers aiming to tap into various communities did so by participating in message boards and forums. More recently they are using popular platforms such as LinkedIn, Facebook, Twitter and even Snapchat. And while that is still a worthwhile way to connect with others, formalizing and scaling a more comprehensive process around social engagement takes that world of potential and breaks it wide open. But it requires a plan.

For starters, knowing what social business actually means is crucial. The term was coined several years ago and has taken on a load of different definitions ever since. And while the topic does not come up that much any longer, it is still important as digital transformation takes centre stage. My personal view on the topic has not changed since 2011:

> Social business is the blueprint for the digital transformation of an organization – bridging external with internal, resulting in a more connected way of doing business, which creates shared value for all stakeholders – employees, customers, influencers and channel partners.

Next, understanding the framework of a social business is equally crucial. If you read my first book, *Smart Business, Social Business: A playbook for social media in your organization* (2011), you have likely already seen the chart shown in Figure 1.1, which categorizes work streams by platforms, processes and people. To fully embrace digital transformation and evolve your organization to be a social business, all three work streams need to work independent of each other, yet also be completely integrated into the DNA of your brand, your business and your culture.

Let's break down these three work streams one by one and review how you can get the ball rolling with each.

Platform, sometimes referred to as just technology

Social business needs proven technology to function, and I don't mean e-mail or an outdated customer relationship management (CRM) system. The challenge is that there are so many software vendors in the space to choose from that it is hard to decide. Many of them promise the same things, but often take months to deploy and ultimately do not deliver the desired outcome.

Figure 1.1 Social business framework

Think strategically before making significant investments in software: consider scale, integration, support and maintenance costs – as well as the current suite of applications that you have behind the firewall. A 360-degree view of all your technical requirements up front will make your choice of technology much easier (and smarter). Another tip? You will want to get your IT group involved from the get go. The last thing you want happening is for them to shut down your project midway due to a security or privacy issue. The following are technology applications that I have used in the past and have the strongest capabilities depending on what it is you need to accomplish:

- **Social Listening:** monitor, dissect and learn valuable insights about online conversations (brand, competitors, general market) – Crimson Hexagon.

- **Audience Analysis:** analysing specific audiences to better understand what they say, share, talk about and general behaviour – Crimson Hexagon.

- **Content Marketing:** manage content creation, distribution and measurement – across channels, teams and global markets – NewsCred.

- **Social Media Experience Management:** listen, publish, engage in real time and build unique experiences for the social media community – Spredfast.

- **Measurement and Reporting:** social analytics and insights of content and campaigns – Simply Measured.

- **Employee Advocacy:** manage, scale and deploy enterprise-grade employee advocacy programmes – Dynamic Signal.

- **Inbound Marketing and Sales:** manage customer contacts, web analytics and the sales pipeline – Hubspot.

- **Web Analytics:** track and learn valuable insights about your web visitors – Google Analytics.

Before you go out and schedule a demo with any of the above vendors, be sure to document a list of your requirements first. Trust me, it's better this way.

And finally, remember that at the end of the day, technology alone will not change your culture, even with the rise of artificial intelligence. You will still need the human touch to build relationships and drive change. There are several other factors you need to consider before you experience true digital transformation, such as process and people, as set out below.

Building simple processes

Here's a hard truth: processes are not sexy and almost no one likes to follow them. Ask my wife and she will tell you that even I prefer to 'cut corners' any chance I get – and then she will tell you all the consequences I have suffered by doing so.

While good processes might be a buzz kill, they are a must-have in all business, especially those embracing digital transformation. Employees sharing sensitive material externally, social media ownership, crisis management and managing product feedback are just a few challenges that you may be dealing with today. Ensuring that you have documentation addressing these issues and evangelizing them internally will be a factor to your success.

My advice to you is this: start thinking through the solutions for all those challenges before building an employee advocacy programme. You don't need to solve all of them, but at least have a plan that you can start working on. You need to make sure you are managing the chaos that exists behind the firewall before focusing on external activities, or you will just have double the trouble. My first book, mentioned earlier, is a good read and will help you to formulate a solid plan of action.

Start with the simple things. Give your teams easy-to-use tools for handling workflows or completing mundane tasks, and they will send fewer e-mails. Increase engagement in your meetings to uncover and address roadblocks before productivity declines, which would also naturally result in more e-mails. No one wants more e-mails. You may not win an award and you probably will not make 'employee of the year' by creating good processes, but I guarantee they will make your life easier in the long run – and the foundation for an employee advocacy programme much stronger.

Several processes that will be discussed later in the book will focus heavily on training initiatives, social media policies and guidelines, moderation policies and expanding your programme globally. Each of these must be documented, approved, rolled up into a larger governance model and then shared with everyone involved. This will ensure that your employees are telling consistent brand stories across multiple platforms, regions and languages, and that there is legal documentation that protects the organization, empowers employees and ensures that everyone is on the same page.

Embrace the people

I have never won a professional award. There are no 'employee of the year' – or month – plaques sitting on my desk or hanging on my office walls. But I have always been proud of where I work, and I am happy to spend 10+ hours a day sitting in an office trying to make a difference for my clients, colleagues and team. It's part of what defines me as a person, it's in my DNA. And just like being a dad, husband and friend, I don't get ornamental acknowledgements for those roles, nor do I need them.

Unfortunately, not all employees feel the same way. It could be a generational thing, poor leadership, or perhaps they have too many colleagues to feel like their individual contributions are making any kind of difference. Whatever the reason, getting a handle on employee morale will undoubtedly be one of the hardest things you do, yet the most important for digital transformation.

Company culture is the foundation of any business, and it needs to be consistently nurtured with the right coaching and leadership. After all, you can have all the technology in the world, and the best processes ever created, but none of it will be effective unless there is a fundamental shift in the way employees think, communicate and interact with one another. And this must start with leadership.

What is the best way to get started? Practise what you preach. Social behaviours must be driven by organizational leadership and practised at every level, from senior executives all the way down to the IT engineer. Otherwise, change will not occur. This means that you and your leaders must not only talk about changing the organization, but exemplify the behaviours that facilitate it. All talk and no action will only make things worse.

It is hard to change people, but most respond naturally to positive environmental shifts. Place a picnic table outside, and some employees will eat lunch outside. Simplify the client billing process, and employees will document more billable hours. Make it easy for employees to participate in a programme and you will see adoption levels skyrocket. Give an employee access to a relevant piece of content and they just may share it.

Digital transformation requires a need for positive business outcomes

Digital transformation can sometimes be a hard sell. Many marketers have a poor attitude towards anything that does not immediately demonstrate value, but the fact that you are reading this book tells me that you understand the inherent worth of these initiatives and wish to use them to improve your business.

Business value can mean a lot of things, but for marketing it means this:

- **Deeper customer engagement:** understanding the behaviours of your audience is critical. If you can dissect their language, sharing patterns and media consumption, you will be one step ahead of your competition. The closer you get to your customers' wants, desires, needs and criticisms, the better you will be in the long run – assuming you take action on them.

- **More effective and relevant content and storytelling:** data-driven stories can break through the clutter and reach your customers with the right content, at the right time and in the right channel. It's a fact. This requires technology and/or a methodology that can cluster audiences' interests and characteristics in a way that can be actionable. (Oh, and you will need smart marketers, too.)

- **Smarter marketing that aligns to business goals:** alignment across the PR teams, marketing, geographies, IT and customer support will ensure that all marketing activities maintain a level of continuity and high performance. When internal barriers are torn down, a higher level of collaboration and integration will result in marketing and business alignment.

- **Integrated and converged media strategy:** telling consistent stories across all channels is the hallmark of integrated marketing. The proliferation of media coupled with the advancements in virtual reality and artificial intelligence makes it even more critical to ensure message repetition across all outlets. It is really the only way to get customers to believe in your brand, take action and tell others about their experience.

- **Integrated influencer and media strategy:** understanding 'who' is really driving the conversation about a topic in your industry is critical. As traditional media and journalists are declining, it is important to identify the 'up-and-comers' or influencers that are gaining traction in your industry. I refer to this group as the '1 per cent', which we will dissect later in the book.

- **Effective content operations and governance:** building workflows and approval processes are important to ensure the quality of all content and digital assets. Much like a traditional newsroom, ensuring the smooth flow of content from ideation to distribution is needed, along with checks and balances along the way.

Present day: modern-day business requirements

Now that we have aligned on all things social business, it should be clear that employee advocacy as a formalized process is a moment we have been building up to for a long time. Table 1.1 shows how today's environmental business requirements have created an intersection of communications that are ripe for mobilizing employees to join industry conversations and influence their peers down the purchase funnel.

We will dive into Table 1.1 in more detail in later chapters, but for now consider a couple of these points. First, think about how empowering employees to engage and communicate with each other has been an

Table 1.1   Internal and external business requirements

INTERNAL		EXTERNAL	
MANAGE MORE EFFICIENT AND EFFECTIVE INFORMATION AND DATA	*Harness the massive amount of available content and data to rethink and re-equip business operations*	**ENGAGE IN A MULTI-STAKEHOLDER CONVERSATION**	*Use new channels to communicate with a wider, multifaceted set of stakeholders – influencers, media and customers*
INNOVATE AT FASTER SPEEDS	*Focus business efforts on innovation rather than continued improvement in order to stay relevant*	**HUMANIZE YOUR BRAND**	*In a world where marketing is driven by data and content, brands must learn to communicate with empathy*
EMPOWER EMPLOYEES	*Equip employees with the right content at the right time in order to increase brand impact*	**EMBRACE THE RISE OF THE INDIVIDUAL**	*Whether you are a B2B or B2C company it's important to remember 'people buy from people.' It's vital to sync the internal with the external*

internal objective for several years now. In fact, the term 'employee engagement' was first mentioned back in 1990 by Professor Bill Kahn at Boston University's Questrom School of Business. He defined personnel engagement as 'the harnessing of organization members' selves to their work roles; in engagement, people employ and express themselves physically, cognitively, and emotionally during role performances' (Kahn, 1990).

Today, ask any company about morale-building goals or how they encourage and sustain a healthy business culture, and surely you will get a growing list of activities in return. Second, think about how engaging in multistakeholder and external conversations has been among a marketer's top priorities over the last several years, and how the pressure to do it with a more authentic voice is climbing. For example, how many initiatives to 'humanize' a brand have you seen, heard about, or perhaps even participated in yourself in the last handful of years? Typically, it involves someone in corporate communications or marketing and three very important external groups:

- **Influencers:** this group shapes the market whenever they talk, Tweet, write an article or record a video. In a business to business (B2B) context, these are the traditional media, analysts, bloggers or technology subject-matter experts. For example, if you study data science or market software to data scientists, you probably already know of Vincent Granville, the founder of Data Science Central. He's not a journalist, he's a data scientist and he's arguably the number one influencer on the topic

- **Ambassadors:** these are paid influencers, and are typical in consumer marketing programmes. You may have noticed the proliferation of DIY videos by vloggers on YouTube, all of whom are influential on platforms such as Instagram and Snapchat. They are everywhere, but the difference is that they are not necessarily experts on a particular topic or technology, and there is usually a monetary relationship required. They have huge followings and are usually entertaining to watch or listen to. For example, Alex Wasabi has a whopping 8 million subscribers on YouTube and 1.9 million followers on Instagram. What does he talk about? Nothing really. He records daily videos and livestreams various activities that many millennials and those born in generation Z find entertaining – at least my 12-year-old daughter thinks so.

- **Customer advocates:** these are people who are already talking about you, your brand or your company. They probably subscribe to your newsletters, follow your social media channels, share your content and buy your products all the time. They have a natural affinity towards your brand. They love you. It is important to pay attention to this group of people and engage with them often. For me, that brand is Apple. I have Apple everything and will never, ever try anything different.

While these initiatives will remain important, the next wave of marketing will require participation not only between marketing departments and external stakeholders, but employees from across departments joining in to share your company's message and stories with their personal networks.

Here's a true story that might be corny, but I'll share it anyway. Years ago, before Zappos was acquired by Amazon, I bought a pair of UGG boots for my daughter. I paid for two-day delivery because I ordered late and her birthday was on the weekend. On day two I panicked when I got home from work because the delivery had still not been made.

Now, I'm not 'that guy' who goes to Twitter and complains about brands for their bad service. I did, however, Tweet something to the effect of, 'I hope Zappos didn't deliver my package to my neighbour.' Instantly, I was bombarded with responses – not just from Zappos Customer Support, but also random employees offering to help, giving me advice and assuring me that my package would arrive. Fifteen minutes later UPS knocked on my door.

Today when I think of Zappos, those unexpected interactions are what I think about, not the fact that it is owned by Amazon. Like most everyone else, I don't relate to logos, I relate to people and I remember personal experiences.

Focusing on people and experiences in every way possible is now considered the golden ticket. The modern business creates an atmosphere where employees are accustomed to engaging with each other. In 2015, Altimeter Group found that 82 per cent of businesses reported being either fully integrated, in the process of, or planning the integration of social with digital. The same report found that interest in employee advocacy programmes has grown a whopping 191 per cent since 2013, with 45 per cent of respondents naming it a top external objective (Altimeter, 2015).

To top it off, employees have a more sincere and trusted voice than an entire marketing department could ever collectively muster. Numerically speaking, Edelman's yearly trust barometer revealed that respondents are increasingly reliant on a 'person like yourself', who, along with a regular employee, is significantly more trusted than even a CEO. So why are we not encouraging them to participate in the external conversation? And I don't just mean for customer support, like my Zappos story, but for other things, like sharing content that could inform a purchase decision (Edelman, 2017).

This scenario should be familiar to most of you reading this. When is the last time you went to a new restaurant or bought a new television? If it wasn't spur of the moment, you most likely spent some time researching online or asking trusted friends for recommendations. This happens in the world of technology as well.

B2B decision makers don't just go to a website and pick and choose which data centres or enterprise security software to invest in. They research, ask questions, ask more questions, and spend countless hours online before deciding.

No one can doubt that purchase behaviour has changed over the last few years. As stated, most searches for a technology provider start online, and usually in Google. B2B decision makers get as far as two-thirds through the buyer's journey before they reach out to a vendor, if the vendor meets the entry-level technical requirements (Consumer Executive Board, 2015).

But reaching B2B decision makers is difficult. They are sophisticated, well educated and extremely sceptical about marketing. They rarely pick up calls from sales, they do not read press releases or company websites, and they avoid any type of human connection with a business until they decide it's time. We cannot blame them, because they are the most marketed-to segment online today. Every technology company with a marketing budget and a brand message is trying to reach this same audience, every single day and in every possible channel.

The role that your business plays online in the B2B decision-making process means it warrants a business strategy to ensure you are getting the most out of it. To put this in perspective, a study with Dell and Carnegie Mellon University's Tepper School of Business found that 75 per cent of B2B buyers were influenced by information they found on social media – showing that having a well-thought-out strategy really can prove to be critical (Social Business Journal, 2015).

One insight we can take away from the research cited here is that engineers trust other engineers. IT people do not want to hear from marketers. They want to hear from other IT people. They want to bounce ideas off each other and talk about how to solve difficult technology challenges. This is why it is critical to find internal subject-matter experts within your company, train them to be content creators and unleash them into the market to participate in these conversations. At this point, it is no longer a luxury but now table stakes if you want to stay competitive.

Social media is changing, and the way we use each platform will continue to change as networks consolidate and new ones are formed. Just because a strategy worked in the past does not mean it will work today. One thing is for certain, though. People relate to people. It is core to our DNA as humans.

Calculating the numbers and understanding what ROI means

Okay, so we have established that engaged employees can significantly increase your company's reach in a manner that is most effective and trusted by consumers, but you need numbers you can hold on to. After all, buy-in from decision makers comes from proven value, not feel-good stuff. Then again, that feel-good stuff is becoming increasingly important so we cannot leave it out.

How about stats that match the feel-good?

Reach and impressions

While these are considered soft metrics to most marketers, they do paint an interesting picture. Terms such as 'reach' and 'impressions' are often miscon-strued or thought of as being synonymous. While it is very easy to group the two together, they do have their own definitions. So before you can accurately create a measurement framework, you first need to understand what they mean.

Reach is a measure of how your content is spread across the internet. You can think of it as the number of unique people who see your content within their newsfeed. In a perfect world, every one of your followers will see every piece of content you post. Unfortunately, that is not reality due to limits of organic reach, which will be discussed in later chapters. So reach is a measurement of your effective audience.

An impression means that content was delivered to someone's feed. A person does not have to engage with the post in order for it to count as an impression, meaning they don't have to like it, comment on it or share it. What many don't know about impressions is that one person can have multiple impressions of the same piece of content. For example, on Facebook a post can be displayed in their newsfeed from the original publisher and appear a second time when a friend or colleague shares the publisher's post. If you saw the content a second time in your feed, that counts as two impressions for the same post so this number can be flawed in many cases.

Engagement

Marketing is all about good storytelling and message repetition, and good content causes action usually in the form of engagement. Daniel Roth, executive editor at LinkedIn, examined 50,000 blog posts published on LinkedIn's blogging platform. What he found was that while only about 2 per cent of employees reshare the content their companies share, they are responsible for 20 per cent of the overall engagement (views, likes, comments and shares) that the content receives. This means that relevant content being shared by employees is not only reaching new audiences, but causing action and, in this case, it is engagement. Highly engaged organizations have double the rate of success compared to less engaged organizations because engaged employees are more productive and efficient, and genuinely interested in making an impact in their role and advocating for their company (Roth, 2015).

Clicks

Measuring clicks generated from employee sharing is easy. If you use Google Analytics or Adobe SiteCatalyst it is as simple as appending unique URLS to employee links. From there, you can track clicks, impressions and leads. Yes, leads. I will drill down on this metric in the case study below.

The maths is easy. Add up all this and a staff that is armed with great content and knowledge to share with their networks is a massive opportunity for business growth. For some, though, even this will not be enough to activate employee advocacy. If you yourself happen to fall into that category, I have one more insight to share with you...

Employee advocacy programmes can and will drive sales

Yes, I said it, and will stand behind my words. If you don't believe me, read the case study below on how a sales team operationalized an employee programme and reaped the benefits of increased leads. Many call it social selling, which I believe is synonymous with employee advocacy.

Don't take my word for it. Read below to see how Jamie Shanks, the CEO of Sales for Life and author of *Social Selling Mastery: Scaling up your sales and marketing machine for the digital buyer* used social selling to feed his sales pipeline, grow his consultancy business and actually demonstrate a real ROI.

CASE STUDY   How Sales for Life used social selling to drive new leads and revenue

Sales for Life is a sales consultancy that specializes in transforming enterprise sales teams to use social selling strategically to increase revenue and leads. Until 2016 everyone on their staff used their personal social channels to randomly share content. Some used Buffer while others preferred Hootsuite. In either case, this was a good thing because all the employees were becoming active and more proficient social media users.

The challenge was that there was no centralization to the programme, which made it difficult to track, collaborate and gamify. So, later in the year, they decided to go big in employee advocacy and invest in technology to help operationalize their programme.

Here is something to consider, which is an extremely important point. Most employee advocacy platforms are typically leveraged by mid-market and large enterprise companies. Sales for Life is much smaller, and they only have 10 sales and marketing customer-facing professionals that are using the tool.

So as you consider the data below, keep in mind that these are numbers from just 10 people. Imagine the impact for an organization that may have 500 or 5,000 sales pros. Also consider that the time frame is only three months.

In February, March and April of 2016, on average, each of their 10 employees shared five articles or pieces of content per day. They typically posted content in the morning, lunchtime, mid-afternoon, afternoon and a few times in the evening:

- February: they added 219 net new contacts and subscribers into their marketing automation platform that are now embedded into their drip marketing campaigns. These folks will now be updated with blog posts and additional content on a regular basis. They have gone from unknown to known users.

- March: they added 163 subscribers.

- April: they added 125 subscribers.

The end result was 507 new subscribers during those three months, all from just 10 salespeople.

What comes spitting out the bottom of this model is that 2 per cent of subscribers become a qualified lead! They are having phone, e-mail and social conversations with the inside sales team to book a next step – a meeting or more information. This translates to 10 qualified leads.

Of all those conversations 30 per cent turn into deeper conversations. Usually this involves a few phone calls where they are learning about each other's business and building more in-depth relationships.

Of every one of those discussions 40 per cent turns into an active deal cycle that becomes a customer – one active deal cycle that is going deep into proposal. Their deals go into six figures, so greater than US $100,000. Remember, this is just three months of data and only 10–12 salespeople participating.

So let's pause for a moment and throw an additional variable in the mix. Typically, most employee advocacy platforms range from $30,000 to $60,000 per year. The price may go up depending on the total number of users that participate in the programme. The price will usually increase when there are more than 1,000 active users, which was not a problem for Sales for Life.

In one quarter, Sales for Life acquired one major customer that will have an active deal cycle with a value of six figures. Even if they had 500+ sales pros on staff, the cost for our platform would not change. Can you imagine if they had 50 on staff?

If the world of sales was linear, they would be creating 50 new active deal cycles every single quarter, worth hundreds of thousands of dollars per deal. By making a small investment of US $60,000 to acquire all those active deals, the ROI is immense. So even a small business like Sales for Life can justify the cost to acquire one six-figure deal, let alone 50 six-figure deals!

The future of work

02

The new office, inside and out

I'll just come right out and say it: the general state of the workplace is dismal.

More specifically, engagement in the workplace is dismal. And while all the hype about the 'future of work' involves an in-depth technology discussion, the future is about the engaged workforce. Gallup, a research-based, global performance-management consulting company, defines an engaged employee as 'being involved in, enthusiastic about, and committed to their work and workplace'. By this measure, Gallup's research revealed that in 2014 less than one-third (31.5 per cent) of US workers were engaged in their jobs, highlighting younger employees as the majority of the group. Even sadder, 17.5 per cent was reported as being 'actively disengaged' during the same period (Gallup, 2014).

The shift in these percentages has since been minimal. In 2015, just one year later, Gallup found only 32 per cent of US workers to be engaged in their job. It is not tough maths but it is still worth highlighting that this is *less than a 1 per cent increase in engaged employees*. This is not a good sign for anyone, employees or the business.

All of this goes to show that you can work in one of the most innovative, highest-paying cities in the world such as Silicon Valley, London or Zurich, with all the latest tools and platforms at your fingertips, and still not see results. If we truly want to have an internal impact, there are a few steps that need to be taken. Again, these are internal and external requirements that are forcing business to change.

Empower the whole workforce

Any marketer knows the importance of equipping their team with the right content – it is what we are here to do. But because employees are now each a part of their own motley crew network, it is extra crucial to expand that gift beyond the confines of your own team if you want to see your business live up to its full potential.

Many companies will tell you they are already doing this. Maybe you are under the impression that your own company is transparent and everyone is on the same page, but research says that this is more than likely untrue. Let's take a look at sales organizations as an example. SiriusDecisions estimated that a whopping 60–70 per cent of all content created by B2B marketing teams is never touched by sales (SiriusDecisions, 2013), a stat their own clients later echoed in greater numbers the following year (SiriusDecisions, 2014). Let's take a look at that stat again:

> 60–70 per cent of all content created by B2B marketing
> teams is never touched by sales.

I'm not sure what keeps you up at night, but it is figures like this that do it for me. Talk about a gross missed opportunity. If there is one group in any organization that should be collaborated with, it is sales. They are the revenue drivers. They are the ones on the front lines of the business talking with customers and prospects, and hopefully closing deals.

Spending time creating content that is not used by the people it is created for is not an ideal situation for anyone. The first step to remedying this issue and ensuring your entire organization is on the same page is to invite them to collaborate on creating content. Once disparate teams are a part of the creation process, they are more likely to buy into the vision and share it. We are going to discuss this in more detail in future chapters.

Second, it is imperative that the content is easily accessible to everyone. And I don't mean just dropping it on the intranet and calling it a day. Yes, the intranet will work assuming it's not 20 years old, but think of other options – the cloud, printing it out and placing it on each employee's desk, blasting it over e-mail, and whatever else you have to do to get all eyes on it. Some companies have a more sophisticated approach to managing a content supply chain, which will also be covered in later chapters.

Try having a bimonthly meeting with team leads to share recently created content. In the next meeting, set aside some time to review how the content covered in your previous meeting has been utilized. Share best practices, failures, whatever. Another approach would be asking a different lead in each meeting to summarize the latest content for the rest of the group. It always strikes me how many marketers do not do something like this. I know most of us are overdoing book reports and such, but being up to date on the latest communications is *crucial* for empowerment.

Remind employees each and every time you meet that you are sharing this information with them, because it is not about just having the right content – it is about having the right content at the right time, and how valuable their participation in the dissemination of that info is to the company. Without their hard work, you would not be able to function as a business. Make sure they know that. Sounds like common sense, I know, but you would be surprised how many people overlook this small detail.

Really, real employee engagement

Somewhere in the maze of the extravagant work perks Silicon Valley has come to be known for, I think a number of us lost our way in terms of what makes a great company culture. And don't get me wrong – indoor tree houses, unlimited personal time off (PTO) and organic, locally sourced meals catered daily are all very, very awesome things. But if we want our employees to be engaged with what they do, they have got to feel good about it. And in order for them to feel good about it, they need more than material rewards.

Brands should focus on building experiences and environments that enable employees to feel like they are a part of something that is bigger than their day job. For millennials in particular, recent research reveals a link between engagement levels and self-worth. In addition to finding steady, engaging jobs, millennials want to have high levels of well-being, which means more than being physically fit. Yes, millennials want to be healthy, but they also want a purposeful life, active community and social ties, and financial stability. Regarding that financial stability, millennials want to be able to spend money on what they want – not just on what they need (Gallup, 2016). I couldn't be more thrilled by this. Retention and engagement backed by making the world a better place? That kind of thing makes me feel great about the future of business and, to be honest, the future of the world.

This is also key to maintaining engagement in leadership participation, so if you've got great cause work going, be sure leaders are partaking, and share that story with the rest of the company. Leadership development experts Brad Shuck and Maryanne Honeycutt-Elliott said, 'higher levels of engagement come from employees who work for a compassionate leader – one who is authentic, present, has a sense of dignity, holds others accountable, leads with integrity and shows empathy' (BI Worldwide, 2016).

Lastly, it is important not to let great, purposeful work, whether cause-related or not, go unacknowledged. The University of Arizona conducted an employee engagement study in 2016 that found that the vast majority of employees who received little or no feedback were actively disengaged from their workplace (University of Arizona, 2016). Engagement went up dramatically when employees received feedback about their weaknesses, and even more so when they received feedback about their strengths. This is good learning and should be used as a blueprint for all employee engagement programmes.

Most companies already have a yearly review process, but I would recommend going beyond that with today's feedback tools and apps, such as 15Five, TINYpulse or Hppy, to name a few. These modern methods encourage more interaction between employees and their managers by having regular check-ins rather than a yearly or biyearly review, and I believe will soon replace those traditional systems.

So the formula is simple:

$$\text{Purpose + positive experiences + celebrating success openly}$$
$$\text{+ ongoing interaction = real employee engagement}$$

Now let's dig deeper on both the internal and external business requirements that are forcing companies of all sizes, shapes and colours to change:

Table 2.1   Internal and external business requirements

INTERNAL		EXTERNAL	
MANAGE MORE EFFICIENT AND EFFECTIVE INFORMATION AND DATA	*Harness the massive amount of available content and data to rethink and re-equip business operations*	**ENGAGE IN A MULTI-STAKEHOLDER CONVERSATION**	*Use new channels to communicate with a wider, multifaceted set of stakeholders–influencers, media and customers*
INNOVATE AT FASTER SPEEDS	*Focus business efforts on innovation rather than continued improvement in order to stay relevant*	**HUMANIZE YOUR BRAND**	*In a world where marketing is driven by data and content, brands must learn to communicate with empathy*

(continued)

Table 2.1   *(Continued)*

INTERNAL		EXTERNAL	
EMPOWER EMPLOYEES	*Equip employees with the right content at the right time in order to increase brand impact*	**EMBRACE THE RISE OF THE INDIVIDUAL**	*Whether you are a B2B or B2C company it's important to remember 'people buy from people.' It's vital to sync the internal with the external*

Innovate at faster speeds

If you are under the impression that you need to be quick to stay ahead of the game, then, well, you're right. There is no getting around the importance of introducing new and relevant ideas as quickly as consumers can consume them, and we can see this reflected in the growing number of successful small businesses that have disrupted the big guys (not to mention each other). If you live in Silicon Valley like I do, it is not uncommon to go into a coffee shop and watch a few entrepreneurs collaborating on their next big project.

Innovating at even faster speeds than we see today will soon become more critical, and throwing money at research and development (R&D) or product can only get you so far. Just like having all the latest tools and platforms cannot control success, neither can a team with cash to burn. Or a system of lean processes. Or carefully chosen metrics. Those are all great and necessary things, of course, but they will not be effective unless the people behind them are fully engaged in their jobs and, as a result, feel empowered to build and create. It always, always comes back to the people.

Speeding things up can seem a little intimidating, but I promise it is not as overwhelming as it sounds. Here is some practical advice for really driving innovation, curated from *Fortune* magazine in 2015:

Accountability + process + collaboration = total digital transformation

There are many, many reasons you should read *The Lean Startup* by Eric Ries (2011) if you haven't already. One of my favourites is that he has some of the best advice I have ever heard on how to begin overhauling the way your organization gets things done. If you work in a large company, you should start taking notes asap.

Speeding up innovation begins with creating metrics for how to incentivize employees, getting new projects funded, promoting employees who take risks and produce the kind of work that gets results. Real results. Next up, identify the teams that will work on new projects and build out the processes needed for helping them to organize and teach themselves new things.

When you have got these small, creative groups up and running, think of them like little sprouting seedlings. In order for them to see their full potential, it is essential to help them grow by doing what you can to encourage a culture that celebrates taking risks and developing new ideas. If you are successful, they will spread this goodness out to the rest of the organization – spread like a virus of innovation.

Seek minimal financing

Throw some money, but not a *ton* of it, into the new projects your teams dream up. Once you have tested their viability, then you can decide how much more to invest. The trick to faster innovation has nothing to do with luck and everything to do with investing in everything in small doses. Ries calls the output of this method a 'minimum viable product', which is basically the most fundamental version of a prototype that can prove whether the idea will work (Ries, 2011). Personal experience tells me that investing not just in projects but people will yield the greatest results.

Embrace the black sheep

Every company has a few employees who are hard to work with. Ries calls them 'black marks', and noted that they do not typically abide by the standard, and are usually quite comfortable with taking risks. I have worked with many who fit this bill and, in full transparency, I have been called a black sheep multiple times in my career. While it can be frustrating to collaborate with people of this nature, these are the individuals who are also often the most passionate about thinking outside the box. In other words, they are the innovators, and an innovative mindset is something you need, and not something you can teach.

While having them around can keep things fresh and new, it is important to note that they do need a particular kind of leadership. Make sure your organization has a senior person who can set and maintain guidelines for these wily workers and hold them accountable in some fashion. Otherwise it could end in a disorganized disaster.

Entitlement funding and complacency are the death of innovation

Just like in a relationship, being too comfortable or complacent can lead to a flat company culture. Ries advises that you keep a look out for practices and processes that are still intact simply because they always have been. I cannot tell you how many times in my career I have heard, 'well, we've always done it this way' when questioning existing processes or procedures. This is the type of thinking that destroys progress.

In particular, make sure you do not have projects that continue to receive funding for no good reason. Ries calls this 'entitlement funding', where a project – regardless of its merits or progress – continues to be backed financially. That type of funding can often lead to the death of innovation, as it requires no risk or incentivizing. Sounds a lot like the US government.

Fail fast and get over it

Most execs don't like to fail. I know I don't.

But nothing is perfect and pretending like it is almost never leads to a good ending. When you set out to change the way your company innovates, failure will inevitably be a part of the process. Sit down and make sure you have a very frank conversation with the rest of your employees about this reality. It will be hard for some to accept that their big ideas will not always work, but if they know that they're not alone, and that failure does not mean they don't get to test their next big idea, they will warm up to this change and all be better for it (Fahrenbacher, 2015). Remember that failure is good for you, it builds character.

Of course, internal improvement is only half the battle. On the flip side, engagement should be happening just as frequently and with just as much gusto on the outside – whether it be with each other, customers, advocates, the media or influencers.

Engage in multistakeholder conversations

If you are on the older side of the millennial pool (or if you have seen a single episode of *Mad Men*), then you know there was once a time when companies did not need to talk to anyone except consumers, and it was not so much a conversation as it was talking *at* people with a thing called advertising. The Don Drapers of the world had it easy: they sent out a message and people listened to it. There was very little market competition and there was no such thing as a 'mobile device', so multitasking wasn't a thing. Consumers rarely questioned the claims made in advertising and never followed up by writing a review on Amazon. No one had any influence except for us, the marketers.

Today's behaviour and expectations are much different. The 'brand message' does not have the same level of influence that it used to. Now, what is said about you by just about anyone on the internet is what tends to hold the most weight, so figuring out how to get people to spread the word of what you do, in a positive light, is an absolute necessity for success. Internet trolls aside, most people who are using social media are influential. Some more than others.

The first step is clear: listen. This is the key to success in just about any relationship, whether it is between a business and their customers or a married couple. Follow that with healthy two-way communication and you're gold. Listen, respond and then listen more. A good rule of thumb is to listen 80 per cent and spend the rest of the time conversing back.

A growing number of channels increases reach, an increase in reach increases the diversity of ears, and the diversity of ears increases the types of conversations your company is expected to have on a daily basis. And let me just say that 'conversations' is the operative word here, because no one, no matter their age, is going to stand for one-way communications of any sort. There must be a dialogue. Have you tried having a conversation with a wall? It's not fun.

In addition to what you do from a brand and a content marketing perspective, you must deploy groups of employees to interact with key groups in a public space. This includes:

- **Advocates:** your advocates are natural champions for your brand, and include customers, partners and employees. These are people who are willing to publicly support your company, products or services in some fashion, whether it be an endorsement or a recommendation. They are already trusted by your target market, so they can significantly influence prospects by sharing their positive experiences through blog posts, case studies, product reviews, video testimonials, social media and so on. Their assistance can include driving referrals, providing product feedback, introducing new products to a marketplace, as well as building long-term relationships with potential customers.

- **Influencers:** industry influencers are people who have an established online presence, and significant pull with an audience in a particular consumer segment. As previously mentioned, these are the 'movers and shakers' of the market. They generally have tons of followers, and these celebrity types can help your company drive scalability via consumer reach, engagement and content. Influencers usually come in the form of thought leaders, experts, bloggers, speakers and so on, and brands should utilize them to create content that increases awareness and loyalty.

- **Media:** for a little while most of us thought that long-form content was on its way out, but recent studies have shown the opposite is true (take yourself, for example, reading a book!). Measuring the amount of time that readers spend on a page is a better indicator of audience engagement than counting clicks per page, so make sure you are still engaging with the traditional media for in-depth coverage of your company. Even with the decline of traditional journalists, they are still important.

It sounds like a lot, and that is because it is. Thankfully, if you have mobilized your workforce and trained them to fight the good fight and participate, it does not have to *feel* like a lot.

Humanize your brand

We often think of organizations as robots: rational and logical. But there are human beings within them, and those humans are just as influenced by emotion as everyday consumers. People – no matter their industry, no matter business to business (B2B) or business to consumer (B2C) – do not want to be treated as if they all think alike. Consumers are seeking value and meaning in just about every interaction they have and, as such, expect to be treated as people first, and as potential buyers second.

A good friend of mine, Bryan Kramer, wrote about this very topic back in 2014 in his book, *There is No B2B or B2C: It's human to human, H2H*. His words were extremely powerful and I almost remember them verbatim. Here is a summary of what he wrote (Kramer, 2014):

> He said that businesses do not have emotion. People do. People want to be a part of something bigger than themselves. People want to feel something. People want to be included. People want to understand. But people are also humans, and with that comes mistakes. Missteps. Failures.

> As humans, it is in our nature to say the wrong thing, get embarrassed and not realize the consequences of our actions. The rise of social media has given a digital platform to the dark side of anonymity, both as individuals and as

crowds. I say it is time to lay down the virtual pitchforks and torches and bring this behaviour back into balance. The delightful side of humanity holds with it empathy, understanding and forgiveness, and when remembered in our communication, it ties us together as a common group.

Communication should not be complicated. It should just be genuine and simple, with the humility and understanding that we are all multidimensional humans, every one of which has spent time in both the dark and delightful parts of life. That's human to human. Human beings are innately complex yet strive for simplicity. Our challenge as humans is to find, understand and explain the complex in its most simplistic form. This means you, marketers, Find the commonality in our humanity, and speak the language we've all been waiting for.

For marketing teams, this shift requires a more human-centric approach than the strategies of yesteryear. While each company will certainly still be able to retain their own voice and tone, incorporating more empathy and emotions – two things that have long been dodged in the business world – is necessary to build a foundation for effective communications.

In fact, research from the Corporate Executive Board (CEB) and Google found that emotions drive buying decisions for even the most stoic of customers. Their survey of 3,000 B2B buyers from 36 distinct brands found that emotions trump rational motivators by a two-to-one ratio (CEB, 2013). The research concluded: 'Not only do emotions matter in B2B buying, but they actually matter even more than logic and reason.' It makes sense, doesn't it?

When you are ready to interact with your customers on a more human level, it is best to start with their mindsets. I like to follow these five attributes, especially when I take my clients through a messaging and narrative workshop:

1 **Beliefs:** discover what your audience cares about (community, family, friendship, activities, ways of thinking, etc) and develop a plan for how your brand can tell stories that coincide with those beliefs and values.

2 **Hopes and fears:** by knowing customers' aspirations, marketers can delight them and gain their trust. Try talking with your loyal customers to understand what makes them feel fulfilled or disappointed. Understanding their pain points will help you to craft a conversation with empathy.

3 **Emotional:** the need for security and self-esteem are often at the root of financial decisions. To find out more about these emotional needs, try

asking open-ended questions such as how do your customers want to be perceived by their colleagues? What aspects of their personal dignity are occasionally at risk? What keeps them up at night?

4   **Expectations**: knowing exactly what it is that gets a customer to trust you makes all the difference. Work to discover both the rational and emotional expectations of your company. Which actions do your customers consider to be unethical? Of what you provide, what gives customers the greatest sense of emotional satisfaction?

5   **Brand perceptions**: analysing how someone would describe your company to others can tell you a lot about their personal values. Remember: you want to capture personal value, not functional value, so work to find out how your brand appeals to customers' self-image and sense of dignity.

The way the internet has changed the buying cycle makes this more important to marketers than ever before. This process enables empathy, thereby humanizing a brand in an otherwise rational and data-driven world. Once you have thought about the characteristics above, you will be able to create *and spread* a message that resonates deeply with your target audience.

(Truly) embrace the rise of the individual

A true one-to-one relationship goes far beyond a nicely personalized marketing message. Whether you are a technology company or sell to consumers, it is important to remember that people buy from people. So get your people out there so they can start making connections.

The process of embracing and building true connection, referred to by Altimeter as digital transformation, represents the realignment and investment in technologies that connect brands to consumers, as well as a business model that more effectively engages digital consumers at every touchpoint of the customer experience life cycle. It sounds fairly feel-good and joyous, but Altimeter's research indicated that while 88 per cent of executives and digital strategists stated that their company is undergoing a formal digital transformation, only 25 per cent had mapped out the digital customer journey (Altimeter Group, 2016).

Undergoing digital transformation without mapping out the digital customer journey is preposterous. I know change can be rough, but talk about putting the cart before the horse!

It turns out that the greatest antagonist to change is company culture (63 per cent). Runners-up include thinking beyond a campaign mentality (59 per cent), cross-functional collaboration (56 per cent) and lack of resources (56 per cent) (Altimeter Group, 2016).

Wrapping your head around the rise of the individual sounds a bit like pushing a boulder up a hill, but trust me when I say the benefits are worth it. Organizations that invest in the complete package (new technologies, people and processes) to compete in digital markets realize business-level returns including market share, greater margins and profits, talent, among others.

Bottom line? Embracing the individual impacts the bottom line. Altimeter's same report found that companies successfully implementing digital transformation saw increases in:

- customer engagement (75 per cent);
- customer satisfaction (63 per cent);
- digital traffic (53 per cent);
- lead general/sales (49 per cent).

You can't miss this train. Start off by synchronizing the internal engagement with external engagement, and then take a good long look at the digital customer experience: what is it that people are going through? What are they doing? How does the information you are providing them assist in that journey? Understand their behaviours, the data they care about, who they influence, who they are influenced by, and then deploy your troops to talk and connect with them in a meaningful way.

Remember, if you can scale and nurture conversations internally with your employees, imagine how effective you will be doing the same externally, with your customers.

But don't just take my word for it. Jacob Morgan, three-times bestselling author, most recently of *The Employee Experience Advantage* (2017), has very similar thoughts on employee experience:

INSIGHT Futurist and thought leader

Contribution from Jacob Morgan, CEO of Chess Media Group

Over the past few decades the investment in employee engagement programmes has continued to rise yet scores around the world barely move, how can that be the case? It turns out that most employee engagement programmes are focused on short-term perks designed to boost engagement scores – basically, employee manipulation. Employees are wise to this and as a result are not becoming any more loyal or contributing any more of their effort. Thus, organizations are not seeing the promised business value. We have done a good job of investing in various perks to keep employees somewhat happy, without actually changing the workplace practices that employees are forced to work within.

Now, with the rise of employee experience, we are finally seeing organizations redesign their core workplace practices around their people. Based on my analysis of over 252 organizations, every single employee experience at every single company around the world is a combination of three distinct environments: culture, technology and the physical work environment. Culture refers to the feeling that employees get working for your organization and comprises 40 per cent of the overall employee experience. Technology is about the tools employees use to get their jobs done and comprises 30 per cent of the overall employee experience. The physical environment is the actual space in which employees work and also comprises 30 per cent of the overall employee experience.

In the past, organizations had the luxury of either not investing at all in any of these three environments or perhaps just making a minimal investment. That no longer works. The game of business has changed and, instead of trying to take market share away from competition or make more money than them, organizations must now focus on outlasting the competition. That is, how does your company stay in the race while others give up? The answer is, by investing in your people.

The interesting thing is that the ROI in terms of productivity, revenue, profit and stock-price performance really only kicks in when organizations do an amazing job at all three things. This is a very exciting time for anyone who is responsible for people inside of an organization. If you want to outlast the competition and create a place where people actually want to show up to work, then you must absolutely invest in employee experience – this means thinking about it from the perspective of culture, technology and physical space.

PART TWO
The business case for employee advocacy

Contextualizing the marketplace for employee activation 03

A business school's definition of a market would be something like, 'the total of all the buyers and sellers in a specific region where you want to sell your products or services'. A region can be the entire world, countries, states, cities or postcodes. But the reality is that a market can be just about anything you want it to be.

For example, if you sell enterprise security software, your market is IT decision makers (ITDMs) from the C-suite (CIO, CTO, CSO) all the way down to security engineers. This group is very important to your business. They are the ones making decisions on whether to purchase your software or go with one of you competitors. Your market might also include media and technology influencers, since they influence the ITDM purchase process based on what they say, write and share. Overall, this is a fairly large market.

Coca-Cola's or Pepsi's market would be exponentially larger. Depending on where you live today, you will notice that their advertising targets different groups of people – millennials active on social media and young families, especially if you live in one of the coastal towns or cities. Their market also includes health-conscious consumers, if you consider their water brands such as Dasani and Smart Water.

On the other hand, if you sell yoga pants and have two retail locations – one in Santa Clara and the other in Palo Alto (both in Silicon Valley), for example, your market is much smaller. It may consist of affluent consumers in these very specific areas who are yoga enthusiasts, drive a Tesla, or people who just love to wear comfy yoga pants around town and in the workplace.

While markets can certainly be simple, they can also be extremely complex. Imagine how segmented a market can be from a political perspective if you consider candidates running for office at the city, county, state and country level. There are several markets and micro-markets overlapping on many levels.

So now that we have defined markets, looked at the concept of participation marketing and the changes that need to be made both internally and externally to make it work, let's focus on one of the primary vehicles powering this mission: social media.

Yes, in 2018, social media is still critical

While many companies are using social media, too many of them are doing it ineffectively – failing to drive awareness, clicks to their website, building a sales pipeline, or increasing engagement with consumers. Their focus is often on how many friends, fans and followers they have or how many shares they can generate from a single piece of content. It is certainly smart to be tracking these metrics but the focus needs to be on translating the value of social media into business metrics and objectives. Still today, I cannot tell you how many people ask me for 'strategies to increase their followers'. We need to start thinking beyond these soft metrics and get serious about making business impact.

And here's a harsh reality. Chief marketing officers (CMOs) and other executive leaders are now questioning their investments into social media and holding their teams accountable for delivering business results. Both marketing and PR teams are now being forced to think strategically on the best way to approach this.

Failure to harness the power of social media is no doubt partly due to its quick evolution from a nice-to-have side effort to the coolest must-have on the block. It has climbed the ranks of popularity with lightning speed, and while you never want to make a marketing decision just because everyone else is doing it, slowing down and taking the time to consider what properly utilized social channels can do for you is absolutely worth it. While the following appear to be basic and more for beginners, it is important to start from the ground up. Here is a quick summary of what you can expect from 'best in class' social media programmes, either from a brand and content marketing perspective, leveraging employees or both:

● **Brand awareness**: companies that regularly engage on social media networks can cost-effectively increase brand awareness (which is a nice way of saying it is dirt cheap to get eyeballs through social media). And when I say dirt cheap, it is really not. It is much less expensive than traditional advertising, but there is always a cost associated with this, especially with the decline in organic reach, which will be discussed in later chapters. Again, this is a soft metric but it is the same metric that billboard ads and television commercials are measured against.

- **Customer education:** prospects actively seek information about you and what you can offer them at every step of the purchase process. By supplying them with the information they want, social media can steer them in the right direction, educate the purchase process and help close the sale. Think of the last time you Googled something along the lines of 'how to hard reset an iPhone 7'. Do you recall what you found in the search results? Well, I tried it and the first result was a post on a message board from Apple's customer community where someone asked the exact same question. Now I know where to go if I ever have to hard reset my iPhone 7.

- Word-of-(digital)-mouth marketing: not a new concept but an important one. We are all influenced by what we find online. We read reviews, ask friends, and Google the hell out of whatever it is we are looking to buy. Consumers love to talk about and review their experience with your brand. A survey from 2016 with SAS Referral Software, Ambassador and Nielsen Research revealed some data points that we fundamentally already know to be true. Word-of-mouth is not limited to specific industries or demographics and the vast majority (more than 80 per cent) of Americans seek recommendations when making a purchase of any kind (Kapadia, 2016). I do it all the time. When a restaurant or a local business goes above and beyond with their service, I go out of my way to write a Yelp review and then share it proactively in my network. I do the same with just about any other product or service that delivers value.

- **Search engine visibility:** content posted to social channels can improve search rankings through keyword focus, links and engagement level. Social sharing and other content forms such as videos and images also aid findability. The B2B purchase decision-making process always, and I mean always, starts with an unbranded keyword search. Ensuring that your content, both long form and social media content, match verbatim what your customers are searching is table stakes.

- **Sales:** yes, the latest buzz word that inundates my feed lately is 'social selling', and while much of the conversation is recycled thought leadership there is a lot of value in looking at this strategically. When sales teams are equipped with good content and leveraging their personal social channels in an authentic way, only good things can happen. Certainly, you will also want to ensure that you have got the basics, such as a clear call to action, trackable links and a streamlined landing page to make closing the deal a breeze.

If that sounds too good to pass up, it is because it is. So let's rewind and make sure you are getting the most out of your social media platforms – by starting at the beginning. The first step to translating the value of social media into numbers your colleagues can appreciate is knowing exactly who your audience is and what they are saying. And in the boundless world that is the internet that means knowing how that massive audience breaks down into sub-audiences.

Understanding the 1:9:90 model and how it affects the market

One of the earliest references to the 1:9:90 model (Figure 3.1) was in 2006 by Charles Arthur from the *Guardian* and it suggests that if you get a group of 100 people online then one will create content, 10 will 'interact' with it (commenting or offering improvements) and the other 89 will just view it (Arthur, 2006).

Since then there have been numerous iterations of market dynamics and influence and how content is created, shared and packaged across the internet. Since 2011, I have been thinking deeply about this subject and have refined the following definitions for each group representing the 1:9:90 model:

- **The 1 per cent:** these are the top influencers, the opinion leaders and the content creators. They essentially 'move the market' when they speak, write, tweet or publish just about anything. There are never more than

Figure 3.1 The 1:9:90 model

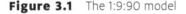

1% – **Influencers** driver the conversation about a specific topic. When they create content, others listen.

9% – **Advocates** contextualize influencer content, provide their own perspective and share with others.

90% – **Enthusiasts** rely heavily on word of mouth, peer recommendations and Google. They are highly influenced by the 1% and 9%.

50–100 people who drive the majority of share of conversation for a very specific topic. They can create new markets. They can launch new product categories. They can do just about anything they want due to their level of influence. This group used to consist of just traditional media and journalists. Today, you can throw just about anyone in this category, depending on the market.

- **The 9 per cent:** these are enthusiasts and the group where most of your employees will fit into. They are highly active online and spend most of their time in social networks. They recommend products, restaurants, coffee shops, clothing – you name it. They share their brand experiences with their networks, whether good or bad. They sign up for newsletters, download content, comment on it, share it, and any other available actions that let their community of peers know what they think.

- **The 90 per cent:** this is the great majority of any market. They lurk and learn and consume content daily. This group is satisfied with using Google search for discovering new products, reading reviews, or consuming the content of their peers without contributing much to the conversation themselves. But don't neglect them, as strength lies in numbers and they decide, based on their purchase behaviour, how compelling the 1 per cent and the 9 per cent really are in telling your brand's story.

The 1:9:90 model applies to any brand, large enterprise or small company. It is important though to realize that each group requires a different marketing and communications approach. You cannot talk to an influencer the same way you would talk to a general consumer. You just can't.

While it might seem a little imbalanced, each of these groups plays a very significant role in the content machine. Here is a common scenario: an influencer in the 1 per cent bracket creates a piece of content. Let's say it's a guide on the modern technology stack reimagined, and includes a number of trends that are currently happening in the workplace as well as an analysis on technology platforms that support them.

Next, a number of technology enthusiasts from the 9 per cent bracket download the guide, read it and share it. Some may write a blog post mentioning the guide while adding their expert opinion. Others just may decide to share it on Twitter or LinkedIn or just retweet the influencer.

Finally, the rest of the market, the 90 per cent, will decide whether or not to download the guide based on the perspective of the 1 per cent and 9 per cent. They may refer to Google to get additional perspectives or ask their work colleagues.

Now, let's say this guide is highly successful and your company offers a tool that is featured in it. Suddenly you've got a load of new prospects. Or, let's say your marketing team partnered with the influencer who wrote this guide and you are doing a lead share. Boom! Suddenly the potential for a slew of new leads is on the table.

The positive impact of social media is endless, but if you want to see great levels of success it is crucial that you are engaging with your audience, every last bit of it, at every step of the process. Next, let's look at the different types of channels where you can activate programmes, tell you brand story and surround sound your audience with good content.

PESO: no, not the currency

The paid, earned, shared, owned (PESO) model (Figure 3.2) is one of the greatest gifts the marketing world has been given. Developed in 2014 by PR expert and CEO of Spin Sucks, Gini Dietrich, the PESO model is an excellent way to organize and segment your marketing activities. The model, slightly adapted from Spin Sucks, truly illustrates integrated marketing and I would consider it an indispensable tool for any marketing professional, regardless of experience or specialty.

PESO enables us to segment all the marketing channels at our brand's disposal into distinct groups so that we can devise an integrated strategy

Figure 3.2   The PESO model: paid, earned, shared, owned media

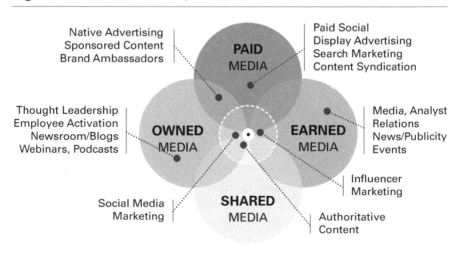

SOURCE Spin Sucks

for our programmes, campaigns and daily engagement. The model also allows us to make sense of the channels in which we are currently investing, develop unique story angles and measure the effectiveness of each tactic.

If you are new to marketing, a recent university graduate or unfamiliar with the PESO concept, the following is a quick definition of each section. And for all of you seasoned marketers, there is nothing wrong with a little recap:

- **Paid media:** exchanging money for distribution. Paid media may be in the form of paid amplification, sponsored content, native advertising, or sponsorships of influential blogs. More specifically, it would be promoting content on Facebook and Twitter, amplifying long-form content using Outbrain or using a network such as Open Influence to activate influencer groups. In a more traditional sense, paid media is advertising. So the billboards you see along the freeway, Super Bowl commercials and display advertising – all paid for. As a brand, you have complete control of this channel. You can increase or decrease your paid investment, control the message and get your brand in front of lots of people very easily with a few clicks of a button.

- **Earned media:** trading valuable content for an established authority's audience. This category represents all media coverage and publicity. An earned media win would be an article in the *New York Times* or *Recode* about your company, published with nothing expected in return. This is your media relations expert leveraging their network of journalists to get a story published or a byline placed on a specific media publication. Nothing comes easy with earned media. You not only need expert media strategists with journalist relationships, but you also need a compelling story to tell. You have complete control of what you pitch, but no control over the outcome, and sometimes hours of hard work can yield zero results.

- **Shared media:** amplifying content through your own audience. Anything and everything that was shared on any social media platform or publishing network for free falls into this category, such as a retweet, share, comment or snap. While you have some control over what you share and create, you cannot control how the audience will respond to your messages. In the early days, large brands learnt the hard way because they jumped right into social media without having an actual plan. What they thought was a 'free way to market products' turned out to be a headache when the audience suddenly expected a higher level of customer support in these channels.

- **Owned media**: creating content on owned channels for the ongoing industry conversation. Blogs, employee stories, customer reviews, webinars and podcasts are all great examples. What is great about owned media is that you have 100 per cent control of the customer experience. So you can be smart about creating unique mobile experiences, optimize the content for search engine visibility or facilitate industry conversations within a hosted customer community using a platform such as Lithium.

What is more important than simple definitions is the need to think strategically in how each of these channels interact with each other. Remember that consumers today have attention-deficit disorder – meaning that they are inundated with a surplus of content, media and notifications and purposely block out what is not important to them at a specific moment in time. It is also important to note that B2B decision makers are 'the most marketed-to' group online today. Sad but true if you are a technology marketer.

For this reason, it is important to have a consistent story across all channels and surround-sound your audience with good stories, multiple times and in multiple outlets. Remember, message repetition is key.

The challenge I see many marketers run into is quality of content. In my second book, *Your Brand the Next Media Company*, I highlight the need for marketers to build their brand narratives with empathy in mind, putting their audience's needs and desires front and centre. The last thing you want to do is inundate your audience with worthless content. They will ignore it, become annoyed and eventually label your brand a spammer. You don't want that.

Don't get me wrong. There will always be a need for branded content because it can drive business value. But imagine a layer of trust and authenticity wrapped around your brand promise. It is already here.

Employee-driven content > branded content

Combining the 1:9:90 and integrated programmes (PESO) for the perfect content marketing plan is an old trick of the trade that requires a lot on the production front. And while it is still necessary for a good chunk of that content to be carefully planned and constructed by the professionals, today your customers will ultimately trust what they perceive to be a third-party reference more than they will the branded stuff.

In fact, a survey in 2015 revealed that only 1 per cent of millennials feel that a compelling advertisement would make them trust a brand more. The same study found 33 per cent of millennials rely mostly on information they find on blogs before they make a purchase, compared to fewer than 3 per cent for TV news, magazines and books. While older generations rely more on traditional media, millennials look to social media for an authentic view into what is going on in the world, especially content written by their peers (Elite Daily, 2015). In 2018, it is (thankfully) a little early to start thinking about generation Z – their predecessors are a clear indication of the direction in which marketing is going: people want authenticity over perfection; they want to talk to people, not brands.

So now imagine the PESO model with the added layer of employee-driven content integrated with the branded content. I often refer to this as 'employees as media' (Figure 3.3).

Giving your employees the driver's seat is a new concept, and yes it can be a little unnerving, but unleashing them is critical. After all, if you cannot trust your employees, who can you trust? IBM is one of my favourite examples of this shift. Years ago, the company built their entire social media policy on a wiki page, with over 300 employees as contributors. The guidelines basically state that 'IBMers' are individually responsible for the content they create and prohibit releasing proprietary information. The document

Figure 3.3 The PESO model integrated with employee-driven content

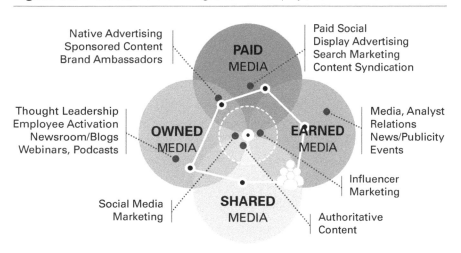

SOURCE Adapted from Spin Sucks

lacks any mention of brand messages or values, and the community itself is self-regulated. Talk about trust.

Do a quick search in Twitter for 'IBM', #IBMer or #ProudIBMer and you will find thousands of IBM employees actively engaged within their communities, delivering thought leadership and talking with customers and partners. The feed is non-stop.

If IBM's bravery is not enough of a sign of the times, the team at Prophet released some in-depth research on the topic in 2016. In their report, 'Social media employee advocacy: tapping into the power of an engaged workforce', they uncovered a lot of the current thinking about activating employees and a handful of interesting findings:

- 90 per cent of brands surveyed are already pursuing or have plans to pursue some form of employee advocacy.
- Consumer response to employee posts often outperform traditional digital advertising results.
- Employee advocacy drives employee engagement.
- Employee advocacy supports employment branding.

Figure 3.4, taken from the Prophet report, clearly illustrates why employees share information about their employers on social (it's a win, win, win):

Clearly, allowing employees to socialize company-related thoughts and information is really working for some companies. But on the other end of the spectrum, you have companies who believe more in the command-and-control model – perhaps because they think giving employees too much freedom will result in disaster. That's fair. I get it.

But Mark Burgess, co-author of *The Social Employee* (2016) claimed (when quoted in a recent *Forbes* article) that the likelihood of that happening is fairly low: he states that when you hear about employees going rogue, it generally tracks back to the company not having a policy, or if they did, they did not train the individual. It really is incumbent upon the company to develop the policy, train on the policy, and integrate the marketing organization and the HR folks (Arruda, 2016).

The reality is that command-and-control companies still exist. And, if you happen to work for one, thinking about employee advocacy may be a little too premature. On the other hand, there are some large and innovative brands that are absolutely knocking it out of the park.

In the case study below, we dive into one of the most creative brands on the planet, Adobe, and dissect their social media journey.

Figure 3.4 Employees are motivated by shared benefits between themselves and their employers

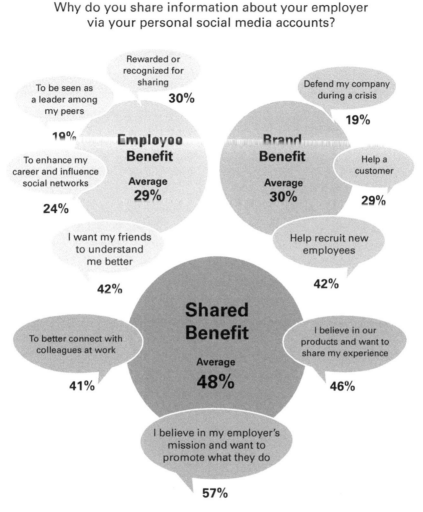

Why do you share information about your employer via your personal social media accounts?

Rewarded or recognized for sharing
30%

To be seen as a leader among my peers
19%

Defend my company during a crisis
19%

Employee Benefit
Average **29%**

Brand Benefit
Average **30%**

Help a customer
29%

To enhance my career and influence social networks
24%

I want my friends to understand me better
42%

Help recruit new employees
42%

To better connect with colleagues at work
41%

Shared Benefit
Average **48%**

I believe in our products and want to share my experience
46%

I believe in my employer's mission and want to promote what they do
57%

SOURCE Altimeter, a Prophet company: 'Social media employee advocacy: tapping into the power of an engaged social workforce', a report by Ed Terpening with Charlene Li and Aubrey Littleton

CASE STUDY How Adobe integrates social media into its business

Lauren Friedman is Head of Social Business Enablement at Adobe. She is responsible for integrating social media programmes and initiatives that empower each of the product organizations and business units. This includes training, technology deployment and employee advocacy. Ultimately, her charter is to integrate social media into every aspect of the way Adobe does business, both internally and externally.

Adobe is not just a technology leader but pretty much a household name. It has historically focused on multimedia and creativity software products such as Photoshop, Illustrator and After Effects, with a more recent foray into customer experience management software, known as the Adobe Experience Cloud.

Lauren has developed Adobe's global social media training programme, including several courses to help employees use social media to achieve very specific business objectives. These include training sessions that revolve heavily around social selling, social for product marketing and social for talent acquisition. Her team also leads the employee advocacy programme at Adobe, where they work to enable all employees to use social media both personally and professionally (Figure 3.5).

Lauren is also tasked with integrating social media programmes and planning across the entire business, not just in marketing. Adobe's goal is to be the most social company in the world and it is doing this by starting inside the organization with a core focus on its biggest asset – its employees.

Lauren launched the social media training in 2014. Prior to this, she was a part of Adobe's Social Media Center of Excellence that consisted of three people doing various tasks. Their social media training began as brief, brown-bag two-hour sessions. It consisted of the basics: how to use social media as an Adobe employee, rules of engagement and platform-specific training such as Facebook, Twitter and LinkedIn. After training over 2,500 employees, Adobe realized that many others wanted to get more involved with social, so training became a core focus.

Adobe's social media model

Adobe uses a hub-and-spoke model. The Social Media Center of Excellence is at the centre and supports social media practitioners across the organization in sales, HR, IT and so on. Most companies today have launched centralized cross-functional groups in order to serve the various business units with a common set of services, objectives, software and knowledge. In the hub-and-spoke formation strategic decisions are still often made in corporate in the hub, with some guidance from the business units in the spokes. Lauren's team guides these departments on governance, innovation and enablement.

Governance for Adobe is all about compliance, using the right tools and beta testing various programmes to establish benchmarks and organizational learning. The 'enablement' spoke of Adobe's social media model helps with industry insights across the social landscape. Its employees are provided with

Figure 3.5 Adobe's road map for employee advocacy

Drive awareness of Adobe's
social programmes and
the value of employee
participation

Mindset
(Awareness)

Teach employees how to
use social media in
accordance to Adobe's
guiding principles (Social
Shift)

Skillset
(Learning and Enablement)

Provide employees access to
curated content and teach
them how to engage and
build relationships online

Toolset
(Usability and Action)

Motivate employees to keep
involved in the programme,
sharing content and engaging
on their social channels

Habit
(Sustained Behaviour)

SOURCE Adobe Systems

social media training, some of which is customized. As an extension of the training, Adobe has launched its employee advocacy programme.

Employee advocacy at Adobe

In 2015, Lauren and her team launched a pilot employee advocacy programme. Once employees had completed internal training requirements known as Social Shift (Figure 3.6), they were given access to participate in the programme. The content that was populated into the system consisted of 20 per cent Adobe branded content and 80 per cent third-party industry content. This 80/20 ratio is an industry best practice when segmenting content for employee programmes.

Figure 3.6   Adobe's Social Shift training model

SOURCE Adobe Systems

Executive support and proving ROI

Initially, Adobe executives were nervous about integrating social media across the business but this was expected. After time though, they recognized the value that employee advocacy had internally by driving employee engagement and productivity. Externally they began to realize how employee advocacy can support marketing KPIs such as by reaching new audiences, brand engagement, customer support and social selling. The key to success for Adobe was starting with a small pilot programme and involving executives early on. This allowed them to collect testimonials, metrics, and proof of the impact of employees using social media from the start.

When measuring ROI Adobe looks to the number of employees that attend training and how many associate with Adobe online. They review what content is being shared in order to gauge interest for the future and track leads that come from social selling. Other metrics also exist that are relative to various business programmes.

In their employee advocacy programme, Lauren's team tracks the amount of content being shared and which content generates web page visits to Adobe. com. They also track overall impressions, which reveal that their employees' reach is larger than the branded channels. Adobe's brand receives over 63,000 mentions on social media each day. Their employees are empowered to respond to any questions they feel qualified to answer to create a better customer experience and help to scale customer service. Way to go Adobe!

The psychology of 'what's in it for me?' and how it affects employee advocacy

Recently, I had a conversation with the chief technology officer (CTO) of a Silicon Valley start-up and we talked about the business challenges he was expecting for the rest of 2017. I was expecting the usual host of today's headlines – security breaches, malware, malicious insiders and so on. I was wrong, in a way.

Hiring top talent was at the top of his list. He said, 'I need security engineers and architects. They don't have to be top of the class or go to MIT or Stanford. I'd settle for the average Joe. Do you know anyone looking?' Even with unemployment hovering close to 10 per cent in many countries (International Labor Organization, 2017), a remarkable number of business leaders are having a hard time finding and retaining talent. This is not just a US problem. Companies globally are struggling with the same challenge.

Because of this, we can now understand why creative employers are getting with their recruiting initiatives. From unlimited PTO, onsite daycare and daily catered meals, to Amazon's recent announcement of a 30-hour working week, it is seemingly a race to see who can provide the best and most attractive workplace (Stahl, 2016).

A recent survey from Glassdoor confirms companies are at least partially on the right track: 57 per cent of respondents said benefits and perks play a major role when deciding whether to pursue a job (Glassdoor, 2016).

And, companies are listening:

- Netflix announced that it added unlimited employee maternity and paternity leave for the first year after a child's birth or adoption.

- Airbnb gives employees an annual stipend of US $2,000 to travel anywhere in the world.

- Asana employees have access to executive and life-coaching services outside of the company.

- Zillow allows employees who are travelling to ship their breast milk home for free.

That's all fine and good for bringing people on, but the reasons employees stay with a company have less to do with the glitz and glam and much more to do with their relationship with the company itself.

The companies that understand that employees are just as important – if not more than – the customers who consume the products and services they sell are the ones seeing the most success. They are working tirelessly to address the varying preferences of three different generations. They know that the rise and transparency of social media means their reputation is highly dependent on what their employees say, and they are taking the right measures not only to provide for them, but also to develop and sustain real connections with them as well.

When is the last time you reviewed your company's Glassdoor's reviews? Were you happy with the results? And if not, did you share that feedback with company leadership?

If you want to see success with employee retention, the formula is straightforward. Build a company culture that celebrates success. Trust and empower your teams, regardless of their level. Be open, transparent and involve them in decision making. And lastly, don't ask your teams to do something that you wouldn't do yourself. It's not rocket science. It's just effective leadership. And the end result looks something like this:

Happy employees = higher productivity = higher quality of work

And there is a business benefit here too because a higher quality of work almost always equals satisfied customers, better products, more revenue, market share, customer retention – you name it. This applies to all businesses, no matter if you are in the service industry, selling a product, a large global company or a local restaurant. Thus, in the context of employee advocacy, the end result can also become:

Happy employees = engaged workforce = army of brand advocates

In other words, it has never been as difficult nor as crucial to keep employees happy. In this chapter we take a look at both the wants and needs of today's employees, and how your company can fulfil them in order to generate effective engagement and participation in marketing and overall employee advocacy.

What employees want, really, really want

'What's in it for me?' A question commonly asked where the benefits are not obvious. I have heard this hundreds of times – previous team members, managers (yes, managers) and even my kids when I ask them to do chores. It is a question that might drive you crazy, but is especially important to answer when it comes to the topic of this book – participation marketing. After all, if an employee was hired as an engineer or finance person, how in the world can we ask him or her to participate in an employee advocacy programme?

During an age when the lines between our work and personal lives are blurrier than ever before, it should come as no surprise that nurturing faithful employee relationships is essentially the same as cultivating loyal customers. Both groups of people want their needs to be satisfied first, and then the needs of the community or broader world. Neither side is more important than the other. Anne Bahr Thompson, Founder and Chief Strategist of Onesxityfourth, illustrates this mentality beautifully in her 'me-to-we-continuum' (Figure 4.1) published in the *Harvard Business Review* (Thompson, 2015).

Figure 4.1   The me-to-we continuum

| 1 Trust | 2 Enrichment | 3 Responsibility | 4 Community | 5 Contribution |
| Don't let me down | Enhance daily life | Behave fairly | Connect me | Make me bigger than I am |

SOURCE Onesxityfourth

An employee may initially work for a company for the artisanal snacks and yearly stipend, but what keeps them are the same behaviours that bring about happy, devoted customers: a laser-focus on the things they care about and a way to help them contribute to the cause. Just as consumers prefer doing business with companies that advocate for causes they care about, employees are looking for employers who advocate for them and on their behalf for causes that matter to them.

Thompson's 'acid test' of a satisfying employee–employer relationship is illustrated by the me-to-we continuum, showing that the best employers help us each achieve our personal 'me' goals, while simultaneously working with us to solve more generalized 'we' concerns. Then, between the 'me' and 'we' extremes, there are a variety of ways that companies can help enrich the lives of employees and communities alike (Thompson, 2015). Let's look at each extreme and everything in between:

- **Trust**: you have probably noticed that trust is a common denominator for most things involving relationships. First and foremost, employees want to work for a company they trust. On the extreme 'me' side, they care that their business lives up to its promises and delivers value to them individually. Fair salary, good benefits and policies that ensure employees are regularly acknowledged for a job well done are the stepping stones to promoting a trusting, healthy and positive work environment.

- **Enrichment**: work–life balance is desired across the board, but each generation has a different idea of what that looks like. Baby boomers are a proud bunch and desire regular recognition for their strengths and skills. Those from generation X seek friendly employers that help them to achieve their goals through simple and streamlined processes. Millennials (unsurprisingly) have the most detailed list of wants: personal and professional development programmes; managers who exhibit supportive behaviours; rewards for good ideas; and a variety of work assignments. Some would say higher wages, but I digress.

- **Responsibility**: fair treatment is a big deal for employees. Everyone wants others to be treated fairly; they want the companies they work for to behave ethically and responsibly. This does not mean they are not forgiving, however. All three generations exhibit empathy, and have a deep appreciation for businesses that are honest about their shortcomings, provided effort to improve is plain. The recent 2016 US election really brought this reality to life. Companies that endorsed certain candidates or policies were held accountable by their employees, with many threatening to quit their jobs. Whether it is right or wrong does not matter. Employees want more, and successful companies are the ones stepping up to the plate and addressing these concerns.

- **Community**: a sense of belonging has always been a huge factor in how engaged an employee is at any given time. Baby boomers feel like a part of the family when they work alongside each other, while gen Xers focus on forming friendships with their colleagues and millennials want an all-round supportive, enriching and connected work environment. Creating or joining a community can easily become a reality in most businesses. It is important that employees feel a commonality with their employers. It can help them grow and expand their personal and professional goals, make new friends, learn new skills, move into new roles in the company or get turned on to new hobbies or interests.

- **Contribution**: on the extreme 'we' side, people of all generations just want to connect and feel a part of something that is bigger than themselves. They want to work for companies that contribute to the communities they care about, and consistently aim to make the world a better place. Employees who feel like they are a part of something more than just the nine-to-five are the ones who are more fulfilled and this is really where employee advocacy can make an impact.

If you are developing and implementing cause-related initiatives within your company, good on you. But take another step and make sure they are a part of a larger plan to support a sense of shared responsibility, and not just one-off efforts. The 'we' side of the continuum must engage employees as a group in order to be effective. Once an employee feels like a part of a family, he or she will be more inspired to interact positively with each other and those outside the company. And that is exactly what participation marketing is all about.

What employees need, really, really need

In 1943, psychologist Abraham Maslow proposed a theory about the hierarchy of needs in a paper titled 'A theory of human motivation', published in *Psychological Review*. The theory is most commonly illustrated as a pyramid, with the most fundamental needs at the bottom. If you have ever attended a business or management class, you are probably already familiar with this model.

It was Maslow's belief that people needed first to satisfy their most basic needs such as warmth, safety and security, in order then to realize their own personal growth and development. According to the folks over at Scancapture (2015), if we think about our employees this way, the theory becomes an excellent model for how to treat them (Figure 4.2), and I agree.

Let me expand a bit more on the parallels of Maslow's theory, employee engagement and employee advocacy.

Figure 4.2   Maslow's hierarchy of needs for employee engagement

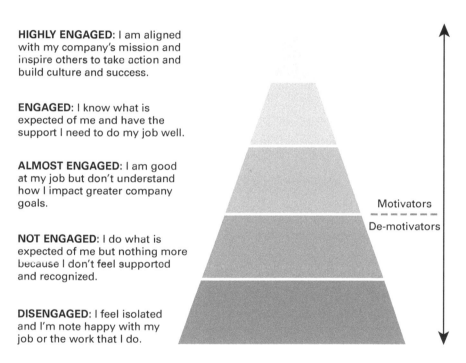

HIGHLY ENGAGED: I am aligned with my company's mission and inspire others to take action and build culture and success.

ENGAGED: I know what is expected of me and have the support I need to do my job well.

ALMOST ENGAGED: I am good at my job but don't understand how I impact greater company goals.

Motivators

De-motivators

NOT ENGAGED: I do what is expected of me but nothing more because I don't feel supported and recognized.

DISENGAGED: I feel isolated and I'm note happy with my job or the work that I do.

SOURCE Scancapture Ltd

Survival = Disengaged

The bottom of the pyramid is a no-brainer: in order to be highly and positively engaged, employees need a salary that allows them to live the lifestyle they are accustomed to. Financial independence is basic survival.

Employees in this stage are at risk. They are already researching for new positions on LinkedIn and are most likely interviewing. If the majority of your workforce falls within this phase of the hierarchy, you have a lot more problems than you think and the very last thing you want to do is invite them to participate in an employee advocacy programme. It will backfire.

Security = Not Engaged

Next, a sense of stability. This is easier said than done since today's job market is so volatile. Employees in this stage may not be at risk of leaving, but you should know that they are likely thinking about it. They dislike their managers and working conditions. They don't speak up in team meetings, don't attend company events, and most likely eat lunch in their cubicles, alone. Simply put, they are just collecting a pay cheque.

You don't have control of how employees feel, but anything you can do to offer security and structure is crucial for engagement. For starters, stop hiring managers. Ensure that you are focused on hiring leaders who can empower and uplift their teams. This can fix a lot of cultural and employee challenges. Listening more and proactively going out of your way to enrol these employees into new projects or initiatives will also help.

While employees in this phase are disengaged, there is hope. But again, it does not make sense to focus your employee advocacy programme with this group. Not yet.

Belonging = Almost Engaged

You can see engagement peeking out over the horizon once survival and security needs are met, and room for belonging is made. Creating a sense of camaraderie (again, so employees can feel a part of something bigger) in tandem with acknowledging individual contributions must be made for employees to feel encouraged to speak about their company in a positive, supportive light.

While employees in this phase are proud to work for you, they don't tell anyone. Change that. This group is ripe and ready for an employee programme.

Importance = Engaged

Finally, engagement makes an official appearance when employees feel not only that their contributions have been acknowledged, but that they have actually made the business better. A survey by Glassdoor confirmed the enormous power of recognition: more than 80 per cent of employees said they were motivated to work harder and stay at their jobs longer when they received appreciation for their work (Glassdoor, 2016). More recent research continues to support this finding, including Dale Carnegie's 2016 survey on engagement across generations (Carnegie, 2016).

Feeling that the work we do is important, no matter the company size or job title, is absolutely vital for reaching the top of the pyramid: self-actualization and the holy grail of engagement – and usually where your company rock stars hang out.

Self-actualization = Highly Engaged

Start here. Put this book down right now and compile a list of employees who are at this level. Employees who have reached this level already love the company, its products and their co-workers. And they are not afraid to show this affection publicly.

These are your internal trailblazers who you can mobilize to participate in your employee advocacy programme. These are your brand storytellers.

Let us not forget millennials

Marketers put a lot of focus on millennials when it comes to content, marketing and advertising budgets, but what about when it comes to their employees? Millennials are about to make up the largest portion of the workforce and they are incredibly unhappy. A 2017 study reported that a whopping 79 per cent of employees surveyed felt undervalued, mainly due to a lack of recognition (TINYpulse, 2017).

Unless you want the bulk of your workplace to be made up of unsatisfied people – or worse, a group of unsatisfied people talking about their unhappiness to all of their networks – learning to work with the millennial style of motivation is a must. Given below are a few things to consider when tailoring your recognition programme.

Recognize often

Millennials really, really want a pat on the back. (Don't we all?) Numerically speaking, 42 per cent want to get feedback every week – twice as often as other generations – and a whopping 80 per cent would like that feedback to happen in real time (TINYpulse, 2015). This is a clear indicator that having open lines of communication with your teams is a requirement.

Shake up tradition

When millennials can sense a gold star coming on, as in mid-year or annual reviews, it does little to increase their engagement. In fact, 51 per cent of employees in one study said receiving a milestone award had no impact on their view of their jobs at all (GloboForce, 2014). Try to make traditional recognition more meaningful by personalizing the moment, and make the reward system social if you can (many platforms enable employees to recognize each other with virtual badges and kudos and such). We dig more into this in later chapters.

Be specific, very specific

Millennials not only want a pat on the back, they want a very specific pat on the back. When you reward someone from this generation, make sure it is for individual projects or initiatives, and be detailed in your explanation of why they worked so well. So ditch the 'employee of the month' approach. Reinforcing every facet of good behaviour will set an example, and help build a culture where doing the right thing becomes the norm.

Make it a learning experience

To some, millennials may be seen as a needy bunch, but they are not without their positive qualities. For example, most people from this generation respond well to mentoring from their more experienced co-workers, and view their manager as a coach who is supporting their goals. Accordingly, they prefer to learn by application over being told what to do. You can be sure you will attract talent from this pool of workers if your company culture emphasizes learning why things work or do not work.

Beyond the psychology fluff

You will not find any shortcuts here. You will need to identify a laser-focused value proposition if you want your workforce to participate in an employee advocacy programme. In addition to the engagement factors discussed at length, there are additional benefits that will attract employee participation, as set out below.

Internal rock-star recognition

Being recognized by your manager is one thing. Being recognized by peers, other managers or even the CEO is another. In the workplace, peer validation equals motivation and the benefits are good for everyone. For the employee, there is nothing better than a kudos or a 'shout out' publicly. It builds confidence and it reinforces their contributions. For his or her peers, it can create a healthy dose of competitiveness and envy. This is great for recruiting other employees to the programme who are on the fence about participating.

Access to exclusive content

A smart employee advocacy programme will ensure that participating employees will have exclusive access to content, product announcements, company news or events. It is similar to an influencer programme but, in this case, the influencer is internal. It is not uncommon for employees to 'live Tweet' a company event or write a wrap-up blog post about a recent product launch or initiative. It happens all the time. I like to think of it more like a newsroom, where you have dozens of beat writers covering an exclusive event and creating and distributing content in real time.

Building external influence

There will always be some employees who gain a substantial amount of influence in the marketplace, similar to the 1 per cent mentioned in Chapter 3. It is not uncommon for them to be quoted in the media, host webinars or podcasts and get invited to speak at industry conferences. This could be your CEO, others on the executive bench or any other employee who has become influential.

There is risk, though. And the risk is losing these employees to your competition. The more influential they become, the more visible they become in the marketplace. This should not be a deterrent, especially if you have built a sound culture. And, if they are misbehaving on social media, which is quite common these days, you will have to refer back to you social media policy and continue to invest in training.

Thought leadership

Thought leadership is for more than just executives. And the truth is that most mid-level managers would prefer to learn from and converse with people like themselves. So in the B2B context, a network engineer would be more keen on engaging with other network engineers. The challenge obviously is that engineers typically do not like to spend time in social networks because it takes them away from their day job, deadlines, code releases, etc.

INSIGHT   Social business expert

Contribution from Carlos Gil, Head of Social Media at BMC Software

Building an employee advocacy model for your brand or company does not happen overnight, it requires careful planning, the right set of tools and technology, appealing content for your employees to share and mass adoption internally, which starts at the top.

If your CEO is not on Twitter, and consistently sharing brand content, good luck convincing 1,000+ employees to do so. Most employees are not marketers, most use social media – specifically Facebook – passively and in between breaks or at home. They view their jobs as what pays the bills but it is not what they are passionate about. So how does a leader create mass adoption for employee activation on social media? Simple. You start with clearly defining the 'why?'

Every employee cares about what is in it for them. If they are in sales, they want to sell more product because it helps them generate a bigger bonus and higher commission. If they are in HR, they want to attract the best candidates and cultivate an open and transparent work culture.

Begin with analysing the various lines of business within your own organization and how employee advocacy directly benefits them. Again, think through the business benefits of the various stakeholders in your company, starting with sales, marketing, HR, customer support, etc. If you can solve that mystery you can gain adoption. Because without adoption, you have nothing.

Next, you have to make sharing easy. Stop e-mailing your entire employee base or posting an announcement on the intranet asking employees to copy, paste and share content externally. It will not happen.

Instead, invest in providing your employees with a turnkey solution, which you can also use to measure effectiveness of shares, engagements and overall employee adoption. Also, it will prove to be more convenient when they can log in using their social media handles and select from a menu of content to share. This leads me to my next point.

Content matters. Employees are not going to jump through hoops to share your latest sale or promotion with their friends, family and network on social media. Instead, provide them with content that excites them to share – why your company is a place at which they are proud to work. If you are looking to engage sales professionals to drive demand, make your e-books, white papers and promotional content live within your sharing platform to make it easier on the employee. Also, keep content fresh and up to date as often as possible. As long as there is a benefit for the employee, sharing is easy, and if content is relevant to them and their network you should be able to scale.

For brands, employee advocacy is a business imperative

05

A single employee's social media network of connections includes former colleagues, classmates and other friends or acquaintances who overlap in skill sets, industries or professional interests. These are the people who can potentially become your next lead, and you have a direct – and, more importantly, authentic – connection to them at any given moment.

Once upon a time we wouldn't think to add these folks to the pot of potentials, because they didn't exist – but today, friend circles are massive and interconnected and continuously changing along with the purchase funnel we wish to usher them into. What was once a fairly straightforward model has now become a very dynamic set of guardrails that requires a variety of different operators. You cannot influence an employee's peers without the help of the employee themselves.

Once you unleash these employees into the marketplace, you will soon realize that there is shared value everywhere. And not just for your company, but each party involved. When your employees share company content and build their own perspectives, the result is truly a gift that keeps on giving – to everyone.

Employee advocacy multistakeholder value model: building shared value for all

The real beauty of participation marketing is its universal benefits. The model pictured in Figure 5.1 is one I've been working on for a little over five years now, and it illustrates the flow of business value from the brand to employees to customers.

Figure 5.1   Employee advocacy multistakeholder value model

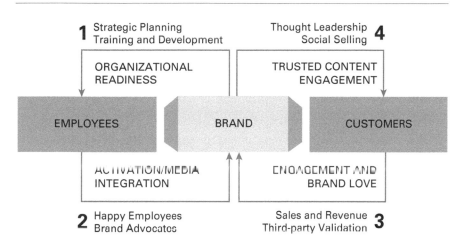

Starting in the upper left of Figure 5.1, the first step is all about making sure you put together your strategy and plan. There are several requirements that you need to think through so collaborating with internal stakeholders is critical – HR, IT, legal, internal communications, marketing and communications. This means enrolling them into the process from day one, not a few weeks prior to launching your programme.

Being really *really* ready, as in ready to build a programme and invest in the necessary technology, means you have done your homework. You have figured out how employee activation fits into your broader HR and marketing programmes, which group or business unit is driving it, and you have implemented a social media policy the protects your company, yet empowers the workforce.

While creating a social media policy may seem elementary to some, you would be surprised at how many companies that were early adopters in social media have not updated their policy since 2012. This should also include training and development initiatives that will be critical in teaching employees how to use social networks, the nuances of each channel, how to engage effectively, participate in industry conversations and how to write compelling headlines (training will be covered in more detail in later chapters). But for now, start thinking about your employees, their level of proficiency in social media and any internal resources you may have to put together a comprehensive training programme.

You have also done your research and started documenting various technology applications or bundle of solutions that align to your business needs as you think about scaling your programme globally. This will include several internal collaboration platforms such as Slack, storage applications like Box, as well as more sophisticated employee advocacy platforms such as Dynamic Signal. Remember to work collaboratively with your IT department when vetting these technology apps. They should be able to guide your decision making, help negotiate contracts and it is also likely that they may already have a technology stack that you can use for your programme.

The most important thing to remember here is enablement. While technology and training play a pivotal role, enablement also means that you are championing your internal teams and motivating them to participate. Once you have got a solid process in place and employees are bought in to your vision, you will move to step two, where employee happiness kicks in.

Enabling employees to be a part of the larger conversation, no matter their department, creates an environment where work is more than just collecting a pay cheque. Even if your office culture is not quite in a place where there is much meaning beyond the hours of 9 am and 5 pm, I fully believe that soon enough it will be. While the workplace experience was once driven entirely by a company, employees – particularly millennials in all of their social magnificence – are now influencing much of how an office functions. And that should come as no surprise; after all, if they are powerful enough to influence consumers, they are powerful enough to influence business process and culture too.

I have already said it but it bears repeating: today's professionals want to be bigger than their day to day. They want to be brought into the vision of the company and the value of your product or service. Once they feel like they are really making a difference, the satisfaction raises the happiness level and suddenly there is better quality work, less turnover and higher productivity. In other words, you have got an army of brand champions on your hands, ready to jump in and engage with each other and the external marketplace.

An army of true brand champions leads to part three: the delivery of effective thought leadership and conversations with customers. This happens in both the expected spaces such as social channels, and in the unexpected such as customer support.

There are a few brands I would like to personally call out for having amazing customer support and service: Comcast Cable and Southwest Airlines. I know what you're thinking. Comcast? Yes. I have been a customer for over a decade. For those of you who are not familiar with Comcast, they provide voice, internet and residential cable services. In many circles, they get a bad rap for their services, but over the years they have done a lot to improve it. If there is ever an outage, or my internal connection stops working, I just tweet at @ComcastCares and they typically respond within just a few minutes. Even if the outage doesn't get fixed right away, the fact that someone responds assures me that they are listening.

As for Southwest, I'm so thrilled with their customer service on a regular basis that I advocate for them all the time – to my friends, my family, my colleagues, and anyone who asks. And here's the thing: not once has Southwest ever asked for anything – not a tweet, a mention or a recommendation. I'm just happy to spread the word because of the value and experience I get from them all the time. They truly care about their customers.

Delivering value is not always being reactive, as in the case with most customer support issues. It can also mean that you are being proactive by providing educational material to people who may be interested in purchasing your product. Many refer to this as social selling, which is more than just a buzz word. The best definition of social selling that I have read is from Hubspot:

> Social selling is when salespeople use social media to interact directly with their prospects. Salespeople will provide value by answering prospect questions and offering thoughtful content until the prospect is ready to buy. (Kusinitz, 2014)

While the term social selling and employee advocacy are rarely mentioned in the same sentence, they are essentially synonymous. Sales people, despite the negative 'car salesman' stereotype are, in fact, employees too and can deliver a lot of value, as demonstrated in the case study at the end of Chapter 1. *Social Selling* (2016) by Tim Hughes and Matt Reynolds is also a worthy read on the topic in case you are interested.

Can you imagine everyone in your company creating experiences like this for everyone in their networks? The result would be 'Part 4' of this book, which is the promised land: an increase in sales and a rise in word-of-mouth marketing.

To summarize the last couple of pages, creating shared value among all your stakeholders requires careful planning and laser-focused execution. By doing so, you will create value to your employees by training them and giving them the tools necessary to be successful, both internally and externally. In return, they will create value to you (the brand) by delivering high-quality work, increased productivity and engaging in 'multistakeholder' conversations specifically with your customers. Then there is value delivered to your customers because they are getting their problems solved (customer support) or making more informed purchase decisions (social selling). That, in turn, creates value back to the brand because your customers are happy, revenue is increasing and your competitors are watching, scratching their heads from the sidelines and wondering what to do next.

Relevant content: the struggle is real

Let's take a deeper dive into how participation marketing can have a positive effect on areas that need it, starting with content marketing. Content marketing is and has been all the rage and hype for several years now, so it might come as a bit of a surprise when I tell you that in 2016 only 30 per cent of B2B marketers said their organizations were good at it (Content Marketing Institute, 2016). Even more shocking: in the year prior, organizations that felt their content marketing efforts were effective was only 38 per cent. Now this makes sense. B2B content is not easy to create because it is more technical in nature. For consumer content, the struggle is less of a challenge since writing 'lifestyle' content comes more naturally for some. In either case, the content must be relevant and you must tell a compelling story with it.

The above data is falling for a number of reasons. For starters, fewer and fewer B2B marketers have a documented content marketing strategy (32 per cent in 2016 versus 35 per cent in 2015), even though there is plenty of research that consistently shows those who document their strategy to be more effective.

Second, too many marketers do not have goals. The same report highlighted that 79 per cent of the most effective marketers have clarity on their content goals, while 77 per cent of least-effective content marketers do not.

So here we have a lack of confidence, no strategy and no goals to measure against. It is hard to believe that, in 2017, marketing is still struggling to document a content strategy. I'm personally still shaking my head in disbelief.

But let's say you're one of the lucky ones. You've hired a rock-star content marketing manager. You have a strategy complete with goals for the year. You have invested in some automation tools and may even have hired an agency with expertise in content marketing. And maybe, just maybe, you have secured additional budget for some lead gen programmes.

If you are still failing to see the results you had in mind, chances are it is because of an inability to create the sheer *amount* of relevant content needed. They keyword here is *relevant*. Because all too often, what companies *think* is relevant turns out not to be so. Irrelevant content, no matter how well written or strategically promoted, goes unnoticed. In fact, I bet most viewers scroll right past it or view it as spam. This means the 'create more, faster' mantra simply does not work, and yet companies are still racing to race and investing just to invest.

For content to be truly effective, it should be targeted, strategic, value-focused and personalized. Only then can it be engaging, and only then can your content efforts really see their full potential.

Throughout the course of this book, we have been talking a lot about employees sharing content. But sharing is just the beginning. There is so much more that they can be doing to deliver value to the business. In later chapters we discuss at length the full employee experience when participating in an employee advocacy programme, but for now let's touch on storytelling, or rather, employee storytelling.

You see, the problem with content sharing is balance. If 100+ employees are sharing the same piece of branded content, it can appear to be spam. It is spam! And that is assuming the content is somewhat relevant. It is still spam even though the content may resonate. While many employee programmes start off this way, it is critical to ensure that employees adopt their own tone of voice, style and content approach. In Chapter 9, I go into depth about training and segmenting employees.

The true value in activating employees is empowering them to tell stories and create content they actually care about. The recipe for success then looks like this potential scenario, which happens all the time in the B2B technology space:

> Jasmine, a security engineer for your company, writes a blog post about the future of network security in 2018. Her colleagues – other engineers – share the content in their individual social networks. They don't just click 'RT' or 'share' either. They provide their own perspective to it first. Some may even write additional blogs about the topic. The sales team sees it and sends it over to a few prospects.

> The result? A ton of engagement on the social networks, and even more clicks to the blog post. Search engine visibility for terms like 'network security in 2018'. Someone in the media is writing a piece on network security and calls your company to get a comment from Jasmine. And maybe, just maybe, your sales team closes deal.

This is another manifestation of the 1:9:90 model, whereby 1 per cent of your employees will become active storytellers or content creators; 9 per cent will package up that content and distribute it out to their networks. The 90 per cent will just watch from the sidelines, and that is completely okay.

I don't think the concept of participation marketing can or should be a complete substitute for a well-oiled content marketing engine, but I do believe that it can certainly close gaps and help you to see the level of efficacy you have been trying to deliver.

Organic reach: the struggle continues

Once upon a time, 100 per cent of your friends, fans and followers would see 100 per cent of your posts across 100 per cent of your social channels. There was no need for promoted tweets or boosted posts. Organic traffic was booming, social communities were growing, everyone was happy and seeing results.

But sound the alarm. Call a doctor. Maybe even the police. Because in case you missed it, organic reach is dying if not 100 per cent dead. Companies now have to think strategically about telling stories across their social media channels and ensuring that their audiences actually see it.

Social networks are all grown up, complete with strict revenue goals and pressure to keep shareholders happy. The result? Paid media is the only option to reach your audience with branded content. To put this in more context, we did a small test in early 2017 to determine the impact of organic reach on Twitter, LinkedIn and Facebook. For starters, we posted for one week organically to each channel and then followed up a few weeks later with identical content and small paid budget (US $100 per post on Facebook, $100 total for Twitter and $100 per post for LinkedIn). The total investment was $1,100. Figure 5.2 shows the results. The data shown is clear. Paid media is really the only way to reach audiences.

If you remember just a few short years ago and think about the search engines, several brands tried to manipulate their content to the top of the search results by paying for links, along with other shady practices. Google and others responded with algorithmic changes that rebalanced the results in favour of quality content. Social networks have also applied an algorithmic approach to the information they prioritize in their users' news feeds.

If you are wondering what this has to do with participation marketing, a few words from Brian Boland, Vice President of Advertising Technology at Facebook, who sums it up perfectly:

> Back in the day, search engines like Google and Bing used to provide a mass amount of web traffic to websites when they first launched. As the search engines began to dominate in usage, there was more competition to rank highly in search results. Because of this, the search engines had to work much harder to surface the most relevant and useful content, businesses eventually saw diminished organic reach. The same is true for social networks. (Boland, 2014)

While Google remains a tough nut to crack, an increase in employees participating and sharing content to Facebook and other social networks on behalf of their employer is a bit of a loophole. Via this route, branded content can

Figure 5.2 Organic reach versus paid media test

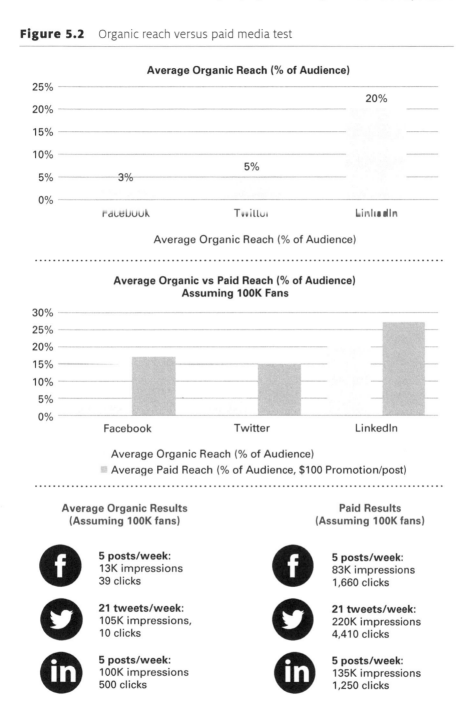

squeeze through the cracks into consumer space and result in organic traffic, reach and engagement. That is, until the smart engineers at Facebook change up the algorithm again.

Know the news feeds!

Facebook: content in your newsfeed will rank with friends and family first, information second, and entertainment third. The more engagement on the post, the higher the organic reach will be.

Instagram: photos and videos in your newsfeed will be ordered by how likely it is that you will be interested in the content based on previous engagement, your relationship to the user posting, and the timeliness of the post. It is still unclear how Instagram Stories are served and shown to users.

Twitter: your feed will be focused on helping you catch up on the best Tweets that you missed while away. Twitter is continuing to tweak their algorithm to figure out which are the 'best tweets' to feature at the top of your timeline.

LinkedIn: your feed on LinkedIn is based on your interest areas, skills, Pulse subscriptions and your previous engagements on content.

Diminishing organic reach is bad news. It is making it more difficult for companies to reach their audiences without making significant investments into paid media. However, it may not be too bad a reality if your employees are posting branded content on their personal profile pages.

Let's dig into some numbers and compare a Facebook fan page with 1 million likes against a company that has 100 active employees sharing branded content on their personal channels. In using the numbers represented in our example, with Facebook delivering 3 per cent reach in an organic post, you might see something like this:

1 million likes × 3 per cent = 30,000 potential eyeballs

According to Pew Research, the average Facebook user has 338 friends and, on average, 33 per cent of those friends will engage with their content within their newsfeed. So that means for every message a Facebook user shares, on average, 113 of their friends will see that post (PEW Research, 2014). There are several conflicting reports on the other social networks and there is nothing official from Twitter or LinkedIn, so let's make some assumptions and apply the 33 per cent reach number above to each:

Facebook: 100 employees × 338 friends × 33 per cent = 11,154

Twitter: 100 employees × 200 followers × 33 per cent = 6,600

LinkedIn: 100 employees × 900 connections × 33 per cent = 29,700

Total reach for one piece of content shared by 100 employees across all three social networks would equal 47,454 potential eyeballs. Of course reach is the weakest metric to measure but this does provide a glimpse into the potential impact of activating employees to be brand storytellers; and it is substantially more than an organic piece of content shared on a Facebook page with 1 million likes.

And remember, there is a huge difference in brands sharing content versus employees sharing content, so these numbers will certainly be larger. Much larger.

The impact employee advocacy has on website traffic

Dynamic Signal is the leading employee advocacy software on the market today. One of their own use cases of using employee advocacy is to drive traffic to their website, acquire new leads and drive brand awareness in the marketplace. Their blog is the pinnacle of their programme and they are constantly populating it with fresh content about the industry and their clients. Last year, they reviewed their overall website traffic for a three-month period and they found some really compelling data: their employees drove some of the best website visits they had ever seen.

Let's begin by looking at the overall traffic for dynamicsignal.com (Figure 5.3). Their top two sources of traffic come from a brand awareness standpoint. 'Direct' traffic includes their e-mail marketing efforts, the typing of the website into the URL, and bookmarks, among many other possible scenarios. 'Google/Organic' includes website visits from those searching for their company, product and our industry. The source 'DySiVS' is a UTM code (tracking code) they created to measure the traffic sent back to the website from employee sharing.

This data gives us many insights about the impact that employee advocacy is having on their website traffic:

- Their programme is sending more traffic to the website than any of their paid channels.

Figure 5.3   Website traffic sources from Google Analytics

Source / Medium ?	Acquisition		
	Sessions ? ↓	% New Sessions ?	New Users ?
	47,451 % of Total: 100.00% (47,451)	**67.89%** Avg for View: 67.86% (0.04%)	**32,214** % of Total: 100.04% (32,202)
1. (direct) / (none)	**11,787** (24.84%)	78.91%	9,301 (28.87%)
2. google / organic	**10,717** (22.59%)	63.46%	6,801 (21.11%)
3. DySiVS / socialmedia	**7,274** (15.33%)	47.72%	3,471 (10.77%)
4.	**5,999** (12.64%)	83.61%	5,016 (15.57%)
5.	**1,383** (2.91%)	99.49%	1,376 (4.27%)
6.	**1,102** (2.32%)	49.55%	546 (1.69%)
7.	**946** (1.99%)	83.83%	793 (2.46%)
8.	**691** (1.46%)	41.82%	289 (0.90%)
9.	**639** (1.35%)	80.91%	517 (1.60%)
10.	**466** (0.98%)	57.30%	267 (0.83%)

SOURCE Dynamic Signal

- Traffic driven by their employees is driving a lot of returning visitors – acting almost like a nurture campaign on social media.

- An argument could be made that their employees are generating brand awareness that is impacting organic search traffic and direct traffic simultaneously.

As any good digital marketer will tell you, it is not about the quantity of traffic but rather the quality of the visits. Let's dig into more data to test this hypothesis.

Their employees are driving website visits with the lowest bounce rate, the most pages per session, and the second-highest overall time spent on site (Figure 5.4). This means that the audience their employees have on social media is not only interested in their content but they are looking for more information about our company, perhaps a demo and/or employee advocacy overall.

A bounce rate in the range of 26–40 per cent is excellent and is a standard benchmark. Their employee advocacy programme generates a 36.42 per cent bounce rate, which is better than organic search and direct traffic.

Figure 5.4   Website bounce rate from Google Analytics

Source / Medium ?	Behaviour		
	Bounce Rate ?	Pages / Session ?	Avg. Session Duration ?
	47.12% Avg for View: 47.12% (0.00%)	2.80 Avg for View: 2.80 (0.00%)	00:01:34 Avg for View: 00:01:34 (0.00%)
1. (direct) / (none)	49.31%	2.58	00:01:21
2. google / organic	42.42%	3.20	00:02:23
3. DySiVS / socialmedia	36.42%	3.62	00:01:35
4.	49.92%	2.17	00:00:46
5.	98.70%	1.06	00:00:02
6.	66.70%	1.55	00:00:11
7.	67.97%	1.83	00:00:52
8.	56.58%	2.34	00:01:23
9.	57.75%	1.61	00:00:15
10.	73.18%	1.55	00:00:34

SOURCE Dynamic Signal

Web traffic coming in from their programme is generating over three page views per session. When they looked at the behaviour flow in Google Analytics they found that their second page visit was to their product page followed by their resources page. These are very good signs of interest into their product.

Dynamic Signal key takeaways

Reaching the right audience

The overlap of a brand's followers and employees' followers is only 8 per cent. By allowing employees to share content, Dynamic Signal has a better chance of reaching prospects that reside within the 92 per cent that are not following our company social media pages but *are* following their employees.

Nurturing the online buyer's journey

The data indicates that Dynamic Signal's employees are becoming a resource similar to a nurture drip campaign. Of the sessions that were created by their employee advocacy programme, 53 per cent of them were repeat visitors. This means that our employees are keeping Dynamic Signal top of mind on social media while their audience continues their buyer's journey.

Employee advocacy can reduce digital marketing spend

The rest of the traffic to their site is mostly paid channels, which in comparison have some of the highest bounce rates and lowest time spent on site. Based on the quality and quantity of traffic, it is an easy decision to invest more in our employees than in paid channels. If you think about it, employee advocacy is about driving organic touch points so the results should beat out paid channels.

Employee excitement and an increase in morale

This data has had one other big impact on Dynamic Signal's employee advocacy programme: it has got their team excited to share even more. By seeing what an impact they have made on their inbound marketing efforts, they understand just how influential they can be to overall success. Plus, they are happy, engaged and also a little competitive internally.

Social selling and employee advocacy = same, or no?

Let's say you need to purchase new software on behalf of your company. You probably start the process by Googling a few keywords and sifting through the search results. You may then check out a few vendor websites just to see what's out there and then cross-reference that list with Gartner's Magic Quadrant (MQ), which are a series of market research reports that aim to provide a qualitative analysis into a market and its direction, maturity and participants.

But when it comes time to form an opinion about one or more vendors, you shoot out a couple of messages to people across your network asking for feedback. I have done this many times in the past and it has always proven to be extremely effective.

One connection reaches back out to you and gives a stellar review of their favourite solution, the value it brings to their business and then mentions the amazing account management they have experienced along the way. Wouldn't you feel immediately compelled to explore the solution further? I would.

You simultaneously notice a blog post shared by one of your connections on LinkedIn that happens to work for one of the vendors you are evaluating. You reach out with a private message. They respond. And the next thing you know you have a software demo the very next week.

I shared this common scenario to make a very specific point. Employees of a company give you the opportunity to reach new audiences that you could not normally reach with your branded channels or by paying for it.

Research from Cisco shows that employees have 10× more followers than corporate social accounts. What's more, a 12 per cent increase in brand advocacy generates a 2× increase in revenue growth (Hawley, 2014). These two data points alone are reason enough to explore employee advocacy programmes for your sales team. But there's more.

Just in case you are not fully bought in or up to speed on social selling, I'll add another tidbit: 72 per cent of salespeople using social media as part of their sales process outperformed their peers and exceeded quota 23 per cent more often. And, there is a direct correlation between closed deals and social selling tactics: 54 per cent of survey respondents have tracked closed deals to engagement on social media (ASG Consulting, 2016).

Now, imagine if not only your entire sales team was using social media to sell, but your entire company was doing the same.

Employee advocacy is the bee's knees when it comes to trust. It benefits everyone, has the power to fuel brand awareness, boosts the effectiveness of content marketing, improves organic reach and drives new revenue. So yes, employee advocacy and social selling are one and the same, and I am not the only one who agrees.

INSIGHT   Social-selling expert and thought leader

Contribution from Jim Keenan, CEO of A Sales Guy

If you are a sales person and care about your clients, your personal development, your career and your company, then I have a message for you: it's 2017, and we're failing our customers, prospects, the companies we work for and ourselves.

In the past 15 years, there have been crazy advancements in the area of sales tools, from CRMs that do just about everything except your laundry to data or insights applications that deliver a full dossier of your client's life straight to your phone or desktop. Shoot, there are even apps that tell you when to call a prospect and what to talk about.

Not surprisingly, advancements in the sales world did not just come in the area of tools and applications; they also came via new organization structures like inside sales, inbound marketing, account-based marketing (ABM) and more, all to make selling more efficient, faster and more predictable. Selling has been turned on its head by technology. It has never been easier to sell.

Yet, I lament, it appears we are doing less selling than ever. We have become slaves to the machine. In spite of all the new tools, new methodologies and insights, our commitment to the craft of selling is waning, and it's time we become the valuable purveyors of change that our prospects expect from us.

Too many of us are operating from 20th-century sales rules that no longer apply, and it is no longer okay or acceptable. Consider the rules below for 2018 and beyond.

Rule 1: care about your customers and prospects

I mean genuinely care about your prospects and buyers' success and business. Put them first, become an expert in their business, be able to bring value to them before you ask for something in return. Your prospects are the ones with the money; they are the people with a problem, treat them that way. I don't suggest you be their bitch, but for sure stop looking at them as an ATM. Put your customers and prospects first. Build your selling methodology around them, and you cannot go wrong.

Rule 2: you don't matter

Your prospects and customers don't care if you are the top sales rep or winning awards. They care about their business and are looking for you to make a difference in THEIR world. They have their own set of goals, objectives and needs that have nothing to do with you. Stop getting upset when they cancel a meeting, don't show up to a call or choose the competition. It's not personal. Neither you nor your product are at the centre of the universe. Pull up your big-boy pants and move on. The truth is, it is probably your screw up that cost you the deal in the first place.

If you want to sell better, just keep in perspective, you don't matter.

Rule 3: stop sending stupid e-mails

The number of stupid e-mails that salespeople send out is at an all-time high. Stupid e-mails are e-mails that do nothing for the recipient. They are selfish requests for time, and rarely offer anything of value for that time. Stupid e-mails unnecessarily interrupt a prospect's day. No, your buyer does not want to give you 15 minutes in their crazy busy schedule to tell you about their organization or discuss how you can improve their business. Just stop.

If you cannot offer something of value in the e-mail that is not product specific, don't send it. Learn how to create e-mails that create value for the recipient. Learn to create e-mails that teach, educate and inform the recipient. Learn to write e-mails that give more than they are asking.

Rule 4: you're not that good

It's time you stop thinking that because you have made President's Club five years in a row and because you are one of the tops salespeople you have nothing to learn. You're not that good. You have plenty to learn, especially if you are over 35. Sales is and has been going through incredible changes, yet too many of you think that you have seen it all and there is nothing you need to know. Sales is a fluid, ever-changing environment and assuming that you have completed the learning journey is a mistake. Have some humility, be open to new things, expand your craft and embrace deliberate learning.

Rule 5: stop blaming the prospect

It is not the prospect's fault if they don't return your call. It is not the prospect's fault if they choose the competitor. You cannot blame the prospect if they continue to push you on price. It is not the prospect's fault, so stop blaming them for your poor selling. Prospects are busy, and they are not beholden to *you*! They are trying to run a business. They have goals they are trying to meet. They have bosses, employees, peers and more all demanding their time. You are not their number one priority. If a prospect is ignoring you, it's your fault. If a prospect is fighting you on price, it's your fault. If a buyer chooses your competition over you, you didn't do a good job selling. Don't blame the prospect. Instead, provide more value, and stop wasting their time. It's not the prospect's fault – it's yours.

Rule 6: ask good questions not stupid questions

'What keeps you up at night?' – that is a stupid question. 'What are you looking to accomplish?' – that is a stupid question. 'What are your goals?' – that is also a stupid question. Most of the questions you ask are stupid questions. Why? See rule 1. You are asking questions to sell your product or service. You are asking questions that benefit you, not questions that help identify and solve real issues, or challenges that your prospect may be struggling to address. Your prospect knows what his or her goals are. They know what they are trying to accomplish, and asking them questions they know the answers to, so you can attempt to sell them your product, is not selling. It is just annoying.

Rule 7: yes, you have to use the CRM

The CRM is there to help you, and if you use it correctly it will be your best friend. If you don't think the CRM is useful, then you are using it wrongly. Today's CRMs do so much more than store a few names and numbers. They are central data hubs that can supply you with everything you need to engage with your prospects the right way. If the data in your CRM is not helping you, if you find the CRM to be a pain in the ass, take a good look in the mirror, 'cause it ain't the CRM. The CRM is a tool, like any other tool. It's only as good as its handler.

Rule 8: you're not ready for a promotion

Hey millennials and wily veterans, you're not promotion material. Just because you have made quota a few times, earned a few rewards or trips to Hawaii, promotion to sales management has nothing to do with your ability to sell. We already have too many unqualified sales managers screwing up sales organizations because they were promoted for being great salespeople. Sales management is about leadership. It is no longer about turning the screw but getting others to turn the screw. If you want a promotion, start learning to lead. Embrace how to motivate, influence and drive people, because that is what sales needs in sales management. Just because you are a badass salesperson does not mean you are promotional material. You're not ready!

Rule 9: you're not exempt from *anything*

Yup, you're a great salesperson, you're crushing it every month. You've never missed quota. Your customers love you. You're Ms reliable. Great, but that does not mean you get special treatment. Put your contacts into the CRM. Show up at the team meetings. Support the other representatives on the team. Share best practices. Be present at company functions. Be a visible, productive part of the team and the entire organization. Just because you are the top rep does not mean you get to operate from a separate set of rules. You're not a lone wolf; you're not special, so stop acting like it. Doing your job well does not entitle you to special treatment. You are not exempt from anything.

Rule 10: stop pushing your product

Feature-function selling is dead. It's not selling, and no one cares about how many features your product has or how fast it can process information. Buyers are trying to get stuff done, and your annoying pitches about how great your product and company are is frustrating and wasting everyone's time. It's 2018. Buyers can look at your site, trial your product or ask others what features you have.

Rule 11: do your homework

Take the time to learn a little something about your prospect. Do the research, know what your buyer does, what the company does, know what division he or she operates in, understand who their competition is, know what their overall corporate goals are, know what is important to them. Your buyer is not an unknown entity; they produce content. They write blogs. They may be public. They have a social media presence, etc. There is no excuse not to know someone before you reach out. Put in the time, stop being lazy and get acquainted with the people and companies that you are calling. It is not their job to educate you on who they are.

Rule 12: elevate your game

Selling is a craft. You are not a carnival barker, working a crowd to find the unsuspecting sucker who will drop the last of his hard-earned money on your rigged game. You're a sales professional and your value is in providing solutions to companies big and small. Your job is to help businesses increase revenue, reduce churn, improve customer loyalty, save money, improve processes, and more. These are not small, immaterial efforts. As a salesperson, you have the ability to substantially change the game for hundreds, thousands or even tens of thousands of individuals – so act like it. Expand your business acumen. Elevate your communication game. Improve your critical-thinking skills. Become a sophisticated sales leader, relied on for insight, advice and direction.

Rule 13: social selling – just do it and stop talking about it

Employee advocacy and social selling are one and the same. Yes, it is a very specialized audience (and somewhat difficult to work with) and the content is different. But at the end of the day, you have to motivate your teams to participate. And the fact that you are reading this book is a very good first step. Companies that are embracing social selling as a business model are the ones that are growing revenue, stealing market share for their competitors and paying mass amounts in commissions as a result.

Now go on, sell that product or service and make your millions. You can thank me later.

Employee advocacy as a business model

06

Employee advocacy happens only when employees feel passionate about what they do, what they are selling and who they serve. It happens when they feel committed to the organization and its mission, and are compelled to share its message because they truly believe in it. And so, the truth about cultivating employee advocacy is that it is far more involved than encouraging employees to look at, 'like' or share branded content. It is not enough to ask, or even to require them to do it – true employee advocacy goes much deeper and spreads far wider. It is dependent on changes that begin at the top and resonate all the way down through the deepest branches of a company's roots.

If the idea of developing an employee advocacy programme seems intimidating, it is worth remembering a few key things: first, the positive impact of a successful, internal brand army has undeniable and unmatched ROI. Second, there are rarely people in a better position than your employees when it comes to understanding intimately your company's mission statement and values, how your products or services work, and why the organization is worth paying attention to. Finally, there are proven strategic business outcomes that any company, of any size, can achieve with employee advocacy programmes.

It is incredibly important that your approach to building an employee advocacy programme be grounded in strategy. Unleashing the power of your employees, if they are unsure of any parameters or goals associated with their actions, is comparable to firing a shotgun instead of a sniper rifle. True, your ammunition may spread wider initially, but it will also fall shorter, you will be unable to accurately predict or follow where it lands, and there's a decent chance you won't hit your target at all.

Driving brand awareness, internally

In their earliest stages, employee advocacy efforts can and should be small. The strategic skeleton of the programme should be built out and solidified – and even beta tested – before it is rolled out company-wide. In fact, you can think of the way you approach developing an internal advocacy programme in the same way that you will later see that employee advocacy succeeds: from a central hub of activity to an outward-spreading trend, kind of like a sunburst.

There are several, very good reasons to start small and scale up, but the best one is that introducing a new process or programme is basically like starting an entirely new business. You begin with a solid, vetted plan; recruit a small group of people who support your idea; collaborate to determine an agreed-upon method of moving forward; and you find more people willing to invest time and energy into your idea. Then, you launch.

While you may worry that these attempts to establish an advocacy programme will be easy for most of the organization to overlook, it doesn't matter. It is not necessary for these efforts to be adopted universally right away, and attempting to force wildfire implementation could completely backfire – you don't want employees to see their participation as an obligation, a burden or an interruption to the work they are there to do.

This is where driving brand awareness with *internal* marketing becomes critical. Sadly, most companies do not have an internal marketing strategy at all, and if they do, it is not done very well. Although the last few decades have shown immense progress in leaders being transparent with their employees about direction, global initiatives, financial data, successes and areas for improvement, the majority also take for granted that their employees believe in the brand and its power. It does not help that the task of sharing information is usually foisted upon people who lack the marketing and communications skills to make those messages resonate (sorry, HR). So, company news and information piles up in people's inboxes – often in the form of overtly cheery newsletters and memos that employees don't read – and zero evolution happens.

Thankfully, there are entire industries dedicated to figuring out how to get people to think a certain way or believe a certain thing. No, not politics: *storytelling*. This is an industry that has spent centuries developing and honing a set of gospel-like principles designed to convince people to think and act a certain way. With a little bit of customization, these same principles can be applied when establishing, and growing, brand awareness and employee advocacy programmes. The primary goal of utilizing this strategy is to build a stronger connection between your brand and its people, much in the same way you do to drive customer loyalty outside of the office walls. There are countless studies showing that employees who care about the work they do will almost always do better work; it follows, then, that employees who care about the work their company is doing will be more likely to support it, facilitate it and talk about it (and with far less urging).

Rule 1: ride the coat tails of unrelated change

Once you have established the basic architecture of your advocacy programme, keep your launch schedule flexible. You cannot, and should not, try to force an initiative so totally dependent on individual buy-in. So, keep an eye open for opportunities where people are more likely to be receptive to new things, such as beginning-of-the-year sales kickoffs, during an acquisition, or when there are changes to executive personnel. And, though the instinct for leadership is to lay low during times of challenge and strife (for example, layoffs, economic issues, legislature changes, failing to hit profit goals), they can actually work really well for the introduction of new processes and tasks.

The theory goes that, during periods of disruption or after year's end, employees are going to be primed to look ahead, and will be very interested in information on how the company is doing, guidance for their roles and security in their positions. They will be more open to revised procedures, additional responsibilities, updated company goals, and improved structures that help them feel assured in their work and confident in the continued success of the business. Leaders who choose to be vocal about innovative initiatives while people are feeling unsure will find that this more nebulous emotional climate is great for implementing strategies intended to further growth. They are more likely to stick, because these new ideas and strategies will be seen as a response to existing ideas that are not working – and are, therefore, worth trying.

Rule 2: identify and enlist existing brand ambassadors

Imagine that you are attempting to convince a person who has never eaten an oyster to eat an oyster. They are interested, but they are also freaked out – maybe because they don't know what to expect, or if they will like it, or if it will make them sick. So they start asking you questions; they want you to describe the taste, the texture, the reason you like them, how often you eat them and what made you want to in the first place. And then they find out that you have never actually tried one, either. Chances are, you're not convincing them to give it a go any time soon. Unless, of course, you tell them you'll try it if they do.

This is one of the reasons that case studies are such an incredibly effective customer marketing tool: you can get decision makers to try a product or service because other companies that are similar to their own have done so, or are willing to. There is something inherently trustworthy about a person or entity that is willing to align their own experiences or reputation with a brand, and it makes the brand seem more credible by association. It takes some of the risk away for potential users, and can also make competing companies experience serious fear of missing out (FOMO), which is great for the company selling the product. No one wants to dismiss a potentially amazing tool that their competitors are using successfully.

The oyster example is also a great way of going about mirror marketing; that is, reflecting external marketing practices in your internal marketing efforts. The days of the customer always being right may not be dead, exactly, but they have at least morphed into 'we should probably ask the customer what they want so we can make that happen, and while we're at it, we should see what our employees think'. There are a couple of key reasons for this, but the biggest one – and the one you should care about – is that many people working in today's growing businesses were attracted to the company they were hired at because of what the company does, why they do it, or who they are doing it for.

Money and perks are always going to be a factor, but study after study of emerging workforces have shown that what employees truly care about these days is being efficient, ensuring the long-term future of their organization, opportunities to advance their knowledge and understanding in their field, and being the best at what they do for a company that is the best in its market (Deloitte, 2016). In other words, they are completely ready to jump in head first and become advocates. They just need a way to do it. And you can begin with these people – easily identifiable by asking a few simple questions – as your brand ambassadors.

These are the beta testers, the walking case studies, the patient zeroes of your employee advocacy programme. They can already explain what your product or service is, what it is like, how it feels to use it, why they love it, and how it has helped them. They are probably already sharing these things with friends, family and co-workers, and because they mean what they are saying, their support will always ring true – especially with those peers of theirs who may not be quite as willing to hop on the advocacy train.

Rule 3: involve employees in the brand definition process

It is an unfortunate habit of many companies to confine employees to their job titles. Whether it is purposeful or completely unintentional, the result is often the same: a vast pool of creativity, innovative solutions, valuable experiences, unique perspectives, and great ideas that go completely and utterly untapped. It is a crushing waste of a totally cost-free resource, made all the more regrettable because, with a little bit of effort, it is actually quite easy to utilize.

In general, there are two primary schools of thought when it comes to asking for employee feedback: the first uses standardized questions to unearth themes that can then be dealt with accordingly. For example, if 90 per cent of responses to the annual, multiple-choice employee survey show that people across the company feel underpaid, or that there is not enough vacation time available, leaders can decide or not decide to do something about it. And if they *do* choose to fix the issue, the task of figuring out how to do it is delegated to a small team, and treated like an open-and-shut case. It is a fairly typical way of handling negative employee feedback, particularly at larger companies with complicated hierarchies.

While that seems a bit dismissive, it is the second mindset that is actually dangerous. In this scenario, the people asking the questions are not really interested in honest evaluations; instead, they are after validation. Surveys, yearly reviews and the like will be formatted in such a way that employees will have a difficult time providing valuable assessments of anything. Many people have, at some point in their professional careers, taken a survey for which the purpose is not to invite constructive criticism but, rather, to give managers proof, on paper, that things are just fine the way they are.

You may have seen this yourself, if you have encountered questions like, 'On a scale of 1–10, how much do you like the new company logo?' or 'True or false: my manager gives me the support I need to do my job.' These kinds of questions seem innocent enough, but they are fundamentally useless if you actually want to know where change is needed and how to make it happen. Why? Because they leave absolutely no room for elaboration or explanation. And, in the case of the first question, responders are not even given the option of 'disagreeing' with the decision they are being asked about – a score of 1 is still a positive score – which essentially means they are being forced, on some level, to say they approve of whatever it is they are being asked about.

Smart, passionate people do not usually take kindly to this type of thinly veiled manipulation, so in addition to being unproductive, this approach to employee feedback can be downright alienating.

All of this is critical to keep in mind if you are serious about instituting a true employee advocacy programme that will grow and benefit the business – because, as you are already well aware, your employees are going to be a fairly crucial part of that process. And you want them to know that. You want them to be invested, and interested, and to know the brand inside and out. So the brand (that is to say, leadership) has to do them the same courtesy.

If you are heading up the development of employee advocacy efforts, ask people open-ended questions about what they think is wonderful and what they think is bad, and leave your own thoughts out of it (for now). Hold focus groups covering everything from logo colours to taglines, the voice of your content, target audiences, product offerings, and everything in between. Do your due diligence, and once you have listened and considered and tested, then you will be ready – not only to make changes where it turns out they are necessary, but to start asking people to actively support what the company is doing.

When it comes time to actually launch your programme, you will be able to cultivate a connection with your people with a thoughtful internal campaign that gets them acquainted with the company message, clearly explains goals and how each employee contributes to them, and then reinforces them by making brand awareness and advocacy a cornerstone of the company culture.

Shifting brand perception

Much of the time, company leaders start thinking about pursuing employee advocacy because a tipping point arrives, usually in the form of unmet objectives, increased turnover, or something else that makes it clear that business as usual is not cutting it. It could be that profits are down, or returning customers are not really returning. Perhaps there is a crisis – remember the fiasco at United Airlines in April 2017? Or maybe the volume of user complaints has increased, or it is becoming difficult to manage workloads because so many positions seem to be unfilled. Whatever it is that is creeping up through the ranks and causing unrest, the gut reaction is almost always to question what is going on *outside* of the company, with competitors, or emerging products, or changing technologies – rather than to take a look at what is happening within the organization itself. That is completely normal. Human, in fact.

We have a collective habit of placing the blame for things going south on environmental factors and other influences we have no apparent control over. And it's true, there are always going to be forces at work that you, your leadership team and your product simply cannot govern. So, sometimes it is useful – especially during the fledgling stages of the process – to think of employee advocacy as psychotherapy for businesses. To do that, you will have to turn investigative efforts inward. You will have to do all of the things a person visiting a therapist must do, like be brutally honest about what the problems are, assess issues that make you extra uncomfortable, realize things you may not want to realize, or take actions that you have avoided in the past. But first, you will want to start with an exercise designed to help you figure out exactly what is causing any undesirable outcomes.

When you begin assessing how your brand is perceived, you may find that you need to start working on shifting that perception. This information can and should come from a variety of internal and external sources, so once again, be prepared to spend some serious time and effort on it, and be ready to make it a priority where it might not have been before. Regardless of your individual position in the company, it is always wise to collaborate on brand perception and revision initiatives – after all, the more input you gather, the more complete the image will be of what is really going on. First, you will need to ask the following questions, bearing in mind that you may have absolutely no idea what the answers are: 1) How do customers, the media or other firms currently perceive your brand? 2) How do you want them to perceive your brand going forward?

As you may have guessed, these are by no means simple questions. There will be research involved in finding comprehensive answers. You may have a few uncomfortable conversations, and many meetings with stakeholders, employees, journalists, analysts or other industry professionals to get to the bottom of it all. You will likely be surprised by some of the information that is brought to your attention, maybe even offended and disbelieving – but it is all for the greater good. You cannot effectively drive change if you don't find out what needs changing.

While you work to answer these overarching questions, you will also want to consider the following in every conversation you have, no matter the individuals involved:

- Are you actually delivering what you promise?
- Has a once popular or useful functionality been drastically changed or removed?

- Has there been a significant focus on one part of the company that has left other elements of the organization behind?

- What about a shift in the way the product works or is delivered to users?

- What practical changes can you make in the short term that will enable the business to deliver on the promises of the brand to customers?

- What long-term changes can you consider?

- Did core leaders change objectives without reflecting those changes in brand messaging or customer deliverables?

As you dig deeper, checking in on how brand information is disseminated throughout the company – particularly to teams and individuals that speak publicly in some way on behalf of the brand – will also become paramount. How are your direct customer-facing teams performing – not just customer service, but community managers, social media managers, bloggers, product marketers and salespeople? Are all of those teams aligned in the message, and does that message match internal communications and top-down edicts? Furthermore, could any of these possible disruptions cause you to miss out on attracting, or retaining, talented team members?

If it becomes clear that a major overhaul is necessary, assess your battles. Be thoughtful about how you execute major shifts in branding language. Recognize that hasty or demanding decisions can be interpreted as a sign of disorganization and panic, and are a great way to inspire false rumours and anxiety amongst employees. Know, too, that most, if not all, of the changes you decide to make can be heavily supported by – you guessed it – an employee advocacy programme.

For instance, the addition of processes to include engagement practices when content is released; a revision to policies that refocus business practices on brand awareness in addition to, and even over, task completion; or, rewards-based activities that encourage brand evangelism within the company and to prospects and clients.

That's not just a theory, either. Organizations that use advocacy as a tool for rebranding knock out several birds with one stone, dramatically improving employee engagement and expanding their army of brand advocates tenfold, at virtually no extra cost (Dynamic Signal, 2016). Research from a number of sources also suggests that companies with thriving employee advocacy programmes experience growth that is nearly twice as fast *and* twice as substantial as companies that do not. They also see an 87 per cent reduction in turnover and a 20 per cent improvement in overall performance (Social Media Today, 2015).

Educating customers the right way

Many company leaders are a little bit afraid of changing things up on their customers, and for a legitimate reason: some customers might not like the changes, and it might cause them to become *former* customers. However, there exists no better resource for determining how to meet customer needs than the very people you are trying to serve. If changes are made at least partially in response to feedback from existing customers – and you clearly demonstrate that fact – the risk of your user base taking a major hit becomes minimal, and well worth it. Understanding customer needs intimately greatly increases the chances that any rebranding efforts will resonate well with the company's user base and target audience. You will enhance people's trust and engagement with the product and overall brand, which in turn will do really great things for your reputation, profits and future strategic opportunities to leverage your customer base. But how can you best communicate that you have listened, learnt and taken action? How can you then get your customers to take action, too?

There are quite a few options to consider, but for maximum returns your best investment should be in educating your customers – not only on how to use your products and services, mind you, but on core company values, your mission, the story of how the organization began, and how they can become involved in the continuing evolution and success of the company. The methods with which you choose to educate your customers might vary a lot depending on what it is you are selling, but there are three things that should always be kept in mind, as set out below.

You always need to meet your customers where they already are (and that means mobile)

There is a super-good reason that all emerging products seem to come with an app, boast about being 'mobile-first', and highlight easy access or usability in every other sentence of their marketing collateral. The average person spends over 10 hours a day looking at screens, the majority of which is spent on a mobile device (CNN, 2016).

That number grows exponentially when meetings and travel are a big part of someone's job, so if your educational materials are not accessible or fully functional on mobile, you are going to miss out big-time on available opportunities to educate people. While you can depend somewhat on customers having an existing desire to learn more about your product and how it can help them or their business, it is crucial that it be easy for them to do so. Otherwise, you are looking at yet another threat to how your brand is perceived.

Remember your audience

Many a glorious product has failed to take off because the people developing and marketing it forgot something frustratingly basic: who their audience is. Granted, any content should deftly reflect the company branding, but when it comes to educational assets, the voice and presentation must be even more carefully scrutinized. Dial down on the marketing speak – the folks interacting with learning content are probably already customers, or interested in becoming customers – but maintain key messages. If the way the product works is complex, beware of getting too far into the weeds. Be concise and candid, but try hard not to sound patronizing (people are there to learn, not be made to feel ignorant). Finally, make it infinitely obvious that there are different options for further learning, training and information – and, of course, make sure those options are readily available.

Content diversity

A single piece of content should be served through several platforms. To educate customers, you need to build educational content. But you also have to consider the effectiveness of different learning media for different people. Some folks like to read at length when they are learning. Others prefer instructional videos and easy-to-digest presentations. Still others want a more interactive, test-and-explore option, or simply want to know what people who have built and used the product think about it. Does that mean you have to create 16 different educational assets from scratch? Thankfully, no. A much more efficient and effective option is to build a small, comprehensive, core set of content and present it in a variety of ways – blog posts, case studies, videos, podcasts, demos, presentations, or whatever format will suit your audience best. And even better? You have already set the precedent for finding out which content is most likely to work, because you have already established a dialogue with your employees and existing customers. Once you have used your findings to build and deliver the content, you can then find out how well it is doing, simply by requesting feedback about its helpfulness (and being willing to iterate where necessary).

Once again, employee advocacy will play a critical role in effectively reaching the customers who are primed to become external brand evangelists. Only with content creators, engineers, marketers, salespeople and other teams that fully understand and believe in your message will you manage to convey it beyond the conference room.

Filling the sales pipeline

Educating your customers does a lot more than help them learn how to use your product, because the focus is not on how awesome your stuff is. Instead, well-executed educational content demonstrates how much better off your customer or prospect will be at what *they* do if they use it. And that shift in approach will help fatten your sales pipeline by: 1) converting prospects into customers; and 2) turning customers into true brand evangelists, who will in turn recruit more prospects.

Enter employee advocacy (again), which, after the initial processes of understanding and implementation, has a great deal to do with the *how*. Most often, the how is social media, which is the most powerful, far-reaching way to significantly drive brand awareness and increase your sales pipeline. In fact, one study showed that about 73 per cent of salespeople engaging in social selling outperform non-social media users, and exceed quota 23 per cent more often (Salesforce, 2016).

What is really wonderful is that the same rules of success apply to all of a company's employee advocates, and it is here that one of the most astounding benefits of an advocacy programme shows itself. Some of the most rewarding advocacy is also the most visible, because it happens when people share news about the company and branded content to their extended personal and professional networks – or, when they use those networks as a tool to tailor their advocacy efforts.

Social channels are havens of information, where customers and prospects do not really hesitate to post personal details, exhibit personality traits, demonstrate identifying characteristics and talk candidly about what they think of the products and services they try. While dedicated research into customer feedback can be time-consuming and require a bit of budget, social media channels regularly act like minute-by-minute, open-source libraries of consumer data. With the right tools in place, you can discover what is necessary to tailor marketing strategies and develop targeted, meaningful campaigns.

There are a few less obvious, but no less strategic, ways to catch a prospect's attention using your employee advocacy programme, too, as set out below.

Identify and utilize covert operatives

Okay, that probably sounds a lot cooler than it really is, but the idea here is to use employees who are not necessarily salespeople to get prospects to pay attention to your company. Share buyer personas, targets, verticals and other information with your employees, and let them be the ones to put company news and content in front of the prospects – either by congratulating them if they show up in a byline, or by studying their social behaviours and sharing relevant content that they are actually likely to be interested in. Neither of these tactics is an obvious bait, but if done thoughtfully will put your company in the prospect's sights.

Co-collaboration on company events and initiatives

This does not sound cool at all but it is certainly effective when you enlist employees to recommend or invite prospects to be an integral part of company events.

This approach may require a sales or marketing person at some point, but not necessarily – and not at first. If your content marketing programme is healthy, you are likely already holding regular webinars and promoting compelling external content alongside your own. Again, you can leverage employee advocates to expand the range of targets with which you have no direct connection. For example, ask people to scour their individual networks and submit recommendations for new webinar hosts, or suggest thought leaders to contribute to your blog. You will continue to show your advocates that they are useful and valued, all while developing important new connections with potential customers.

Show off your product to employees and existing customers

You might be wondering why razzle-dazzling the people who already work for your company and use your product is a useful way to spend your time. It seems a little counterintuitive if what you really want to do is expand your sales pipeline. But remember that passion leads to investment, which leads to loyalty, which in turn leads to support. Sometimes you have to remind existing proponents of why they love what you do, and why they should keep sticking around. So, whether you decide to make reinvigoration a regular task or something that is only necessary when a new feature is introduced, rest assured that it is one of the simplest and most effective ways to ensure continued dedication. Which leads to enthusiasm. Which then leads to sharing. And then a bigger sales pipeline.

Solving customer support issues

With an army of employees on the front lines of the internet, one thing you will want to turn your attention to is streamlining and correcting customer support issues. It is certainly possible that you have a killer customer support team that responds to queries instantly, handling them deftly and only escalating problems that they just cannot solve. But even if that is true, participants in your employee advocacy programme can serve as an extension of that service. If it's not true, they can help you fix what's broken.

First things first, though: it is actually fairly important that employee advocates think of themselves as part of the customer service and support process, whether they are in engineering, finance or marketing. Simply put, advocates are brand representatives in everything they do and say that could, in some way, end up in front of a customer or target. So part of their evangelism should focus squarely on keeping an eye out for any rumblings that indicate someone is dissatisfied with your product. If they can help, wonderful – if they can't, or don't feel that it is appropriate, they can at least connect people with employees who can.

In extension mode, non-customer service employees can do a couple of really valuable things. They can unearth issues that are cropping up outside of the official customer service realm, and they can help lighten the customer service team's workload. They can even galvanize the problem-solving process. You see, customers and prospects do not have a negative experience and then spend time thinking about which part of the company or product was responsible for it. They associate whatever they encounter with your company as a whole, so even if they have had a jolly time up until the software malfunctions, the subsequent customer service they experience is going to colour their entire perception of your brand. And since all of us have, at some point, been the victim of a product not functioning quite right, it is universally known that the biggest factor in whether you consider customer service to be good or bad is not actually dependent on how knowledgeable the agent you speak to is, or whether the outcome lives up to your expectations. Rather, it is how fast your problem gets acknowledged in the first place. Remember, disgruntled customers don't care what department you work in. They just want the problems solved quickly and efficiently.

Employee advocates can give you a massive advantage here. Because they have ears to the ground for any and all dialogue going on about the company, there is a very real chance that they will find out about product bugs, login issues, or downed web pages long before anyone hits up the customer service chat box (which sometimes doesn't happen at all). With the right training and understanding of the product and messaging, they can reach out directly to the people having issues and give them a hand. Knowing that someone from the company is taking care of them is the absolute best way you can start out a customer service transaction on a positive note, even if the employee who reached out is 'Jenny from the design team' or 'Michelle from marketing'. No one cares about exactly *who* has acknowledged that they need help – what they do care about is the reassurance and feeling of connection that comes from an actual person saying that they will make sure the problem is handled.

With employee advocacy, the customer experience becomes everyone's job, which will make your organization's ability to deal with issues exponentially more powerful and swift.

Providing insights for innovation

Given the way that employee advocacy works, it is fair to say that it is quite a bit like crowdsourcing. You are getting input and effort on various aspects of the company from a much larger group than is solely dedicated to those things, and it can dramatically alter how you do business. More people means more perspectives, more experience, and way more ideas. And when you start crowdsourcing ideas, you also start to see major breakthroughs in innovation.

Lots of companies confine innovation to a small team, or hold the misguided belief that product 'experts' are the only people able to catalyse change. But when you task everyone with developing innovative solutions – whether for improved product functionalities or to figure out what your next physical mailer should look like – you get to see how different people perceive the business challenge at hand. You also get to take advantage of any unique solutions they suggest for dealing with it.

Involving your entire employee base in innovation also surfaces more opportunities to accelerate and test processes, learn from the different ideas you try and implement viable suggestions more quickly. Transparent, collaborative problem solving between disparate teams – but teams that are well-versed in brand guidelines and company initiatives – allows new ideas to be mulled over, vetted, dissected and evolved almost simultaneously. This greatly reduces their chance of failure, and can also influence people to think more broadly about their work as individuals and as a representative of the company.

Additionally, there are some highly useful by-products to making innovation a central part of your employee advocacy programme. At the top of the list is strengthening engagement across teams. Much like customers want to know that their feedback is being heard, employees want to know that their experience, opinions, ideas and intelligence are respected and welcomed. By asking for their input, you are demonstrating that they hold value to the company beyond their ability to write code or use professional design software.

Expertise in a particular area, though, can actually be a hindrance to innovating for that area, which is why collaborative ideation is such a beneficial exercise. When employees are given the chance to think outside of their specific roles, they can provide wonderfully unique insight into what is working and what is not, even if they cannot tell you exactly why that is. It is the same reason focus groups always involve a hyper-diverse group of people: how we use things and why we like them (or don't) is heavily dependent on our personal experiences, existing knowledge and perspectives.

For example, an engineer might not be bothered that a certain app requires six different pieces of information to work, because they inherently understand the complexity behind intersecting data points; a copyeditor, on the other hand, probably does not – or if they do, they may not care. They just want the app to work, and no amount of explaining why so many details are necessary is going to make them like it any more. By putting these two opposing perspectives together, under the umbrella of overarching company goals, a viable, working solution can take shape. Think of how much more precise and powerful a solution could be if it is born from 10 perspectives, or 100.

Another fantastic benefit of applying employee advocacy to innovation is maximizing opportunities while mitigating risk. With so many smart, creative brains working together to improve and expand ideas, inspiration and further ideation is going to happen at rapid-fire speed. People will naturally consider how all of the ideas before them may or may not succeed, what can be done to make them work, or why they simply won't. Opportunities and dangers will surface, only to be crushed, supported or modified so they make sense. This diversification of idea generation and analysis ensures that you are discovering a complete catalogue of insights that will help you do business better.

Once you have established a solid internal process, you can even begin leveraging your customer base for innovation, further broadening the pool of potential that you are able to tap into.

Influencing peers to purchase

Marketers and brand managers spend a lot of time, energy, resources and budget trying to understand what messaging via traditional media will resonate with their target audiences (which calls to action will spark the most clicks, conversations, etc). Millions of dollars are spent on media that aims to create marketing messages in each of the phases – awareness, consideration, preference, purchase and loyalty. And smart marketers also create metrics models for each phase of the purchase funnel to measure the effectiveness of those messages. However, the purchase funnel is no longer a funnel, it's circular.

Employee advocacy is now at the centre of the model. It is meant to illustrate the power of social media and how employees can potentially aid and influence their peers and micro-communities down the purchase funnel via authentic messages (or everyday conversations). The model (Figure 6.1)

Figure 6.1 Employees can aid and influence peers to purchase

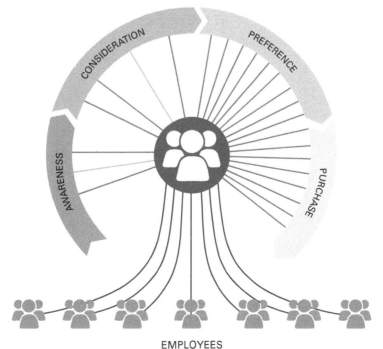

EMPLOYEES
(EXECS, SUBJECT MATTER EXPERTS, AMBASSADORS)

is now circular and the lines below represent industry conversations with others in the market.

As you consider employee advocacy a part of your business model, your employees have the opportunity to influence others at various phases of the purchase funnel – creating a cycle of influence and advocacy that you are facilitating through your employee advocacy programme. To bring it full circle, over 84 per cent of consumers place more value in recommendations from friends and family above all forms of traditional advertising – and, consumers are 77 per cent more likely to make a purchase after hearing about a product or service from a person they trust (Nielsen, 2013). While this data point is somewhat outdated, one could argue without much rebuttal that it is even more true today. The awesome thing about these statistics is that, when it comes to employee advocacy, the message being shared very rarely comes off as manipulative or pushy (unlike direct sales lingo, which too often appears to be both).

Part of the reason for this is that, when employees are truly invested in a company product and message, they internalize their support. It becomes part of their personal value system, so when they share information about the company, it comes out of a genuine belief that the person or entity they are sharing it with will benefit from checking it out.

A more businesslike way to think about this concept is through the lens of 'lateral leadership'. Lateral leadership happens when an individual or group has influence over outcomes and decisions without actually having positional authority over anything. An employee advocacy programme is a stellar example of this, since it consists of several people who are collectively supporting a product or brand. For people who are not familiar with a product, the more individuals who seem to trust it, the greater the likelihood that they will see it as more trustworthy, even if they know absolutely nothing else about the brand.

Internally, this means that initial employee advocacy efforts should first focus on converting people who are most likely to be impacted by any changes to the company or product. Once the programme expands and is being used for customer and prospect outreach, the same concept can be applied to reach out to influential prospects and existing customers with robust peer networks.

Employee advocacy is, it turns out, a lot more than just getting employees to 'retweet' or 'like' branded content. There are many business implications to think about, too, from changing the top-down approach for gathering and implementing feedback, to integrating employee advocacy into the company culture, and finally, to extending your advocacy efforts beyond the company's walls and putting it in the hands of your users.

And while there are numerous strategic imperatives to think about, the most critical thing to keep in mind is that having a strategy is imperative. You can neither anticipate nor track performance of any programme without first plotting what success looks like – for your business, your employees and your customers.

INSIGHT Social business expert

Contribution from Lauren Friedman, Head of Social Business at Adobe

Employees are essential advocates more than ever before. They are the number-one source of information, and guess what? They are trusted. It's not the boss, senior executives or media spokespeople. Consumers want to hear from people like themselves – engineers, product people and innovators. They want to hear from the baggage handler, not the head of baggage at an airline company. They want someone who has all the detailed information (because they are working on it every day), doesn't have an agenda, and can tell it to them straight. That someone is an employee. They are more like you, they are peers, and they understand what you actually want better than anyone else.

Trust is even more important in the age of the millennial consumer. Millennials are not influenced by advertising. They read blogs, Amazon and Yelp Reviews and Google everything before making any major purchase decisions. And, they value authenticity as more important than anything else. That is why your most trusted, valuable and most likely untapped marketing assets are your employees.

At Adobe, we have a social measurement team that is dedicated to determining the marketing metrics that matter and providing us with actionable insights into how our content is performing. What is interesting is that the top-performing social accounts are not always our Adobe-branded accounts, but rather individual employees. On LinkedIn, for example, our cumulative employee connections are seven times greater than the number of followers we have on our corporate LinkedIn pages. And they are engaged. In fact, 91 per cent of LinkedIn members who engage with our employees' content about Adobe are not engaging with Adobe content anywhere else on LinkedIn. What does that tell us? People want to see more from and engage with our regular employees because they know them and trust them.

Below are some things we have learnt along the way.

It's not just about a tool

Yes, the right tool will help you scale your employee advocacy programme. A tool will make it easy for employees to share content, build their community and monitor their performance. However, it is important to remember that employee advocacy is more about helping your employees build their personal brands than it is about creating an army of corporate bots. Building out a full-fledged programme with training, best practices, tips/tricks, webinars, speakers, exclusive events, and more, will not only inspire them to be true brand advocates, but will also help build that authenticity that is so important in today's trust economy.

Set clear key performance indicators and know which metrics matter

There are dozens of metrics available to measure the success of your employee advocacy programme. Think about the specific business objectives you are working to achieve, how employee advocacy can play a part, and only measure what matters. For example, say your objective is to drive more traffic and leads. You will want to measure click-through rate and lead-generation actions taken on your website (signing up for a newsletter, a webinar, white paper downloads, etc). Or maybe you want to increase brand awareness and positive perception towards your brand. In that case, you can measure the number of pieces of content shared, engagements and sentiment. What is most important is that your employee advocacy objectives feed directly into your existing business objectives.

Executive buy-in at every level is critical

Executive buy-in is one of the most important components to deploying an employee advocacy programme. And it starts at the top. If senior leaders support the programme, their management team will support it as well. Employees have enough on their plates and if their managers are not encouraging them (or even requiring them!) to participate, it is unlikely they will. Executive support stretches beyond just buy-in to the initial rollout of the programme. We have found success at Adobe when leadership is also an active participant in the programme, regularly communicating and encouraging their team in team meetings or one-on-ones.

Leaderboards with actionable insights inspire employees to engage more

Everyone likes a little bit of competition, right? Employee advocacy is no different. Employees want to see how they are performing against their peers. It creates a sense of comradery and incentivizes them to build actions from the programme into their everyday routines. Habit is key in sustaining an employee advocacy programme and leaderboards are one way to build that habit.

However, it is important that employees know how to improve. Providing them with a score and a standing is step one, but providing them with best practices and tips on how they can improve their scores will inspire them to continually improve and stay active.

Employee advocacy does not need to be a generic corporate programme

In fact, you could argue that it *shouldn't* be. In many cases, employee advocacy can be even more successful when it is tailored to meet the needs of a specific business function. For example, Adobe's Social Selling programme is an extension of our employee advocacy programme. It is geared towards our sales organization and we have tailored our training and employee advocacy goals to that specific team. Or perhaps consider using employee advocacy as a recruiting tool for talent acquisition teams. The opportunities are endless and these individualized programmes are ultimately all part of employee advocacy, but help employees personally to use their social presence to better accomplish their specific day-to-day jobs.

Remember, what your employees share is entirely their prerogative

At Adobe, we have an open philosophy towards social media. We work to enable and empower our employees to be active on social channels, while providing them with the right information to protect their own brand, Adobe's brand, and customer information. But we also understand that employees who opt-in to participate in this programme are using their own personal social channels to share Adobe news. This means we have to focus teaching on our core social media principles – authentic, responsible, involved and respectful – and trust our employees to act with integrity while representing themselves and the Adobe brand online.

PART THREE
Blueprint: launching your employee advocacy programme

Employee advocacy: a model for disruption

Employee advocacy works. There is no doubt that when planned and managed with care, an internal evangelism programme has the power to give companies the competitive edge necessary to move beyond boundaries that have previously held steady.

But as with so many business imperatives that do not have hard-and-fast rules or a universal template, executing an employee advocacy programme will require leaders to build a flexible, tailored and strategic approach that can unleash the full range of benefits within their particular organization and industry. But how do you do it? What overarching themes, challenges, roadblocks, risks and parameters do you need to consider? How can you mitigate these factors for the best chance of success? Furthermore, when you do start to see shifts and returns, what do you measure, and how do you measure it?

It is often these questions – and the hundred others that accompany them – that can stop a promising advocacy programme from taking root. It is intimidating to take on, especially if your existing company culture is hierarchical, siloed or otherwise divided by goals and policies. Even here, though, bringing all personnel into the fold of brand awareness can act as both a balm and a tool for eradicating outdated practices or a divisive organizational structure. By increasing engagement internally, you will give employees a feeling of committed brand ownership and vested interest in how the company is performing.

With this in mind, know that a solid foundation for advocacy can only be built when the people it will impact most are its top priority, and when their experiences, challenges and skills make up the core from which everything else is shaped and developed (Figure 7.1). Unlike most strategic undertakings, employee advocacy programmes cannot be created from the outside in.

Figure 7.1   Employee advocacy architecture

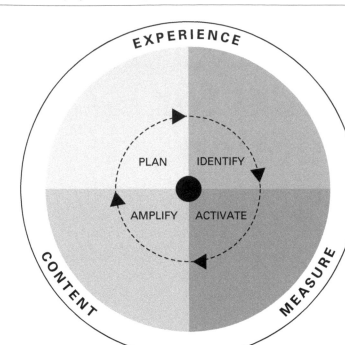

You cannot begin with customer needs and pain points at the forefront, and product features dominating everyone's time and space. Rather, as is implicit in the name of the initiative, you have to start at home.

Customize the employee experience

The tangible aspects of employee advocacy are all about storytelling, sharing, engagement and reach – or, more specifically, being able to drastically increase all of those things. Your company message, as well as the multitudes of content and sales assets that have been painstakingly created across teams, are the obvious external deliverables. But what about the internal ones?

It is crucial that you provide a tailored, personalized experience to your employees. Remember that there are two key layers to getting people to share and create branded content even after you have established the base and expectations of your employee programme. The first is ensuring that people will feel engaged with the way you ask them to participate and contribute. Your approach cannot be identical for every segment of employees. Rather, it should be aligned with their different interests and goals, cater to their various job functions and, if applicable, be available in their local languages.

If you work for a global company and have rolled out an employee advocacy programme, you would need to ensure that employees in Germany – as an example – would receive a unique experience. This means that the content and usability of a software platform must be tailored to their specific language, German. It is the same with sales or customer support and just about any other segment of employee that is participating. The experience must be unique and personal. It's not a one size fits all.

This takes work. Quite a bit of work, actually. It is not as simple, perhaps, as sending a company-wide e-mail with some blanket instructions and calling it a day. It could become more complicated as you scale. You might not get it right the first time, or the second. But just as your customers don't all reflect the same persona or point on the buyer's journey, your employees do not view the company mission, brand and its overarching strategies in precisely the same way. Your advocacy programme should reflect who your employees truly are as people and as representatives of your brand, and encompass what they do in their work.

It is really not all that different from the marketing and branding efforts you have in place for customers; you are still crafting communications that are designed to appeal to a target audience. It just so happens that this audience is internal – which, unlike your client base, comes with some very valuable added benefits.

Namely, accessibility – if something is not resonating, you can simply ask why and change your approach. Plus, you are far more likely to succeed early on because: 1) there is already a relationship between the brand and the employees, which significantly decreases the guesswork involved in figuring out how to speak their language; and 2) you have the luxury of being able to observe their behaviours from a front-row seat. This will be instrumental as you develop the language and processes for your advocacy programme, including the types of content you ask advocates to create and share, and the way you ask them to do both. You will also need this information to plan the timing of your requests in regards to what different teams are working on, when company events or conferences are taking place, and other influential, time-sensitive situations that may exist.

The second key layer of enticing employees to be and stay involved is the content itself – the assets and messaging you are asking them to share with their different networks. You may be wondering exactly how this works or why it matters. If it is branded content, and you need it disseminated, programme participants should just share it, right?

Wrong. Never forget that the only way employee advocacy works, and continues to work, is if employees are invested in what they are doing and believe in the value of what they are sharing. Their loyalty will quickly waver if they start to feel like they are being pushed to share content that doesn't mean anything to them, or that makes them appear to support something that doesn't gel with their outlook. This in no way means you need to create entirely new content or revise your messaging, but it does mean you will have to take a long look at the way teams in your company function and the dynamics they exhibit.

The content that companies create typically falls somewhere between sales and marketing, and since it is part of those teams' jobs to promote branded assets and messaging, it can be much trickier to get this right for personnel that live outside of those two camps. But there is a way, and it is actually fairly simple: align the content you choose as closely as possible with the goals of the people you want to see it and share it. For example, if your advocate is an engineer, they likely care deeply about your company's product and its functionality. They also understand how it works more intimately than other employees might, and since they have a great deal to do with how it is used, they will identify most with content that focuses on the way that your product or service helps users to be successful.

At the other end of the spectrum, employees on the creative side of things – designers, videographers and the like – are passionate about your company's (and product's) aesthetic, its interface, its message and its face-value differentiators. These folks may care less about how a product actually functions, but find its usability and purpose extremely important. Fittingly, content that helps clients better understand what they will get out of a product, how easy it is to implement, or that tells the stories of users who have had success is what the people on these teams will connect with most (see Table 7.1).

Table 7.1 Align sharable content topics with the right internal audiences

Job Function	Shareable Content Topics
Executives	industry-related topics, thought leadership
Sales	customer case studies, research reports, white papers
Engineering	in-depth technology and product material
Customer Service	how-to guides, proactive customer support topics
Marketing	general company news, announcements
HR	cultural, company news, hiring
Business Unit(s) or Brand	product-specific news, thought leadership
General Employees	all of the above

Profiling your various employees and vetting content that makes sense for each group is not a one-time exercise. It is necessary, for the health of your programme, that these personas remain flexible and that you do regular assessments of content as it is created or retired. After all, neither employees nor assets are unchanging. Branding and messages shift and industry disruptions happen. Your advocacy programme should not only be strong enough to withstand these inevitable business challenges, but also serve as a tool to help you weather them.

That means broadening your concept of advocacy, which as we have mentioned goes far beyond just getting employees to share content via social media channels. It also means involving people who are not normally content creators in the ideation and development stages of bringing new assets to life. As a rule, people are tired of company leaders, marketers and salespeople being the only voices of an organization. To limit your focus to selling, promoting and validating products and services is to become complacent. And, unfortunately, leaving the creation of customer-facing messages and assets solely to the people whose jobs revolve around those goals can do some real damage. In particular, it devalues everything you publish, because people are not fools. They know when they are being sold to, and they can tell the difference between a thinly veiled ad and a worthwhile read.

If the only person being bylined in external publications is your CEO, or every single blog you put out centres on the exact same message and perspective, it will not be too long before your audience – including employees *and* the people who actually use your stuff – disappears. The quality and integrity of your content matters at least as much as the number of times it gets shared, and usually quite a bit more.

Again, the solution to this problem requires nothing more than an open mind and a little faith in the uncommon: invite different teams to create content. Ask team leaders and supporters to author blogs, answer questions for videos, suggest survey topics, or brainstorm ideas for e-books and infographics. Encourage them to seek out opportunities to speak at conferences or on industry panels. Make media training a requirement for everyone. Above all, always remember that the greater the diversification of your advocate pool, the broader your reach will be, and the more extensive and rich your network will become. It doesn't hurt that people are inherently more dedicated to the success of things they have helped create, and are about 10 times more likely to share it with their networks (Link Humans, 2016).

Naturally, involving the majority of your employees in the development of assets is a process, and should be treated much the same way as you manage the distribution of existing content. Remember, it is the employees' experience that is paramount – so, you will want to align the types of content being developed with the people you are asking to be involved in developing it, and focus it on the work that they do.

Ask a data scientist to author a blog post about the way your software processes information. If they are not comfortable writing it, ask them for an outline. Have salespeople conduct customer interviews for case studies; and then help them make it a part of their normal client check-in process. Or, sit down with your engineering team to pick their brains about product intelligence so that your sales and marketing people can use the findings to shape new resources.

The most imperative piece here is to empower your employees to become storytellers – even those who are not at all used to speaking about the brand, let alone on behalf of it. As this practice expands across the business, and the conversations surrounding your company swell to include more diverse perspectives, the brand itself will become more human. People inside and out will start to see themselves as a vital part of it, see their values mirrored and their voices heard. The possibilities are enormous and the resulting benefits are immense – boosted loyalty, new connections between teams and individuals, deeper insight into how your products work and your organization functions, more innovation throughout the business, better collaboration across the company, new avenues with which to reach customers, and more valuable content to boot. Oh, and companies that place a premium on this type of open communication with employees are 20 per cent more likely to drastically reduce staff turnover (Winfrey, 2014). Since US $11 billion is lost annually due to employee turnover, that is some fairly indisputable ROI if you ask me (Everson, 2015).

There is one more aspect of the employee experience that should not be left out – and that is asking for their feedback. On everything. From the messaging you use internally to encourage participation in employee advocacy to the platform you use to make it happen. From where you ask them to share content to the sample social media posts you provide. From the types of content to the content topics themselves. From what your overall objectives are for the programme to how they will be measured, and how that will influence individual goals.

Anything and everything that impacts how employees experience an advocacy programme should be subject to their scrutiny, and it is critical that you are ready and willing to hear it. It is the only verifiable way to ensure the continued adaptability and success. And to do that, you also need to think about the business impact of your advocacy programme.

Establish your measurement framework

As mentioned in this book already a few times, it is important to recognize that your brand is regularly engaging in a widespread, multistakeholder conversation. Driving brand awareness or changing brand perception involves interfacing with customers, prospects, media, board members, investors and, of course, employees. New business requirements are forcing change to happen in areas that previously appeared steadfast. The demand for solutions that are not only innovative, but that are also built at the speed of light, is toppling companies that would rather try to make what they are already doing work, instead of reassess their approach entirely.

Resistance, as they say, is futile.

As you go about building your advocacy programme, keep in mind that people buy from people. Your internal communications about brand evangelism need to speak to employees where they are, perhaps even more so than the messaging you reserve for customers and the need to convince them that your product is better than the competition. This is particularly true when it comes time to measure the success of your programme, an intimidating exercise since participants are, essentially, volunteers. And volunteers can walk away at any time.

However, defining needs, goals and logistics up front can greatly improve the retention power of your programme. It sounds obvious, and maybe even a little dull, but you can think of it kind of like you would if you were preparing to bake a layer cake for the very first time. You have to have an idea of what you are trying to achieve in terms of taste and texture so that you can find the right ingredients, and the right tools, in order to properly follow the correct steps that will lead to the creation of a glorious dessert that will then be eaten and hopefully talked about for many years to come. Process before execution is vital to evolution – and you cannot bake your first cake without a recipe. You must define your goals, and those goals need to be clear and agreed upon before you can justly hold anyone to them.

That is why developing a solid, but still flexible, blueprint of success is the most practical initial step you will want to take. Below are a handful of key elements to consider as you begin building out the measurement framework that you will use to understand how your employee advocacy programme is performing. And it starts, like many things in life, with figuring out exactly what it is that you want to accomplish.

What does your brand want to achieve?

This is not always an easy question to answer, but start small, and look first to areas of the business that you know could do better. If you have an exceptionally high turnover rate, or are finding that work is being duplicated – or not done at all – the real issue may lie in how things are being communicated across teams. If your worries are external, such as a series of bad reviews from an influential analyst, or a decline in product ratings, product functionality may be to blame. Brand perception may be the thing you want to focus on fixing if you have noticed an uptick in negative social chatter. Or, if you work for a company with strict sales goals, perhaps the target is mobilizing the sales team through employee advocacy to increase the sales pipeline.

What you want to achieve could be even more quantitative: bigger returns, lowered expenses, shorter time to market, sales. Maybe nothing is wrong, exactly, but you want to grow and are not sure how to do it. Whatever the case may be, figuring out *why* you are trying to implement employee advocacy is the absolute first step to defining a framework for its success. We will explore this topic in more detail in Chapter 8.

What business and marketing outcomes are expected?

After you determine all of your concrete reasons for turning to employee advocacy, it is time to tie those reasons to outcomes. In general, these will probably be both qualitative and quantitative to some degree, but you should assign tangible values wherever possible. Reduced turnover, bigger profits, a larger customer base, increased share of voice, more enterprise sales, or more media mentions are fairly easy to measure. But something as seemingly ambiguous as 'happier employees' is still a wonderful and totally achievable goal – you just need to define what that looks like for your specific organization.

Taking a granular look at measurement and KPIs

Before going into too much detail about measurement, key performance indicators (KPIs), analytics and all the things that maths geeks love to talk about, let's visit a quick data point from an Accenture study back in 2014. According to the study, 78 per cent of CMOs believe that marketing will undergo fundamental change over the next five years. This change will be driven by analytics, as well as digital and mobile technologies (Accenture, 2014). More importantly, the same study revealed that 42 per cent of CMOs believe that analytics skills will be a core competence of marketing.

So as you read the rest of this book, ponder this question: do you have analytics capabilities within your marketing organization and is it a core competency? The five-year mark is right around the corner so it is not too late to learn how to be data driven. In today's competitive environment, it's table stakes.

The time for assumptions is over. Marketers must know the impact of their programmes and campaigns. In order to determine success you must have a baseline of data that backs up your story. This data will help you to understand exactly what tactics are producing a desired action from your audience, and which ones need to be modified in order to generate the results you are looking for. More importantly, the data you are measuring – clicks, share of voice, engagement, traffic – will then allow you to determine what outcomes you are achieving and how they align with the business objectives of the company.

Your employee advocacy programme is no different than any other marketing programme or campaign. It is critical to track every send, view, click, share, like and reaction, and more importantly, you will have to tie those data points back to your business goals. You must be able to easily turn your data into a compelling business story, and explain it in a way that your colleagues and executives will understand. Doing so will allow you to declare your programme a success and obtain the internal buy-in should you need to expand and grow.

Capturing data is easy, understanding data not so much. Most employee advocacy platforms provide the basics – high-performing content, active users, adoption, etc. However, telling a story with that data requires a deep understanding of the information you are collecting. Because of the difficulty in that, your story is often left untold, making it hard to realize and justify how successful your programme is, and potentially leaving business value on the table.

There are three pillars to measuring an employee advocacy programme that contribute to overall programme success. Each of these pillars, although independent, are highly correlated and require upfront planning to ensure your infrastructure is in place:

- **Measuring programme adoption**: how many employees joined the programme?
- **Measuring participation and engagement**: how many employees are viewing, sharing and creating content?
- **Measuring real business outcomes**: are you achieving your business objectives?

Most employee programmes today focus solely on the first two pillars of programme measurement – adoption and participation – and often forget to align KPIs back to actual business objectives. There are three reasons for why this happens:

1 The current technology application is not capable of tracking enough data both within the platform and/or on social platforms (eg Facebook, Twitter, LinkedIn).

2 The current technology is not integrated with other enterprise services such as Eloqua or Google Analytics.

3 They don't even think about it.

What happens with the first two options is that data is limited, or your data is fragmented amongst different enterprise services and it is difficult to connect the dots to tell a broader story. You don't want to be in a position where you are unable to measure success all the way to programme objectives. This is why upfront planning is so important as you will be able to identify and assess your specific business needs and make sure the dots are connected from beginning to end before launching your programme. Reading this book is a very good first step.

And to address reason three, well to quote a famous hip hop artist from New York who is no longer with us, '… and if you don't know, now you know!'

Measuring programme adoption

Early success consists of giving your employees access to the platform and making sure they are able to successfully discover, view and share your content, and making it easy to do so. You want to focus on a few things:

1 How many employees have easy access to the platform.

2 How many employees have actually accessed the platform.

3 How often these employees are returning to the platform on a continual basis.

Example company data: measuring programme adoption

- 60 days ago you invited 1,000 employees to participate in the programme.

- Since then, 800 employees registered (80 per cent registration rate).

- 500 employees access the platform each day (50 per cent daily active users).

- 650 employees connected their social channels, giving your company a total potential reach of 936,000.

Examining and tracking this data allows you to watch for any trends, monitor potential drop-off and answer a few very specific questions: did employees not join the platform or did they register and just never return? Also, it can give you direction to better align your content strategy based on the users that have authenticated their social accounts. Again, if your total potential reach is 936,000 but 850,000 is on Twitter, you will need to optimize your content into short, shareable and clever pieces of content for Twitter. These seemingly small insights will allow you to adjust, in real-time, to account for any potential roadblocks and increase overall efficiency. Now that you know who is in the platform and who you have access to, you will then want to understand what you can do with those who are actively participating.

Measuring participation and engagement

Participation, and high-level engagement metrics, are where the majority of employee advocacy programmes start, and unfortunately finish. Knowing how many shares your content is receiving and how many clicks on those shares is a great start, but it doesn't tell a story. You need to know what your employees are viewing, enjoying, sharing, and what their audiences are doing with that content as well. For example, if you only track shares and clicks, you may see 15 clicks on one piece of content, but what you won't see is that it was shared to 15,000 followers and therefore only 0.1 per cent of their users engaged with that post.

Example company data: measuring participation and engagement

- The white paper discussed in previous chapters, 'Trends on enterprise security in 2018' was viewed 3,000 times in the last 30 days.
- The white paper was shared 2,500 times by 350 different employees.
- The 2,500 shares generated 30,000 clicks, 10,000 likes, 8,000 comments, and reached a potential audience of 450,000.

Now that you know exactly what content your employees like and, most importantly, what content their audiences like, you can easily adjust the content strategy to maximize your efforts.

Within the above example, it is clear that content similar to the white paper is most likely to be shared and, when it does get shared, generates the most engagement compared to other types of content. This helps you to understand what content is resonating with two of your most important stakeholders – employees and potential customers.

Measuring real business outcomes

The last and most important pillar is understanding how your employee advocacy programme aligns to meet tangible business goals. For example, if you are managing a social selling initiative, it is incredibly important to know if you are actually making an impact and selling products. Alternatively, if you are aligning your programme to support a brand awareness campaign, you will need to be tracking share of voice, topical share of conversation and brand mentions on social media.

Surely, knowing how many of your employees have joined the programme, how many times they have shared content and how many clicks they have generated is important, but you cannot quantify the success of the programme based solely on those metrics alone. With a few maths calculations, you can know specifically how much money the programme is saving or generating for your company. You can also know how much time you are saving in getting your content in front of your prospects and customers.

Example company data: tracking leads and sales

- In a two-month period, 70 per cent of website traffic came from employees creating and sharing content, all trackable using unique URLs or tracking IDs.
- From that traffic, 4,500 people downloaded the white paper and became an active lead in your CRM.
- The amazing sales team turned 42 of those leads into paying customers.
- This resulted in $600,000 in net new revenue.

The examples mentioned above only describe a few ways to extract value from an employee advocacy programme, but there are several more use cases that are critical to your success:

- **Brand awareness**: with 1,000 employee advocates SAP has generated over 500,000 clicks, 200 million impressions, and are driving 30 per cent of all web traffic to their corporate blog.

- **Company culture**: Cathay Pacific created a content hub focused on travel, which has inspired over 1,000 employees to become storytellers and share their experiences with the brand in a more personalized way.

- **Event promotion**: VMware drove 14 per cent of the event registrations for their annual conference by empowering their employees to share content on social media about the event.

- **Internal communications**: New York Sports Clubs has hundreds of gyms, with thousands of trainers on the floor who are generally hard to reach. With their employee advocacy platform they are now keeping over 5,000 employees informed in real time via mobile notifications.

Each part of the overall success of the programme is important, but the connection from beginning to end is crucial. So, when your CMO sends you an e-mail asking about the ROI of your programme, you will have a definitive answer and be confident with the numbers too.

There's an app for that

These days, there is an app for basically everything, and that includes employee engagement and advocacy. As you hunt for a solution that makes sense for your company, you will need to consider all of the aforementioned pieces of the puzzle, so you can determine essential functionalities, nice-to-have additions, reporting capabilities and integration possibilities – all of which are detrimental to track adoption, participation and business outcomes.

Do you need a platform that syncs with your content management hub? Would you ideally be able to segment employees by role or other qualities? What about the ability to translate internal messages into different languages, provide a leaderboard to incite friendly competition, or offer rewards to high-performing advocates that they can either display or use for real-life items? What matters to you most – accessibility, mobile integration, fancy functionality?

Above all else, participation in employee advocacy should be easy for people to do, so in all respects – including your enablement platform – you should be confident that both the mission and the expectations are clear. Employees should know the value of the programme and know why they are doing it. Then, when they are given insight into the full scope of how their participation is being evaluated, they will be able to connect easily the actions they take with the changes those actions facilitate – both inside the office walls and within the larger marketplace.

Storytelling: developing and leveraging content

In a world where business success is so often dictated by deep data and unique content, brand leaders must understand how crucial it is to communicate with empathy. And that means developing content that resonates with people personally and professionally; that is, it tells a story that sells *and* sticks.

The thing is, everyone loves a good story. It is an act that binds us together, connects us to ourselves and our actions, and makes us real. We all spend an enormous amount of time writing and telling the stories of our lives, and shaping the various chapters becomes more important to us, perhaps, than moving on to the next one. There are very few things that are more essential to a person's humanity than their own story and the stories of others that impact their own plot. Stories are saturated in emotion and rooted in experience; when we hear them and tell them, they open up new neural pathways and inspire images for us to connect to. When the content we consume is a story and not just a sales pitch, we remember it – for the same reason we remember fairy tales, legends and our favourite movies. It changes us.

Unfortunately, over half of marketers report that having enough content, or at least content that is viable, is the biggest challenge they face when designing employee advocacy programmes. It is for this very reason that it is so necessary for you to construct an editorial approach to brand storytelling that is specific to your employees, and that you do not simply rely on existing sales and marketing bullet points. The following outline uses the same principles as external brand storytelling, but has been adapted so it is more suitable for employee advocacy.

Make use of whatever existing, available content and data you have

This includes white papers, infographics, blogs, webinars and other assets that either already align with your current branding initiatives, or can be revised relatively quickly so that they do. It also includes any information you have about your clients, prospects and targets that can be used to educate employee advocates or inform the creation of new editorial content, or creative 'social' content leveraging various data points about your business or industry.

Equip employees with the right content at the right time to increase impact

True, you should give your employees access to your content library, or at least a curated selection of content that they can feel free to share whenever the mood strikes them. But that's not the end of it. There will be times when a world event, industry trend or company announcement gives you a limited opportunity to leverage your content in real time. If your company has an executive speaking at an upcoming event, for example, give employees the information they need to spread the word. If everyone is suddenly talking about the very topic you published a blog about two weeks ago, give your people the link and encourage them to jump into the wider conversation. Know your content, and pay attention to the channels it is shared on – employee advocacy is a fluid endeavour, and you should be ready to strike whenever the iron is hot.

Provide talking points for your advocates

Your participating employee base is not going to consist only of people who are comfortable with social media, knowledgeable about different types of content, or who would inherently know how to answer questions about the content you are asking them to share. So help them out. Provide a clear breakdown of the brand's message in language that doesn't sound like an advertisement. Encourage them to ask questions when things don't make sense. Where applicable, provide context for posts on different platforms that they can use verbatim, but encourage them to adapt the content and share it using their own voice.

Whatever you do, don't just hand them a piece of content and run away. Help them tell your story the way you want it told. And empower them to tell stories in their own words.

Help employees to guide new stories as they unfold in real time

A major component of employee advocacy is having an army of brand ambassadors monitoring social networks of clients and prospects. There are many reasons this is beneficial, but one of the most useful is how much influence this gives your brand over how its story gets told. You cannot control what people say or think about your company, but you can certainly keep an eye on it. Employees are your eyes and ears, amplified; and, with the right training and resources, can help guide the stories happening about your company while they scroll through their feeds and engage in industry conversations.

Don't dictate – motivate

Just like you cannot control what the outside world thinks about your brand, you cannot force employees to be advocates either. And you really shouldn't try. It won't work, and in most cases, it will completely backfire, causing people to resent the extra work that you have tasked them with, and doing only the bare minimum to meet whatever requirements you have tried to set. Remember the 'flair' in the film *Office Space*? That is what you are setting yourself up for if you become an employee advocacy dictator. Instead, continually communicate why this programme is so important, and what makes it worthwhile for the people who help it grow. Value begets value; force inspires spite.

Don't be intimidated by the potential for mistakes

How many times have you heard that failure is a necessary part of success? Probably quite a few – so it doesn't really bear repeating. But even so, implementing employee advocacy is going to cause some anxiety. After all, you are handing over the reins to your brand to a lot of different people, and that kind of dispersed activity invites a considerable number of variables. Mistakes are probably going to happen – but if you have done your due diligence, your research, planning and training, the possibility that any of those mistakes will be catastrophic is fairly low. And when something unfortunate does happen, you will ideally have such a widespread of supporters that it will not cause much more than a ripple.

As you unleash your employees on the world, it is, of course, not just about having them share and promote content that already exists. They should also be part of the development process, which includes internal efforts as well as becoming involved when opportunities present themselves outside of the company proper. Whenever possible, be sure to make use of the three core types of employee-driven content, which have the dual benefit of spreading brand awareness *and* placing your employees in clear positions of brand authority.

The first is something you have definitely heard of: thought leadership. In this context, your employee is the topic expert. They are speaking, writing or commenting on something in a way that demonstrates their advanced knowledge of a particular subject – perhaps digital transformation or the future of work – both of which are topics that every technology company is trying to align themselves with these days.

While this avenue is most often reserved for the executive suite, it absolutely does not have to be. There are plenty of experts behind the firewall that have no intention of becoming vice president of anything, and that has nothing to do with how skilful or educated they are in a certain area. Find these people and use them whenever possible – while your company may only be mentioned in passing, it will be solidly connected to talented individuals that people want to listen to. Plus, it has the potential to help further the employee's career and expand their network, which is good for everyone involved.

A second type of beneficial content includes a company representative as one character in a broader story about an industry trend, event or other issue. Typically, the overarching topic is not specifically about your organization, but includes an employee as an expert who can provide their perspective on the subject. This type of article, webinar or event has the same benefits as an individual thought leadership piece does, but it also does something else that is truly awesome: *it places your employee alongside other industry experts, and positions them as someone with authority.*

Thought leadership does not always do that, since it is so often written in a heavily opinionated way and published by the company itself. But to be considered as someone whose input on a situation is valuable is one of the most invaluable advocacy wins in the game.

Finally, the most flexible type: an employee offering their perspective on an external event or topic that is in some way related to your company or the broader market. This is not content in the same way that a blog post is content, but it is an exceptionally useful form of advocacy. As employees become involved in conversations with other people who are talking about things that can affect your brand or product, they are not just absorbing information that could be useful, they are also in the middle of a thicket of people who care deeply enough about something to start bantering about it, and are uniquely poised to get your brand involved, offer their own expertise and thought leadership, or even drive others to learn more about your company or its products.

Regardless of what type of content you've got on hand, are planning to create, or are pushing your employees to interact with, it needs to be useful to the people who engage with it, and relevant to the employees who are leveraging it. It doesn't matter how well it is written or how prettily it is designed if it is nothing more than an extended advertisement. Every single piece of content you put your name on, whether article or video or infographic, should fall under the umbrella of at least one of the following eight core values (and how your audience should perceive each):

- **Utility**: it is useful; it explains how your product works, why your company is talking about something, or helps your customers understand or solve an issue they may be having.

- **Education**: it teaches people something about a topic, product feature, company leader or industry trend.

- **Entertainment**: it is light-hearted, inspiring and highly memorable; the ultimate use of storytelling in enterprise content.

- **Access**: it connects others to people like themselves – people who share the same interests, passions or reasons for being there.

- **Emotion**: it incites a passionate reaction, either because they strongly agree with it or because it is controversial.

- **Exclusivity**: it makes them, as a customer or industry member, feel special and invested in the topic.

- **Information**: provides news, insider information or useful viewpoints that are relevant.

- **Promotional**: it gives them more information about products before they actually buy. This is where content creators can pretend to their heart's content that they are on *Mad Men*. Promotions and advertisements are par for the course when you are running a business; it is when these mini sales pitches try to masquerade as a valuable asset that things start to feel dirty.

Whether internally developed or externally generated, amplification does not happen without you making an effort to integrate stories and content across the broader digital ecosystem. With employee advocacy in place, much of this will occur organically, but there is no shame in using whatever resources you have at your disposal to help your company rise above the noise. Don't be afraid to syndicate employee-driven content to other relevant sites, pitch thought leadership content and bylines to relevant media, or put some budget behind the content you are publishing and promoting on branded social channels.

Employee advocacy programmes can push your content's reach outward by nearly 700 per cent, but that does not mean you should completely ditch the available broadcasting methods that have worked for you in the past. In any case, you can be certain that your competitors are doing it, so always protect the networks you have worked so hard to build.

Executing an employee advocacy programme that works means constructing an adaptable, customized strategy that encompasses every possible opportunity and leverages every potential resource. Is it hard? Yes. Does it take time? Yes. Planning? Absolutely. But with a thoughtful and strategic approach to employee advocacy, the return on your many investments is all but guaranteed. The calculated game plan illustrated above will help leaders to create an incredibly solid foundation on which to craft metrics for success, explore untapped markets, and shape a company culture that is driven by collaboration, shared goals and employees who are passionately invested in the future of the business.

INSIGHT Social selling expert

Contribution from Koka Sexton, Industry Principal at Hootsuite

Employee advocacy when done right should ultimately drive business value for your company. But when launching an employee advocacy strategy for your company, the mistake I have seen is that companies are spamming the community – only pushing their news, as if there is value in doing that. Though this may be the ultimate goal, the company needs to think of their employees in a larger context.

I believe the ultimate goal is really empowering your employees to build a habit of sharing on social media. Habits take time, some say 21 days, so be patient. But if you can achieve that, they will naturally be more inclined to share information about your company because they would have already shared updates about the industry and other topics that they, meaning your employees, find interesting.

When I have discussed employee advocacy strategies for companies, the first thing I asked them was 'what topics are most interesting to your employees?' and 'what do they care about?' Every marketing organization will know what content, assets and sources they would want employees to share, but what really matters when building an employee advocacy programme is to front-load all of the other types of content that employees will naturally want to share first. For example: a company could have four main internal use cases for employee activation:

- **Recruiting talent**: the best candidates are usually referrals, so activating employees to partner with your staffing teams are a win–win for everyone involved, especially if you have an employee referral programme.

- **Driving brand awareness**: empowering employees to help increase share of voice. This is especially effective if your company is a challenger brand or start-up.

- **Driving traffic to website**: use employees to share blog content that would bring in new readers and subscribers to the corporate blog.

- **Drive lead-generation**: using the same thinking as driving traffic to a website but taking another step and capturing their e-mail addresses.

But in order to make the employee activation programme sticky, they need to add in more than these business drivers, starting with content related to:

- **Leadership**: topics that help others to become better leaders, applicable to every industry in the world.

- **Entrepreneurship**: topics to help both entrepreneurs and intrapreneurs be successful at growing their business or programme.

- **Marketing**: how to think 'out of the box' when marketing products and services.

- **Life hacking**: topics related to being more efficient and productive using apps.

- **Industry news**: topics related to your industry or related industries.

- … and so many others.

Many of these topics become interesting to your employees as something they would want to know, as well as share within their own audiences. By giving them these larger topics to share, you are helping them build their own social footprint, add to their credibility in the social ecosystem and become influential in certain topics. Then, you are able to drive behaviour of your employees going into your employee activation platform in order to increase the habit of sharing.

As you are adding content from these other topics, you can sprinkle in company/product news or thought leadership into the mix. It is a best practice to follow the 80/20 rule, whereby 80 per cent of the content is industry-focused and 20 per cent is company-focused. Most companies are doing the opposite.

The best employee advocacy programmes empower their employees to be brand ambassadors as well as offer them a way to develop their professional brand online. Do this and you will be successful.

Building your employee activation plan: who is responsible for what?

It is fairly difficult to accomplish anything without a plan. It doesn't matter whether you are attempting to build a treehouse or a business, projecting the ideal outcome and identifying what tools and other components you will need is necessary in order to actually make anything happen. A blueprint, a risk analysis, a schedule – all of these things (and many more) are essential to achieving your goals efficiently and with as little resistance as possible.

There are endless reasons why a thoughtful, cohesive planning process is critical to the success of your employee advocacy programme, too. After all, you are basically pulling together a brand new business unit that requires resources, investments, stakeholder buy-in, growth strategies and an appropriate core team with the right mix of talents and skill. Before you even start recruiting people, though, you have to think about what you want to happen in the short and long term, what you can ideally execute in-house versus what you cannot, and exactly what value you are offering up – in this case, both for employees and the company overall.

A plan helps you plot a strategy, and a strategy helps you allocate resources, surface unexpected needs and locate disconnections. But most crucially, it will help you to guide the growth of the programme, pinpoint organizational responsibilities and sort out priorities.

If this strikes you as overkill, it is worth reminding yourself that implementing an employee advocacy programme is no small undertaking. It is not simply a side project, or an assignment to be handled by a single person. Because of its breadth, and because of what may be at stake, there are many business principles – not just planning, but within the planning itself – that should be taken into consideration while you are still in the early stages.

Since 'small business' is a perfect way to be thinking about your advocacy programme, one of those overarching principles to utilize is a highly practical, small and medium-sized business (SMB) concept known as displacement. Displacement means what it sounds like: whatever you do is equivalent to something else that you don't do. This is key to planning, and a wonderful framework to adopt for high-level programme outlines as well as the deep, detail-oriented stuff. This is because whenever you catalogue a need for your advocacy programme, you should simultaneously assess your ability to meet it: do you have the resources to make it happen? If not, how will you get them? Why do you want it in the first place? And finally, if this truly is a necessity, what will you have to sacrifice for it? By determining what pieces of your plan are worth giving up so that other things can happen, priorities, goals, objectives and logistics will start to emerge organically and take shape.

And that is when you can really start making things happen.

Define your goals and business purpose

Naturally, the absolute first thing to put down in writing is what you are trying to accomplish by weaving formal employee advocacy into the fabric of your company. A critical piece of figuring this out is fleshing out primary objectives. In this initial part of the process, it is smart to really unleash your creativity and ambition. Thinking well beyond the box is encouraged; long-term, big-time future payoffs and ideal circumstances should be discussed and noted, and any information you might have about potential investors, major target prospects, untapped markets or revenue growth trajectories should play a role.

In other words, if you know the CEO plans to go public some day, or has promised a 40 per cent year-over-year revenue increase, let that inform your objectives. But go even further than that; let go of practicality and probability for the time being. Imagine where you want to see the business go and what you want it to become, both in terms of physical growth and in relation to the overall culture. Do you want to some day partner with the three biggest sales software providers in the world to create a new product? Write it down. Do you imagine some day walking through the doors of new headquarters in Milan, or being able to send employees on a yearly company trip? Make note of it. There is good reason for this: it is much easier to scale down from grandiosity than it is to climb incrementally towards it (especially if you haven't really defined what 'it' is). Overarching objectives are akin to explanations; they are the why and the where. The goals that you link to them are the what, who, how and when.

So, as you may have guessed, goals are a bit more conservative than objectives, and should be thought of as the stepping stones that will help you reach those big, bold ideals. To facilitate setting these goals and be able to accurately connect them with objectives, it is always smart to divide and conquer as much as possible. Specifically, you should split goals into two segments based on whether they are qualitative (conditional) or quantitative (calculable). You want to be able to attach numbers to as many of your goals as possible, because that will make them concretely measurable.

For some things, that will be fairly easy: participation rates, shares and engagement on different social media platforms, an increase in customers/leads, or a decrease in turnover. Others not so much; the general satisfaction of employees before and after the implementation of the programme, for example, or how well the messaging is being received. However, the success of goals that lean towards the qualitative end of the spectrum can be gauged if they are properly outlined. Never be afraid to utilize survey tools to regularly assess different elements of the advocacy programme, particularly before it even launches. This will at least give you somewhere to start, a benchmark, and a metric with which to compare future findings.

Spending time exhaustingly projecting goals and metrics can be tedious, and you may be tempted to leave it for another day. You may assume that, over time, new missions and needs will emerge and you will be able to adopt them then; they will, but without a basic understanding of most of the probabilities and risks that could occur, you are putting your programme squarely in the path of disruption. It is not just for your own knowledge, peace of mind, or ability to analyse progress that you are doing this. You also need this information in place to help other people throughout the company understand what you have in mind, what value it holds, and why they should want to be a part of it. This idea is at the heart of another business principle known as valuation, which is basically a term that means 'figuring out what your business is worth'. In this case, you want to know, and be able to demonstrate, how an employee advocacy programme could benefit both your brand and the people who bring it to life every day.

Mapping out these objectives also gives you a unique chance to uncover areas of your business that are suffering, even if they are not precisely tied to the programme (though we like to think employee advocacy can help improve anything that is not going quite right, even if just a little bit). You will likely find that no matter where you decide to start, you regularly end up somewhere unexpected – and that's okay. In fact, it's more than okay; it's awesome. A major reason that creating a programme like this is so intimidating, and causes so much anxiety over how to begin, is because leaders don't always know their businesses as intimately as they probably should. And if they are being honest with themselves, they know it.

Most executives and managers are perfectly aware that the people guiding the future of the company – themselves included – are not always in touch with employee and customer relationships, culture characteristics, communication challenges, or other problems that are quietly eating away at success. Worse, they are not always attentive enough to notice the individual brilliance of different team members, or to facilitate killer ideas.

We get it – leaders are busy. They don't want to be seen as micro-managers and they very rarely have a minute to spare on issues that appear mostly harmless. Still, the depth that is necessary when planning an advocacy programme is going to expose at least some of the stuff that is eroding the foundation of the company. So, while acknowledging that there is trouble afoot is not easy to do, it is the right thing to do. Besides, identifying issues is really the only way to stop them from growing.

Thankfully, many of the more common problems that result from inattention can be reversed completely with a well-executed employee advocacy programme. Once you have spotted the problems you want to tackle, it can be very helpful to visualize them. It will help you to start assigning them to existing goals, develop new goals and, finally, link each of the goals to the objectives you have identified for your programme (and company). However you decide to create this map of connections – with some type of software, or with a sketch on a whiteboard – try to keep yourself (and your team) from thinking of anything as permanently fixed. There is no single or perfect way to solve a problem, and there is no guarantee that the precise path one business takes will work exactly the same way for yours. In any case, write down your goals, make them flexible and run them by colleagues to see if they make sense. But always know that they may change multiple times before you launch your programme, and be okay with that. It is going to happen. Here are a few example goals and objectives to help you get started:

- Increase website traffic by 26 per cent.
- Increase leads by 26 per cent and decrease cost per lead by 13 per cent.
- Increase brand awareness by 14 per cent.
- Increase company content reach by 20 per cent and engagement by 30 per cent.

- Drive 20–50 per cent of overall event registration.

- Increase employee optimism about company future by 27 per cent.

- Increase employee productivity by 12 per cent.

Please do not use these numbers just because they are printed in this book. They have no meaning whatsoever, other than some of them represent days of my birthday, 12/26. You will have to develop your own goals that align to your culture and that will ultimately deliver business value for you. You can do this effectively by starting at a very high level and then drilling down into department-specific goals. Here are some considerations when doing so:

- **HR and company culture:** let employees endorse the company as a great place to work and help with recruiting candidates. Employee referrals are almost always better hires.

- **Social selling:** establish and extend relationships with prospects and customers on social media.

- **Lead generation:** increase sales, leads and conversion by having an always-on, human-centric marketing channel.

- **Brand awareness:** humanize your brand and increase awareness through your employees' authentic voice.

- **Event promotion:** drive more registrants and attendees to webinars and events with real-time sharing and engagement.

---

20 questions to help you identify your goals and business purpose

1   What does your company do best, and what is it worst at?

2   What made you think your company might benefit from an employee advocacy programme?

3   How do you expect your programme to help address those issues?

4   Think of any current or past programmes that have relied on employee participation. What worked well, and what could have been done better?

5   How will you differentiate this programme from other employee-centric initiatives in the company?

6   Who will be the key stakeholders in the advocacy programme?

7   Of key stakeholders you plan to identify, how invested do you expect each of them to be, and why?

8 How big is your company, and what percentage of the employees do you expect to participate at first?

9 Who will you be targeting initially – team leaders, certain departments, specific individuals?

10 Which of those departments do you expect to join in immediately, and which will be more hesitant (and why)?

11 What approach will you take when creating internal marketing, promotion and communications materials?

12 Where will initial launch budgets come from?

13 How much money will you need to get your advocacy programme up and running?

14 What data, materials or other information do you need to request or allocate budget?

15 What needs to happen with the programme for you to consider initial budgets well-spent?

16 Will you start the programme using a technology platform?

17 If so, how much time and budget are you able/willing to invest in an advocacy platform?

18 What percentage of their working time do you expect participants to spend on employee advocacy?

19 How long will the beta phase of your programme last?

20 Finally, what needs to have been accomplished by the end of the beta phase for you to consider continuing and growing the programme?

Logistically, how do all the pieces work together?

Once you have settled on a comprehensive set of objectives, goals and metrics, it is time to start plotting the logistical aspects of the programme that will help you to reach them. Defining the systematic characteristics of your advocacy programme is primarily to identify who owns the programme overall, who owns various elements of it, and what dependencies are needed to ensure success. In this phase, even the best-laid plans will sometimes be forgotten, so it is always useful to develop a mantra that can keep you motivated and headed in the right direction. Base it on the following principles:

1 Always manage priorities and expectations.

2 Strategy equals focus.

3 Resources should always be allocated where they will do the most overall good.

4 Capitalize on your strengths and work away from your weaknesses.

5 Always target priorities according to their ability to help you meet long-term objectives.

While setting goals, the culture of your company no doubt came up in conversation, and it is now that you need to place it top of mind. It should stay there, too, for as long as you are building any key programme assets or messaging. The reason for this is that your employee advocacy programme needs to be an extension, and a reflection, of the overall experience people are accustomed to, so that it can work in tandem with other company initiatives and, moreover, remain familiar as participation increases over time. Ensure that your programme does this well by adopting and adapting existing core business values, and consistently verifying that you are not drifting off into totally unrelated territory. What you are doing is already challenging enough; there is no need to make it more difficult.

With culture in mind and goals established, you will want to begin outlining how different pieces of the programme will work. Because the majority of the programme's measurable actions will have to do with creating and sharing content via social media, creating some rules for how to do that should be done as early as possible. There are two major benefits here: participants get a template for how to do what you are asking them to do, and you can remain confident that branded assets and messaging are being communicated appropriately. And while there will no doubt be many specificities that emerge as you lay down these rules, there are a handful of things you should not leave out. These include:

- **Social media guidelines**: the importance of avoiding abusive or intolerant language, and what you consider that to be. Reminders of not sharing confidential company information, or bashing competitors or competitive products.

- **Content mapping and narrative**: content pillars and storylines that define the brand and products. A library of keywords, phrases and hashtags that should be used to ensure relevancy and visibility in the Google search results.

- **Rules of engagement**: where employees can find the resources they need to properly respond to external questions and comments. How to escalate issues that they are unsure how to handle; or deal with negative conversations or comments they may encounter about the company or executives.

It is important, too, to note the key differences between a company or programme's social media guidelines and its social media policy. They are not exactly the same thing, though they are certainly connected. Guidelines are more flexible; these are principles to inform educated decision making and behaviours, and are often communicated as suggestions and best practices. When it comes to creating a set of social media guidelines for your employee advocacy programme, they may differ slightly from those of the company at large. There may be specific initiatives or campaigns that come out of the programme and are separate from other efforts happening at the corporate level, so it is certainly a good idea to leave room for any necessary adjustments.

However, policies are strict, and typically mandatory for everyone. Your advocacy programme will almost never be different from the social media policies that are in place for teams regularly handling external or customer-facing communications. You don't mess with a policy without facing consequences, either – no matter who you are or what position you hold in the company. Handle both guidelines and policies with care and clarity, and always guarantee that they are easily accessible and regularly communicated.

While social media is a gargantuan piece of any advocacy programme, it is not the only thing that requires some boundaries and set-up. It is also important to determine how people's actions on social media will impact their success in the programme itself – and that is where incentives come in. It has surely occurred to you (many more times than once) that you are going to have to figure out a way to encourage participation without demanding it. And, even after onboarding the first wave of employee advocates, you will need to maintain their interest and commit to demonstrating regularly the value of the programme (much like you do with customers). That said, there are some things that are really important to remember, because as easy as choosing incentives may sound, an alarming number of companies fail to make them work properly, let alone in a sustainable way.

First and foremost, do your research

I know, I say this a lot and finding reasons why research is important may seem like a no-brainer. Sadly, many would rather avoid getting involved in research because of the time it takes to get answers and put a plan together. But it's worth it so don't skip this step.

When people set out to create new business models or breakthrough products, it is nearly always because they are aware of a need that exists.

They know that somehow, somewhere, there is a gap in the market that they think they can fill. Even with that assumption in place, it is just plain silly to go forward with creating something unless you have some proof of concept – some evidence that what you intend to do is actually a good idea.

The same rules apply when you start thinking of ways to motivate employee advocacy, so do the obvious: ask them what they want. Learn what has and hasn't worked for your company in the past, and at other companies who have advocacy programmes in place. Then you can use that information to develop your own incentives, and with at least some confidence that they will do the trick. Know, too, that it really does not always come down to finite, tangible rewards. Public recognition and awesome experiences often work even better than money and gift cards, and you should never underestimate how powerful it can be to see your name at the top of a leaderboard.

Make the path to winning easy to understand

You want your employees to take certain actions in exchange for perks. That concept is common enough, but defining exactly what you want them to do, and how it will earn them those returns, can be difficult. It can be tempting here to get extra prescriptive; after all, if you need to meet a goal of 1,000 Twitter shares in a week, it would make sense to offer bonuses to the first 20 employees to tweet 50 pieces of branded content in that time, right?

Well, maybe – if you don't care about the consequence of spamming the entire internet. Or the pressure that would put on your content creators to provide an astounding number of assets in a laughably short amount of time. Or if you don't care about a high level of repetition, a lack of meaningful engagements, or really anything at all besides hitting an arbitrary number.

But of course you do care, right? You care about all of those things. So rather than try to cheat the system this way, stay flexible with your goals and offer comparable prizes for top performers. Most importantly, clearly state what it takes to reach them, and give employees the freedom to choose what they go after and how they do it.

Offer different employees different incentives

We cannot emphasize it enough: people are different. Teams are different. They don't have the same goals, individually or collectively, and they certainly don't assign the same value to different motivators. For some employees, money is all they are interested in. Offer them a gift card to their favourite store and they will post anything you want, no questions asked. Others have executive dreams, and want to be in the CEO's inner circle. Still others just really, really want someone to listen to their latest amazing idea and help them make it a reality. This goes back to doing your research. If you have done it well, you already know that a single set of incentives is not going to work universally, so create levels of achievement, instead of offering hyper-specific awards. For example, top-tier advocates get to choose between lunch with the C-suite and a catered lunch with their team; median performers can take off early on a Friday or scoop up a $25 gift card. The more all-encompassing your incentives, the more people they are going to motivate.

Be generous and frequent with payouts

This is a major part of a successful, incentive-based anything, and it is useful to think about it like a pay cheque. It may not always be monetary, and it may not directly impact someone's livelihood. But an incentive needs to be enticing enough to justify the work you are asking for. In other words, don't ask for 80 social shares per month in exchange for a pen – unless, of course, that pen doubles as tickets to a Lakers game.

Timing is utterly crucial too when it comes to rewarding someone for their work, and can easily be the thing that keeps a person dedicated to employee advocacy *or* keeps them from participating at all. Because your programme is strategic and well planned, you are going to have a schedule attached to growth milestones and goals – you will need to do the same thing here. Providing the right type of incentive is only half the battle; it also matters a great deal to people that they get what they are due in a timely manner.

Again, think of actual compensation, and imagine: how long would you continue to work, and work your hardest, if you had been promised a pay cheque for a specific amount, but had no idea when you would get your hands on it? Would you keep doing your best, or would doubt eventually creep in and cause you to wonder what you are doing it all for in the first place?

The final key piece of your programme logistics is about ownership. Clearly, there are multiple moving parts to a working employee advocacy programme that are necessary for everything to function, and keep functioning, well. As with anything, particularly in relationship to your programme, it is smart to play to people's various strengths, as well as the roles they hold within the company.

Your social media team should serve as the expert consultants for how you use different channels; your resident blogger can help you to craft internal messaging with the right voice and tone. Engineers should be an integral part of choosing a technology platform, and salespeople can provide a lot of insight into the right way to motivate and choose incentives. This approach is a superb way to involve people through showing them what value they hold individually, which will make them more invested in the outcome of the entire programme.

As a result, you will end up with a clear path towards assigning those first advocacy champions – who will no doubt play a crucial role in the expanding adoption internally and throughout the company.

Which employees do you start with?

What makes an employee a great candidate to become an advocacy champion is dependent on a few things, some of which are far more obvious than others. It will take some observation on your part, as well as some digging. It is actually quite a bit like the customer prospecting process for salespeople, albeit more personal. First, you might wonder exactly what a 'champion' does that is different from what a participant does – or at least, different from you (and anyone who is involved in the most nascent stages of development).

And that's just it: they are not you. They are not the people who thought an advocacy programme would be a super idea, because they probably don't have as much constant exposure to how the company is doing (and therefore, any reason to start looking for solutions). They are not necessarily people who have the positional authority to make new initiatives happen. True, employees higher up on the totem pole can indeed become advocacy champions, and it is important that they eventually do. But it is far more critical that you identify leaders within the most predominant group of employees, because they are automatically going to be more trustworthy to their peers. *Because* they are peers. So, what do you need to look for in potential champions?

They have natural leadership ability

This is not always integral, but it can be very useful. People who are vocal, charming, charismatic and more outgoing than the people around them tend to be born storytellers. They tend to be inherently good at communicating, mediating and understanding the possible outcomes of different actions and events. You want people like this in your corner, who can interpret the real-life impact your messaging and needs may have on the people around them. These are the connectors, mavens and salespeople that Malcolm Gladwell describes in his book, *The Tipping Point* (2000).

They demonstrate empathy

This is perhaps the most important quality an advocacy champion can have. Empathy is the ability to truly understand the emotional state and perspective of another person, to the point where they can share them. They can easily imagine themselves in another person's situation – or are thoughtful enough to know when that is simply not possible. This matters for your programme champions because people with empathy are able to encourage participation by changing their tactics, language and approach, depending on who they are trying to persuade. And because they are doing this by being genuine rather than manipulative, they don't run the risk of sacrificing their trustworthiness. Empathy is also an attribute that makes external engagement with customers more impactful.

They know how and when to listen

Anyone who has ever been in a long meeting has mastered the art of looking like they are paying attention – when really, they are thinking about what to eat for lunch, or how much time has to go by before they can fake a bathroom break. There is no avoiding this phenomenon in the face of a truly dull presentation, but if someone is almost always off on another planet, and cannot respond appropriately when they need to, they are not the best person to spread the joy of employee advocacy. Instead, look for people who are actively interested in how the company is doing, are involved in conversations about improving things, and who talk about new ideas without a ton of prompting. More than that, locate people who respond to the things other people share thoughtfully – not as though they were just waiting for their turn to speak.

They are open to change

Change can be truly alarming for some people. For those who prefer the predictable, incremental shifts are about the best you can hope for, since springing new rules and processes on them is likely to leave them floundering. And, because launching an employee advocacy programme is not going to be a quiet, unassuming initiative, you will need a buffer between it and them (also known as advocacy champions with enough empathy to coax them into participation). Champions should already possess the disposition to handle ambiguity and disruption, since they will not only have to face it, but bring other people into the fold.

Social media and technology are already a part of their daily lives

Because social media is the primary route you will use to enable employee advocacy efforts, your champions should already have a fairly firm grip on how to use it. These days, it is par for the course, but there are always going to be varying levels of aptitude. These folks should also be fairly adept at learning how to use new software, as you will likely be implementing an advocacy platform prior to launch, if not very soon afterwards. Your champions need to be able to act as point people for the programme itself, as well as the things necessary to participate in it successfully.

When you begin your hunt for advocacy champions, keep the above in mind, but don't treat it as gospel (except for the parts about empathy and listening – those ones are crucial). There may very well be a number of quiet, shy, low-key social media users who would make amazing advocates but have not otherwise been given the opportunity to shine. Always keep your eyes and mind open.

Employee planning and segmentation

As mentioned in Chapter 7, the core focus of building an employee programme should be grounded in the employee experience. This means that every facet of the planning and preparation should be calculated with your employees at the forefront of your thought process. One way to do this is to segment them into distinct groups. I like to break it down as follows, but feel free to do it your own way:

- **Executives:** all members of the executive C-suite. In larger companies, this would be the CEO, CTO or any other employee with 'chief' in their title. In smaller, start-up-type companies, this could be anyone with a leadership position.

- **Subject-matter experts (SMEs):** these are the wicked smart employees who are building and developing products. This group can include engineers, scientists, product managers or even the founder of the company.

- **Sales:** it can't get any more straightforward than this. This is your sales team.

- **Ambassadors:** these are employees who don't fit into any of the above categories. This group can include just about anyone from marketing and finance, retail employees, or even the summer interns.

Part of the planning process should map out a few things, like what it is you want each group to do and where you want them to do it. Figure 8.1 offers an example of how you might want to communicate this on a PowerPoint slide.

As you can see in Figure 8.1, you will need to map out the desired action, content type and channel for each group. In this case, executives are responsible for creating thought leadership content and sharing it on branded social channels, the LinkedIn blogging platform, and submitted bylines to third-party media sites such as Forbes, Entrepreneur or Inc.com. SMEs are also responsible for creating content, but with a little different flavour. Their content focuses on technology and/or the technical specifics of what they do for a living. Your sales team is responsible for sharing content created from your executives and SMEs, and they will use their personal social channels to do so. Meanwhile, your ambassadors will also share content in

Figure 8.1 Segmenting employees' desired action, content types and channels

	ACTION	CONTENT	CHANNELS
EXECUTIVES	Content Creation	Industry and thought leadership	Executive branded Twitter handle, branded blogs, LinkedIn, bylines
SUBJECT MATTER EXPERTS (SME)	Content Creation	Brand, product and other technology-related topics	SME branded Twitter handle, community, engagement in industry forums
SALES	Shares	Industry and thought leadership	Branded LinkedIn profile and/or personal social channels
CHAMPIONS	Shares	Pre-created content from brand, thought leadership, cultural, job openings	Personal social channels

their personal channels, such as job openings or cultural-related content, as an example.

Before we go any further, please know that I am not asking you to take Figure 8.1 as gospel. Every company is different so yours will not look exactly like the diagram shown. Start here and adapt it as necessary.

Document roles and responsibilities

Once you have identified all the key players in your company, it is time to figure out how your team will support the programme and be able to scale at a rapid pace. You will have to figure out who on your teams will curate and post the content to the technology platform. As yourself: is this the same person who will coordinate with internal stakeholders in marketing and PR? What about training? Who will be responsible for creating and delivering the training programme? And you cannot forget about measurement and reporting. Is there a team or agency supporting you? Or, are you doing it all by yourself? Seems like a lot of questions, but having a plan will ensure success.

Figure 8.2 gives an example of how a more innovative employee programme operates behind the scenes. We dig very deep into this process in Chapter 10, but for now you can see that there are a lot of work streams and areas of responsibility – from audience research and analytics, online monitoring and content creation. Each part of the process requires specialized skill sets and substantial time commitment, so identifying resources early on is critical.

Figure 8.2   Real-time listening and employee activation

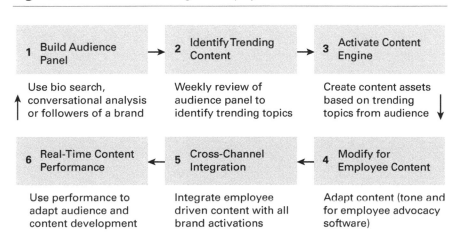

No pain, no gain (so train, train, train)

More often than not, there will be a fairly large influx of questions about your employee advocacy programme directly after it launches. It doesn't matter how well you have prepared or how detailed your resources are; people will come straight to the source for answers. But since no one has time to answer a slew of one-off FAQs, it is very important to be clear about the training component of participating in the programme. If nothing else, it may prevent people from becoming anxious about what is going on, because they are certain they will soon have a forum in which to get the information they are after.

The materials you develop to train participants need to be diverse, and work well for everyone from your glorious, ready-and-willing champions to people who flat-out refused to get a Facebook profile until one of their friends made it for them. You will also want to remember (again) that the people you are training come from a wide variety of backgrounds and experience, so it is smart to have modified training processes in place depending on those differentiating factors. Of course, the overall message and approach should be cohesive, but you cannot (and should not) appeal to engineers in the same way you appeal to someone in marketing. If it sounds like a lot of work, rest assured that it is necessary work – at least if you want your advocacy programme to do well from the start. Research shows that training programmes that address all experience levels and roles have a direct impact on employees' performance over time, as well as their quantitative and monetary value to the company (Academia, 2013).

Once again, your training programme is contingent on how well you map your goals to outcomes, and the easiest way to start laying that out is to solidify a schedule. So, if your primary goal is to get everyone well-versed in the social media policy, sharing guidelines and how to use the enablement platform before any advocacy really starts (hint: this should be your primary goal) – determine when you want that done by. Begin working backwards from the date you have selected, and pinpoint days and times where it makes sense to pull people out of their regular roles and tasks.

Speaking of roles and tasks: remember all of that intelligence you gathered while looking for advocacy champions? It becomes extremely useful here, too. Prior to finalizing your list of training topics, objectives and materials, you will want to revisit what you know about your audience so you can properly segment them into different training groups. By understanding their roles, expertise, existing level of advocacy readiness, social media knowledge, involvement in content and branding, and expectations about the programme, you will be much better prepared to tailor trainings to meet their needs. You don't want to put someone who runs your company's social strategy in the same training as people who need help setting up Twitter accounts – it is a waste of time for them and for you, and is a surefire way to demonstrate laziness.

Additionally, recognize that the way a person is trained can have a major impact on what they retain. Some people are visual learners who go blind in the presence of text blocks; others require some form of written instruction in order to process information. Be sure that your training materials and resources are available in a variety of ways; or, at the very least, find out what the majority of employees prefer. You may not be able to cater to each person's individual preference, but you will at least give yourself a leg up with the majority of the group. Just be sure to know the impact of the options you offer, both in terms of budget and bandwidth. Videos typically cost more than written instructions, but if 82 per cent of your trainees prefer to learn this way, it is probably worth it. All of this information will prove essential as you decide on the appropriate method for each group and training topic. It will also help you to develop training materials that make people feel supported and ready to go forth and share – instead of confused, resentful and unprepared.

Consider Edgar Dale's Cone of Learning (Figure 8.3) as you build out assets for your training programme. Dale was an American educationist who developed the Cone of Experience. He made several contributions to audio and visual instruction, including a methodology for analysing the content of motion pictures.

In Dale's model he builds a hierarchy of various learning experiences. The percentages given relate to how much of the content that people retain. Essentially, the model shows the progression of experiences from the most concrete (at the bottom of the cone) to the most abstract (at the top of the cone). The model clearly illustrates that after two weeks most people tend to remember 10 per cent of what they read, 20 per cent of what they hear, 30 per cent of what they see, 50 per cent of they see and hear, 70 per cent of what they say and 90 per cent of what they do. As everyone learns and retains information differently, you will have to ensure that your training assets are complementary to these learning styles.

We explore employee training in depth in Chapter 9.

I hear and I forget. I see and I remember. I do and I understand.

Xunzi

Figure 8.3   Edgar Dale's Cone of Learning applied to training employees

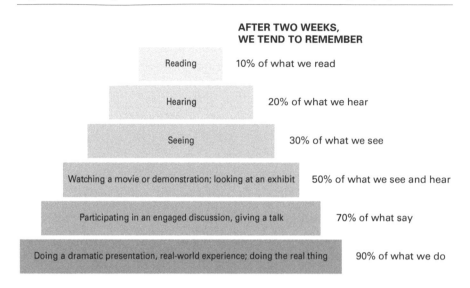

Finding the right technology

Chapter 11 is dedicated entirely to technology but it is worth mentioning now. After all of this intense research, planning, goal setting and training, it would be an incredible shame for your employee advocacy programme to dribble into nothing because there is no viable tool in place to enable your employee's efforts and scale. For advocacy to deliver desirable, trackable results, your employees have to be backed by the right platform.

There are many platforms on the market, each with a unique array of features and functionalities that guarantee success. But of course, by now you are well aware that it takes far more than a fancy piece of technology to breed success, so you will want to select a platform that makes sense for your company, your programme, your people, your ideal outcomes and your budget.

Beyond everything else that an advocacy technology platform should do for you, it must enable growth. It must help you to guide the direction and expansion of your advocacy programme, so you can move proactively towards objectives and metrics instead of simply reacting to events as they occur. Your absolute most powerful and valuable asset is your base of employee advocates; make it as simple as possible for them to help you deliver results.

Build your marketing plan

At this point, it is time to start finalizing how, and when, your employee advocacy programme will officially launch. With support from people closest to the existing company messaging and culture, you can shape and vet the programme's mission statement; plot how you will introduce the programme; how and what you will initially communicate about it; where you will house resources; how participants will access assets, trainings, educational materials and guidelines; and what kind of calendar you will follow to keep enthusiasm and participation growing. You can do this most effectively by treating the launch of your programme in the very same way that you would the launch of a new product or service: with a dedicated (internal) marketing campaign.

In this scenario, your company is the market, and employees – whose participation you are depending on – are the targets. Their teams or departments are the verticals. You have done the research, you've developed the messaging, created and housed the resources. You have even handled the first phase of the buyer's journey (awareness) by figuring out why your company needs employee advocacy, and spending ample amounts of time assessing challenges, risks and potential roadblocks. Now it is time to take your employee leads through consideration and help them decide why they should be a willing and active participant of the programme.

Choose the right way to announce the programme

Base your choice on how internal communications are done already, and then take it up a notch. If the normal approach is a single e-mail from the CEO or HR, do that – but tie it to a brief launch meeting as well. Already doing regular all-hands meetings to communicate with everyone? Build up anticipation to this one with a series of e-mails or other in-house efforts to spike people's curiosity and enthusiasm. Don't forget to brand launch materials in a unique way, too. Your employee advocacy programme is basically its own product, so treat it like one.

Activate your advocacy champions

Those people you worked so hard to pinpoint during the research and observation phase should be a part of your pre-programme and day-of-launch efforts, not just everything that happens afterwards. Coordinate with them on how everything should go down, and always listen when they bring up potential issues with your plans. Remember, they are influential; and they are your direct line to your internal targets, and are highly likely to find out important information before you do.

Make a big deal out of it

Launching an employee advocacy programme is an event, an ongoing one. You have put months of effort into building it and doing everything you can to ensure that it is successful, which most likely includes spending copious amounts of time and money. Do not treat the long-awaited arrival of implementation like any other old directive. If it does what it is supposed to do, this programme will have massive impact on the future of your company, its profitability, its growth and partnerships, and the overall success and happiness of its staff. Communicating the magnitude of this opportunity is not just fair because it is true; it is also strategic, because enthusiasm breeds interest, and interest will breed participation.

Keep propelling the programme forward

What happens after you launch is just as important as what you do beforehand, so keep reminding employees of what they stand to gain by being a part of the programme. You are not going to convince everyone to join from the start, but as they continue to hear about the successes and benefits related to employee advocacy, and watch their colleagues join up and stay involved, most will come round. But it is up to you not to forget about latecomers, or they may never come at all.

Revisit your success metrics (frequently)

Now that things are moving along, it is time to start striving for goals and checking off milestones. No achievement is too small – particularly in the beginning. After some time has passed and the programme has started to really take shape, you will be able to take a clearer look at the objectives and metrics that you defined in the beginning. You will be able to ask yourself crucial questions about where your programme is doing well and where it could use some improvement, as well as document things you are learning or did not anticipate along the way. This will be an ongoing process, so make sure that whatever you are using to track metrics and milestones is a living, evolving document.

Refocus on retention and growth

After so many long hours spent planning and running towards the actual launch of your advocacy programme, it can be an exhausting dose of reality to realize that your work is in no way over. It is, however, a little bit different, since you will need to shift your attention to keeping the advocates you have and scaling the programme overall. This means continuous training, updating resources, rejigging metrics and adjusting other elements of the programme – such as communication tactics and incentives – as the need arises.

Documenting the plan of action for an advocacy programme is perhaps the most daunting of all aspects you have had to consider, but it is well, well worth the time and effort. It helps you bring complete clarity to your idea of what the programme should be, and lets you track who is responsible for what and when. It provides a path to follow, and signposts to guide you while you travel. A plan helps you do what you need to do when you need to do it, and recruit the people who are most likely to help you reach your goals – no matter how lofty or far away they might seem. But the best thing about having a plan of action is knowing that it will help you turn your big, bold vision into a reality – a reality in which you can grow that ideal into something more incredible and valuable for your company than you ever imagined was possible.

CHECKLIST

Table 8.1 Checklist while documenting your plan of action

GOALS AND OBJECTIVES
Have you documented your goals and objectives?
Do they align with your overall business goals?
Have you defined how you will measure your employee advocacy programme?
Have you shared these goals with your colleagues, direct reports and other leaders in the company?
Have you re-reviewed your social media policy?
PROGRAMME LOGISTICS
Have you designated an owner of the programme?
Have you collaborated with all of your internal stakeholders (IT, HR, Privacy and Security, Marketing)?
Who will fund this programme? (Remember there are technology and human capital costs)
Have you decided on a name for your programme?
If you have decided on a name, will it be shared externally?

(continued)

Table 8.1 *(Continued)*

EMPLOYEE SELECTION CRITERIA
Have you decided which employees will be invited to participate in the programme?
Have you segmented your employees based on job function, location or business unit?
Have you identified your internal 'advocacy champions'?
TRAINING AND REWARDS
Have you built customized training programmes that speak to your employees' participation levels?
Have you built your training assets that align to different learning styles?
Will the training be on-demand of available for remote employees?
Have you identified a trainer?
Have you decided on one company leaderboard or several leaderboards?
Have you allocated budget for other rewards (eg gift cards)?
TECHNOLOGY
Have you identified the right technology partner or set up demos?
Have you outlined all the requirements you need for your programme to be successful?
Have you identified budget owners of the technology?
Have you involved the IT group before making your final decision?
MARKETING PLAN
Do you have all the resources available to launch (eg e-mail from CEO, intranet, HR announcement)?
Will the plan involve a launch event?
Do you have content pre-populated in the platform?
Do you have a team ready to manage the content curation and distribution process?

INSIGHT Health-care social media expert

Contribution from Vince Golla, Director of Social Media at Kaiser Permanente

Don't be surprised to see employee brand advocacy perfected first in health care. Why? Because health-care professionals practised advocacy long before it became a hot topic in marketing communications. And, if you must cut to the chase, we have very strongly started that journey at Kaiser Permanente, where our amazing teams care for close to 12 million Americans.

Work here for just a day and you will hear the same two words repeated: 'the mission'. In 2017: to provide high-quality, affordable health-care services and to improve the health of our members and the communities we serve. Make health care better, more accessible, more affordable. Help make lives better.

It is measured not just in lives saved but in lives made healthier, richer, longer. This is the purest distillate of a mission, performed countless times a day in every hospital and every medical office. Are there stories to be told? More than ever can be shared.

Yet there is a dichotomy here: health-care professionals do not always tell their stories because they put patients first, and among those responsibilities is protecting their patients' privacy. They are as methodical about privacy as they are about delivering care – not just because it is the legal thing to do, but because it is the right thing to do. Snap a pic in the hospital and share? – wait, is that a patient's name on that whiteboard? That pic will not see the light of day. Spontaneity can fuel brand advocacy; however, spontaneous storytelling presents challenges here that do not exist elsewhere.

So how do health-care companies empower their employees and physicians to tell their stories both safely and effectively? These people are busy improving health care, and health itself – anything that slows them down will not get done.

The way to do this is to invest in building the infrastructure – and the trust – that enables these mission-driven people to share great stories about their organizations. This means that we have to make it as easy as possible for them to participate. Create policies that are brief, clear and thoughtful. Launch tools that are nimble, mobile and convenient. Create structures and guidelines that protect patients and organizations. Curate content journeys so it is easy and convenient for them to share stories and celebrate the mission.

I'm happy to say that working at Kaiser Permanente we started building a formal employee business acumen and brand advocacy programme in 2014. Today, 'Be KP' consists of a robust training and education programme, regular updates tailored to inform and delight our employees, and a 'Be KP Champions' programme through which our most energized employees can represent the brand at key events and in their specific workplaces.

In 2016 we launched a social media brand advocacy platform through which close to 2,000 employees are already sharing Kaiser Permanente content in their personal social channels. Our Be KP training, plus our Social Media 101 curriculum, are prerequisites for using the social media app. Thousands of social posts – each hashtagged #BeKP – help show that the people of Kaiser Permanente are engaged, mission-driven and motivated to share our story and our mission.

I love sharing a case study about one of our sales vice presidents who was clearly motivated to share about the brand in his social channels, but often found himself running out of time in the day for that 'one more thing' to do. We measured that he shared 12 times about Kaiser Permanente in the six months prior to launching the app – and 40 times in 40 days following the launch. His comment? 'Well you made it easy and convenient for me to advocate and share. Why wouldn't I?'

Serving my modest role enabling this is both a passion and an honour. You will no doubt feel the same way when you launch your programme. As I think about what happens next in this space, I return to the same sobering stats:

- The number of newspaper employees in the United States has plummeted from 410,000 in 2001 to 173,000 at the end of 2016, according to the Bureau of Labor Statistics (https://www.bls.gov/opub/ted/2017/newspaper-publishers-lose-over-half-their-employment-from-january-2001-to-september-2016.htm).

- Fully 62 per cent of US adults say they get news on social media, and 18 per cent say they get their news from social media 'often', according to the Pew Research Center (2016) (http://www.journalism.org/2016/05/26/news-use-across-social-media-platforms-2016).

- Only three of 10 employees say they are fully engaged in their employer – but 50 per cent say they already post content about their employer in their personal social media channels, according to the Weber Shandwick study 'Employees Rising' (2014) (https://www.webershandwick.com/uploads/news/files/employees-rising-seizing-the-opportunity-in-employee-activism.pdf).

- Overall trust in corporations, governments and organizations declined in 2016, and 'search engines' have become the most trusted source for news, according to the 2016 Edelman Trust Barometer (http://www.edelman.com/global-results).

- One glimmer of hope: the same Edelman Trust Barometer found that a company's employees were the most trusted spokespeople to communicate about topics ranging from treatment of employees to views on industry issues.

All of this could spur heartburn in the hardiest communications strategist. And yet I see opportunity. What if we trained and inspired our employees, equipped them with important and easily digestible information, and then trusted them to share in their circles of friends and colleagues, both physical and virtual?

Today it sounds like the next best thing. A year from now it might be table stakes. What if two years from now it is too late?

Identifying, segmenting and training the workforce for brand engagement

Once you have officially launched your employee advocacy programme, it is time to bring it to life – which means sharing your vision and your strategy with the people who can help make it happen. That means training, ongoing training.

If you have thoroughly mapped your programme goals to desired outcomes, you can use the projected timelines for reaching those outcomes to dictate your training schedule. Remember that those outcomes need to be prioritized, though; you may be eager to hit a 20 per cent increase in overall social shares across channels, but that kind of result is a symptom of a working, well-executed programme. It is not something you can just throw at people as a success metric without telling them how to get there. Be practical, and determine what your employees need to know, what they need to be able to do, and how large the learning curve for those things may be for different people, before pinpointing exact dates that goals need to be met.

Then, once you have selected those milestone dates, you can easily work backwards from them to shape the schedule for your training programme. As you do this, though, it is imperative that you be considerate of people's primary roles and job functions. Remember, employee advocacy does not work if you demand it – if you make participation a huge, disruptive inconvenience, people simply will not do it. If you make participation mandatory, resentment will build, and many people will do the absolute bare minimum that is required of them to keep from getting hassled. That's not a great way to start off your programme.

Before you finalize the logistical stuff, such as training topics, objectives and materials you will need to provide, look again to the information you gathered on different teams and individuals prior to launch. Ideally, this goes beyond what their company role and team are, and includes deeper insight into what they are passionate about, how they prefer to learn new information, and how they currently feel about the company's initiatives and culture. Other things to investigate include their existing social media aptitude, involvement in content and branding activities, and what expectations they have about participating in the programme. Whatever data you manage to gather will prove helpful as you divide people into different training groups and prepare the materials that are most likely to help them succeed.

With that in mind, it is critical to understand that all training methods are not created equal, and the approach and assets you use can have a huge impact on how well people retain the information you present, as suggested in Chapter 8. Moreover, not everyone digests information the same way. There will always be a wide variety of experience, for one thing. Some folks will need help setting up social media accounts, whereas others may have already developed a solid following on a few social channels. And, where some people excel with written instructions, others will require visuals, hands-on activities, verbal guidance or some combination of these in order to reach their full potential.

It is unlikely that you will be able to perfectly cater a training system for each individual person, but with a quick survey of trainee preferences you can get close. Additionally, consider the options you have relative to those preferences and your overall budget for training and asset development. Sure, creating a training e-book may not cost as much as filming a video. But if the majority of employees tell you that they learn better with visuals, that matters more than the added cost. Offering a small variety of options can be well worth the additional time and effort (and budget) you may need to put into developing them – especially if it means you can get your programme up, running and expanding more quickly.

Connecting your curriculum with employees' learning styles

Learning experts have, through many years of research and observation, determined that there are seven primary styles of learning: visual, physical, aural, verbal, logical, social and solitary (Ferriman, 2013). Typically, these styles are collapsed into only a few – but learning is a very complex process, so understanding the nuances of each is a great jumping-off point for finding out how to execute the training and devise the resources for your employee advocacy programme.

Visual learners

You guessed it. These employees learn more effectively with visuals. But there is more to it than just pictures and graphs. On average, visual learners remember about 75 per cent of the information presented to them in diagrams, graphics, charts, symbols and other representative images (Visual Learner, 2015). People who do best with these tools also depend a great deal on spatial awareness, or the relationship that objects have to each other – particularly when there is a change in their positions.

Digging even deeper, there are actually two types of visually oriented people in this category: analytical visual learners and global visual learners. Global visual learners are what nearly everyone imagines when they think of learning visually, because they process iconic, or pictorial, information before they digest any associated text. However, analytical visual learners process the printed word first, which many people do not even connect to visual learning. But in the end, both types of information, whether written or drawn, are symbols that represent information and therefore appeal to the visual learner.

Physical or kinesthetic learners

Thankfully, you do not have to plan an extended game of charades to appeal to physical learners. Also known as kinesthetic learners, these people need some type of tangible connection to information for it to effectively stick; they need to do, to make and to be involved. For example, they might be perfectly able to glean data from a chart, but *creating* that chart themselves will be the most impactful for them. They like to be on their feet, use their hands, and to move around while they think about and explain things. In other words, they learn by doing; they benefit from using their bodies, role playing, utilizing physical objects, drawing figures, making models, or trying out products and platforms for themselves. In the case of your employee advocacy programme, this group will learn the most quickly once they actually get their hands on your platform.

Aural learners

Aural learners listen. Obviously – but it is not as simple as just paying attention when someone is talking. They are the kind of people who hear songs once and remember all of the lyrics; they often use or come up with clever memorization tricks and acronyms so they will not forget important info. Sounds and rhythmic patterns evoke an emotional response in them, and they like to listen to music when they work or study, because it helps them to stay focused. Aural learners prefer to attend webinars, play podcasts or use audio books to explore and study new concepts. They are bound to ask if the trainings they attend will be recorded, as they are likely to return to it many times as they become more involved in your employee advocacy programme.

Verbal learners

You might think verbal learners do well when other people tell them what to do, but it is kind of the opposite. Verbal learners actually like to act as their own teachers, reading instructions aloud, taking detailed notes to review later on, and are big fans of key terms and phrases. As you might expect, their vocabulary is usually quite advanced, and they are very good at communicating information and articulating what things mean. Consequently, they make great writers and public speakers. When participating in a training, they will be scribbling or typing away to keep track of what is happening, so they too will likely benefit from written and recorded materials.

Logical learners

These are the people who ask 'why' and 'how' more than anything else; they often appear as reluctant to try new things, but it is only because they almost never make snap decisions of any kind. In order to be able to use something or apply it effectively, logical learners need to find out how something works, or why it is necessary, before they can truly understand it or support it. They are all about processes and systems, and they have to be able to connect actions to viable outcomes in order to do the action in the first place. What is relatively unique about logical learners is that, as they are presented with the pieces of the puzzle, they will quickly grasp the larger picture of why an initiative is taking place – so long as it makes sense, that is. You will be hard pressed to get logical learners to do anything if they believe it is useless or poorly thought out.

Social learners

Social learners love a good brainstorm session. They are masters of collaboration, and do a lot of thinking out loud. Because they prefer to work in teams or partnerships, they are adept at building off other people's ideas. Having their own ideas challenged or modified does not upset them, because most of their thought process happens as they share concepts with others. When they learn, they do very well in intimate (but not necessarily small) group settings, and are likely to ask a lot of questions during the process.

Solitary learners

Call them introverts, shy as a violet, or quiet as a mouse – solitary learners do best when left to solo time and self-study, and will feel too anxious and distracted to benefit much (if at all) from group training. They typically need to work at their own pace, rather than within a time frame set by someone else. While you probably are not going to let people out of joining a training session because they are solitary learners, do bear in mind that they will do better in small groups, and will get more use out of whatever assets you provide than they will from a session itself.

Most of your employees will not fall squarely within these descriptions, because the vast majority of people benefit from a variety of learning approaches. But you don't just want them to attend a training session or two – you want them to make your employee advocacy programme a success. That means figuring out not just which approach will work for different groups of people, but identifying which will work *best*.

And so, determining how to move forward with the creation of your training approach and assets requires that you figure out what your employees need. A quick survey is the most efficient way to do that – here is what you need to ask. You don't need to word your questions in exactly this way, or limit yourself to only these 10 questions. However, they are designed to help you get straight to the core of your employees' learning styles, and make your training programme as successful as possible – so they make for a good starting point.

---

10 key learning questions and why they matter

1 If you had to choose one, what kind of learner do you consider yourself to be?

   a) Visual: I prefer to read instructions and study associated images, graphs or charts.

b) Aural: I prefer to listen to someone tell me how to do something.

c) Verbal: I prefer to take notes or read instructions aloud in order to understand.

d) Physical: I prefer to learn by doing.

e) Logical: I prefer to understand why and how things work before I use them.

Why this question matters: even if people don't know exactly what learning style they technically adhere to, they are the best resource for information about themselves and how they like to do things. This can help you segment your training groups more accurately. In the event that someone's personal assessment does not gel with the rest of their results, you will at least know which training sessions and materials to offer to them, and why.

2   Do you prefer to learn in groups or on your own?

a) On my own.

b) In a group.

Why this question matters: it is the fastest way to split up social and solitary learners. Most people who work well on their own choose to do so; people who rely on others' energy and support may feel intimidated by the idea of a solo, do-it-yourself training programme.

3   What is the best way for you to study for a test?

a) Review reading materials, pictures and graphs.

b) Have someone ask you questions that you can answer aloud.

c) Go over the detailed notes that you took during the lectures.

Why this question matters: this is an incredible way to assess what kinds of resources you need to have available, and which ones may not be necessary. It is tempting to cover all of your bases and translate every bit of training material you have into a variety of mediums, but asking this question can keep you from wasting your time on assets that might not get used very much.

4   What is the best way for you to figure out how something works (such as a new software platform or tool)?

a) Ask someone to show you how to use it.

b) Read about it or listen to someone else explain how it works.

c) Give it a try and figure it out by myself.

Why this question matters: this question provides a lot of insight into how people will behave when they first start participating in post-training employee advocacy efforts, and can help you shape follow-up sessions.

5   What do you find most distracting at work?

   a) When people walk past you or chat with others near you.

   b) Loud noises or other abrupt interruptions.

   c) Being asked to attend an immediate meeting that you had not planned on.

Why this question matters: this is a great question to help you determine the appropriate environment for your various sessions (eg a standup, meeting room, or off-site), and you will find out how much flexibility you will be met with if you have to change the time or date of any trainings.

6   When you find yourself in a new place, how do you learn your way around?

   a) Walk around until you find different landmarks.

   b) Ask someone to show you around.

   c) Try to find a map or floor directory that will tell you where things are.

Why this question matters: aside from the obvious (that a person's answer supports what kind of learner they are), this is another chance to solidify different assets and approaches that need to be available after initial trainings take place, such as point-people, slide decks, recordings, or a written guide.

7   What is the best way for you to remember an important number?

   a) Picture the number(s).

   b) Say it aloud several times.

   c) Write it down or immediately make note of it somewhere.

Why this question matters: there are going to be a lot of numbers shared with the participants in your employee advocacy programme, from goals and metrics to leaderboard positions, shares, percentage changes and conversions. This question will help you determine how to make people aware of those numbers and what to emphasize about them.

8   When working on an important project, do you tend to:

   a) Sit in relatively the same position while you work, only taking necessary breaks?

b) Stay focused, but get up and walk around every once in awhile to shake up your energy?

c) Work in spurts and, in between, spin around in your chair, multitask or check social media?

Why this question matters: training sessions are not often as quick as we would like them to be, so this question should give you a good understanding of how long to make them, how often to offer breaks and how to manage the time spent on different aspects of the training.

9   When learning new information via a presentation, do you:

a) Listen carefully to what the presenter is saying?

b) Read the slides that accompany the talk?

c) Think of questions you have about what is being presented?

Why this question matters: this one should be fairly apparent. Knowing how the majority of people answer this question will give you more insight into how well your training presentations and instructions will be absorbed, and how many times you should offer the same kinds of sessions.

10 When your boss asks you to do something, do you:

a) Get it done?

b) Ask them to explain why it needs to happen?

c) Tell them you will get to work, but come back to them often with questions?

d) Begin researching how similar projects have been executed?

Why this question matters: for some people, the initial training sessions they attend will be enough for them to jump right into the advocacy programme and get sharing. But others may need a little more preparation. This question should give you a decent idea of how many people might attend optional training refresher sessions, so you will know whether you should plan for them.

After you receive the results of your assessment, you will need to start applying your findings, taking into consideration a person's individual role in the company, what stakes they hold in the outcome of the employee advocacy programme, and their personal experience with content, social media channels, branding and networking.

Considerations for executives, subject-matter experts and ambassadors

Many companies group people into trainings based on their department or positional authority. The above section shows that, while you can occasionally predict how someone in a particular role will learn, it is certainly not the only factor, or even the deciding one. That said, you still need to consider how your training approach and schedule will work for people who operate from different viewpoints within the company. They will see the programme as functionally different if they are someone who is simply participating, versus someone who is also actively tracking the participation of others.

The executive C-suite

Perhaps the most challenging group of employees to onboard will be people who are members of the executive C-suite. And if you are one, I am sure you can agree. In general, they are not as focused on execution as they are on strategy, and statistics have shown them to be the most sceptical group to leverage social media as a communications tool. This can make it harder to sell them on how valuable their own participation is for the overall advocacy programme.

Although reports have shown that about 80 per cent of CEOs around the world are utilizing social media, of those top execs, newer CEOs are 52 per cent more likely to participate than those who have held a top-tier seat for a long time (Weber Shandwick, 2015). However, even those seemingly social media-savvy CEOs are primarily using LinkedIn to monitor customer engagement depending on activity generated from their own company's sites and channels. While that is great for providing transparency into how their brand is doing in certain social media spaces, it does not help them share thought leadership, brand wins and content with their own peer networks, or expand opportunities for new customer channels. Social media is also so pervasive that it should be viewed as an utter necessity, simply because it allows companies to actively tell new stories, drive more successful customer service, find new talent, and investigate competitor activities and strategy.

So, training your executive team to participate in employee advocacy may have to focus on the 'why' a little bit more than the 'how', at least at first. It is for this reason that you should seriously consider a separate, pre-training presentation specifically designed to convince your execs that their participation is, in fact, likely to be the most important when it comes to overall programme momentum. There are a few obvious reasons for this – namely, their position in a company makes them automatically more likely to be considered an authority in their industry. Plus, behaviour is imitated; so when execs are actively participating, everyone else in the company will follow. But that's not the end of it.

In addition to being able to monitor customer engagement, they can use their networks to actively look for new touchpoints and connections for prospects and customers that may not be accessible to other employee groups. These channels can also help them solidify their authority on topics that are relevant to them, which will in turn grow their individual following. This is actually true for all employees, but executives have a leg up because of their existing status internally and also in the market.

This is especially important because, whether they realize it or not, listing an employer on a social media profile and being active on social media is an advertisement for the brand. Anything you say or do via these channels could, then, be a reflection on the company at large. Most people are unintentionally acting as (low-key) brand advocates already, but augmenting these efforts requires a leadership team that is willing to take charge of the way those efforts unfold. They need to support and participate in advocacy by guiding the content distribution process and making sure that anything that comes out of the programme is beneficial, rather than worrisome, for the business. It is the difference between a proactive story about the brand versus a reactive statement in response to what your competitors are doing.

Executive participation is the only way to truly demonstrate the importance, value and power of employee advocacy programmes, and that management understands how impactful cultural shifts within the company can be. Besides, it gets fairly difficult to entice employees to do something that their leaders are so clearly unwilling to do themselves.

Executives often live their lives by numbers, so it may take exactly that to solidly prove the necessity of their participation in the programme. Here are a few facts that you can share with them that might be helpful to garner participation. And if you're a sceptical executive, please read on. First let's explore some numbers.

Companies that increase employee engagement are 21 per cent more productive than companies that don't. And, execs can indirectly drive employee productivity simply by showing that engagement matters to them, therefore boosting overall profitability. On top of that, a single disengaged employee can cost an organization an average of US $10,000 in profit per year (Gallup, 2013). I'm sure that number goes up every year too.

Second, if a company the size of IBM with close to 400,000 employees can do it, so can you. They initially launched their employee advocacy programme with just 200 subject-matter experts (SMEs). During the first few months after launch, these 200 employees drove 146,000 shares, resulting in 188 million impressions and 603,000 clickthroughs to various IBM web properties – an estimated cost savings on media spend between $300,000 and $1.2 million (Emerick, 2014). If this doesn't demonstrate a compelling ROI, I am not sure what does.

Employee advocacy makes a huge – and positive – impact on how businesses succeed, that much is clear. But if executives don't lead the charge and take up the mantle themselves, a programme's potential can be greatly diminished before it is ever even close to being realized.

SMEs and their importance in advocacy

So, on to subject-matter experts, often referred to simply as SMEs. You probably already have a fairly decent idea of who these people are and why they have the title: they have a great deal of experience in a particular job or extensive knowledge on a topic.

These are the employees who are building products and creating experiences for your customers. Innovation is their middle name. They pour their heart and soul into the company and are constantly thinking of how to improve – the products, existing processes and the company as a whole. These are the engineers, product managers, data scientists. Or, just about anyone else who is crafting new, exciting customer experiences, or just trying to disrupt the market with new ideas.

SMEs know how their particular department, product or company works from the inside out and bottom up. In many cases, they start off in entry-level positions and rise up through the different tiers, always staying on a relatively straight path. This is not always the case, of course, but typically it is this trajectory that leads to such a deep understanding of their role, how it functions within the company, the processes associated with it and, most importantly, expectations that work – and those that do not.

SMEs are an incredible resource when it comes to predicting how changes will impact their teams, as well as how to best introduce new initiatives so they are most likely to be well-received. This is the primary reason these folks are so important to your advocacy programme, both internally and outside of the company proper; they can act as translators and liaisons to people, networks and channels that your brand (or programme) may otherwise be unable to penetrate.

Because SMEs have such intimate knowledge of what they do and how their peers think and work, gamification and leaderboards will only get you so far. They are masters of their craft and disruptive initiatives – or at least those that have the potential to upset the order of operations they are so used to – will be met with resistance unless their benefit is clear. And that does not mean explaining how the company will profit; it is highly necessary to help them understand how participating in the employee advocacy programme will help them be more effective and efficient in their own roles.

In addition to helping you convince SMEs that their participation is mutually beneficial for both them and the business, this detailed explanation will provide them with the tools to compel other people in their departments to join. They can also be instrumental in helping you figure out how the processes and tasks portion of employee advocacy can be most easily woven into their daily work.

While it is true that you should identify the SMEs throughout your company and regard them as such, it would be a major mistake to reduce them to that aspect of their abilities alone. Do not rely entirely on them to tell you each and every way that advocacy efforts could challenge their normal activities. Do not depend on them to want to lead training efforts for their teams, or to want to be charged with executing the functional responsibilities involved in your programme.

Encourage them to be point people, certainly; they will be more adept than anyone else at fielding department questions that have to do with advocacy. But SMEs require many of the same considerations you will need to give to employees in various other roles, especially when it comes to figuring out how they learn and what types of resources can help them go beyond advocacy and become the brand ambassadors you want them to be.

From advocate to ambassador

Though used interchangeably quite often, there is a subtle (but important) distinction between an employee advocate and a true brand ambassador. Functionally, they will do much of the same work as everyone else in terms of sharing content and disseminating information to their networks. But as they grow within the programme, certain qualities and behaviours will emerge that can clue you into their ability to become leaders within the advocacy initiative. Eventually, they will begin to have a fairly heavy influence on how it grows and changes.

They will, like all of your employees, be trained on how you anticipate the programme working, and which tools and resources you will expect them to use. In fact, you likely will not even be able to figure out who is ready to become an ambassador until the programme has been launched and running for some time. The real magic of turning employee advocates into brand ambassadors is being able to recognize and identify them based on their initial participation in the programme. Those people who are in the best position to go beyond general advocacy will demonstrate enthusiasm early on. They will do more than what is asked of them without prompting, and were probably doing some form of advocacy before you introduced any type of formal programme.

Grooming them not only to continue doing what they are already doing, but to help engage additional employees and even customers, will involve advanced training sessions that you offer down the road. Though you already know that some type of rewards or perks system is going to be necessary for everyone in your formalized programme, a crucial part of creating brand ambassadors is acknowledging their unique and inherent capacity for advocacy. It will keep their momentum from slowing down, and make them even more likely to want to grow individually as brand advocacy leaders.

With a significant understanding of the diversity of your employee base, its nuances, its widespread challenges, and how different teams function, you will be able to create custom training experiences that will do far more than just teach your employees what advocacy is or how you want it to work. Training that is squarely based on highly specific, in-depth knowledge will help your employees to shape an advocacy initiative that has very little risk of failure, and a massive chance at driving unprecedented success.

Creating custom training experiences

As you move into the training execution phase and begin boosting your employees' collective social IQ, you can take all of that exceptionally detailed information you have gathered and start strategically applying it. But first, there are some things you should know about what it means to train people in a company environment.

The four learning elements: earth, air, fire and water (not really)

Don't worry, this has not suddenly turned into a book about the zodiac, and you don't need to ask employees what their birthstones are. But the quintessential four elements of earth, air, fire and water can help bring some context and further understanding of how adults learn in corporate environments, so that you can make the best use of your data and resources. This section is less about exactly what you use to train and who you use it for – rather, the four elements of learning should affect *how* you train, period:

1 **Reinforcement** (earth): uncomfortable as it may be when annual review time rolls around, there is always a part of us that really, really wants to know how we are doing. If we are doing awesome work, we want to know it is being noticed; if things are not going so well, we want the opportunity to figure out why. The same is true when we are learning a new skill or platform, or trying to understand why a new initiative is being implemented where we work. For the people actually hosting employee advocacy training sessions, it is important to recognize how grounding both positive and negative reinforcement and feedback can be. Both essentially work to keep people focused and in line, because they will naturally seek to avoid unfavourable comments while looking forward to approval. Verbal encouragement works best in training sessions, since it is immediate. However, if you need to share negative feedback about how a person's training is going, it is best to share your comments with their direct manager and trust that they will pass along the message. This strategy is also how you should handle individual feedback about someone's participation and performance once they have dived head first into advocacy.

2 **Transference** (air): as discussed, most people want what they learn in a training session to weave directly into what they do on a daily basis. When they are able to do that successfully, it is called positive transference – they are able to apply what they learn to what they are doing without much disruption. But with any positive comes the negative, too. Negative transference happens when people cannot or don't use what they learn. To minimize negative transference – in this case, employees not seeing any reason to participate fully, or at all – employee advocacy training must centre primarily around how it will benefit the individual person in their role, with less emphasis on what rewards the company or brand will see. This is not to say you shouldn't explain why it matters for your brand, because to pretend it is not a factor is dishonest. But the greater the clarity around why each participant is valuable, the better chance you will have of convincing them of their unique part in the process. It's a classic give and take, but a very necessary one – much like breathing.

3 **Motivation** (fire): you already know that you need to motivate employees to join in on your advocacy programme, even if you do make the training portion mandatory. But mandatory or not, you still want people to want to be there (as much as anyone ever wants to go to a meeting, that is). There are a handful of ways to do this, but again, the one that will likely work for the largest number of people is personal benefit and achievement. If it is made clear that participating can have a tangible, positive influence on their current role, overall career, social following and other aspects of their

professional life, you will have better luck keeping them interested. And, although trying to force employees to become brand advocates is almost always futile, it doesn't hurt to remind them that the leadership team is invested, expectant and planning to check in on progress and participation.

Another great motivator is that, through both the customized training sessions you will offer and the advocacy programme itself, people will have major opportunities to collaborate with people and teams they may not normally interact with. This does not work for everyone (remember solitary learners?), but many people like the idea of being a part of something larger than themselves, especially if it includes opportunities to get face time with executives or make new acquaintances.

Additionally, new initiatives and the work that goes into them are bound to light the fire of people's inherent curiosity and desire to gain new knowledge. Finally, the training itself – though most would not admit it – is a great way to stimulate employees' minds and creativity, because you are giving them a nice break from their daily work routine. That is true of participating in the programme, too (at least at first, so definitely take advantage).

4 **Retention (water)**: obviously, a big part of training someone to do something depends on whether they retain the information. It is necessary for them to contribute effectively to the advocacy programme and start realizing the personal benefits of doing so. But retention requires repetition; trainees need to practise new skills until they become familiar and comfortable. It is for this reason that scheduling initial training sessions in waves, and offering follow-up or refresher sessions on a regular basis, is so critical to long-term success. You should always think of your employee advocacy programme as a living, growing, flexible entity; think about the way you prepare people for it this way, too.

Every company and their employees are different. Different culture, different DNA and different perspectives. And it is not always going to be an easy road to travel. You will get pushback and negative feedback. But don't let that stop you. If employees are complaining about the training, perhaps it is a question about relevance. Perhaps they don't want to jump head first into the programme. Maybe they just want to get their toes wet, see how it goes, and then decide from there.

One way to think about training is to create a training curriculum based on 'levels of participation' (see Figure 9.1; Table 9.1). This approach is effective because it addresses the employees who are unsure about how much they want to commit to the programme. As their commitment level rises, your curriculum will address various steps that will increase their knowledge

Figure 9.1   Build training experiences based on levels of participation

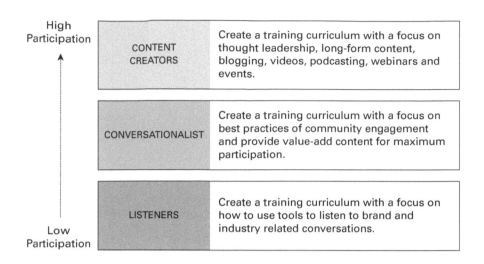

High
Participation

CONTENT CREATORS
Create a training curriculum with a focus on thought leadership, long-form content, blogging, videos, podcasting, webinars and events.

CONVERSATIONALIST
Create a training curriculum with a focus on best practices of community engagement and provide value-add content for maximum participation.

LISTENERS
Create a training curriculum with a focus on how to use tools to listen to brand and industry related conversations.

Low
Participation

of social media. If you are lucky, a high percentage of employees will make it to the top and become brand storytellers. And don't frown upon those that don't increase their participation over time. It is completely normal for some to stay where they are comfortable.

Finally, it is time to take all of these things – the survey data, learning styles and relative resources, elements, and everything else, and set the schedule to execute the training for your employee advocacy programme.

As you dive into preparing your employees, you probably now have more information to consider than you ever thought possible. Because of that, it is tempting to go beyond feeling confident and to start feeling invincible – as well as highly protective of all of the work you have done. But for your own sanity, try to be open to the idea that, even with the extensive effort you have put into making your employee advocacy programme a reality, there will be hurdles. And those hurdles will likely take the shape of people who neither know nor care that this is vitally important to you and the company you work for.

This is no reason to panic, or to throw your colour-coded training manual into the trash. Return to your metrics; you never expected every single person in the company to join up right away, or total and unwavering retention of participants. Your success is not fully contingent on the volume of employees you entice to join, just like it does not hinge on your ability to somehow execute a training regimen so perfectly that historians write about it in the future (although, that would be pretty cool).

Table 9.1 Employee training – titles and descriptions

LEARNERS	
How to set up Google Alerts to monitor news	Step-by-step instructions on how employees can set up and use Google Alerts based on certain search queries
How to set up a Twitter account	NA
How to use Google Advanced Search to monitor conversations and hashtags	Step-by-step instructions on how to leverage Twitter to find relevant information about the company or industry topics
How to optimize your social profiles for maximum engagement and visibility	Techniques and best practices on how to use the functionalities and capabilities of each social network to improve brand visibility
CONVERSATIONALIST	
How to find and source relevant content	Techniques on using tools like Feedly, Buffer, BuzzSumo or LinkedIn Pulse to curate and share relevant content
The anatomy of an effective social post	Techniques on how to write effective post copy, use hashtags and images for Twitter, LinkedIn and Facebook
How to become a Twitter Power User	Using tools like Hootsuite, Buffer or Tweetdeck to be more efficient in social media
How to effectively engage with influencers	Tagging and engaging with industry influencers
CONTENT CREATORS	
How to write effective headlines	Techniques on how to write headlines that drive more sharing and click throughs
How to write effective stories	Techniques on how to write good blog posts, emphasizing the key fundamentals of storytelling
How to write content for search engines	Techniques on how to incorporate industry keywords into blog post titles and content
How to use emerging tools for employee storytelling	Techniques on how to use Snapchat and Instagram to tell good stories

Much like the training you have lost blood, sweat and tears over is designed to give your employee advocacy programme the best chance for success, the dedication you put into developing a thoughtful, deeply researched training process will determine how successful you are at executing it. What matters most is that you give employee advocates the tools, skills and information they need to effectively bring your programme to life.

Remember the 1:9:90 model? That rule applies here too: 1 per cent of your employees will be completely active, engaged and motivated to tell the brand story; 9 per cent will package those stories, provide their own context and share within their networks. The 90 per cent will sit back and just be observers – and that is totally fine.

Susan Emerick, our Insight contributor below, is not only a personal friend, she is also the co-author of *The Most Powerful Brand on Earth: How to transform teams, empower employees, integrate partners and mobilize customers to beat the competition in digital and social media* (2013). She is an IBMer who spearheaded several of the company's brand advocacy initiatives.

INSIGHT   Bestselling author and thought leader

Contribution from Susan Emerick, IBM Marketing

For those of you who have followed me on Twitter (@sfemerick) or read my book, *The Most Powerful Brand on Earth*, you know I believe the most successful brand advocates are those who gain visibility and trust by sharing their expertise, and the most successful brands are those that build systems around these experts to align and scale impact for the brand.

IBM has done just that

Before I get into the details I would like to establish a common understanding of how we define employee advocacy – meaning: *brands empowering employees to support the goals of the brand, using content and employee-owned social* – as explained in my book, this could also be extended to business partners or even customers.

But why should brands care?

Well, for starters employee advocacy is the fastest-growing and most effective means of driving brand engagement and advocacy at scale. Second, customers trust your experts and regular employees more than anyone else in your company.

In fact, people trust regular employees as credible spokespeople more than official brand sources like the CEO, as shown by the 20 point gain since 2009, in Edelman's latest Trust Barometer study (Edelman Public Relations, 2017). In addition, the study reveals that employees rank highest overall 36 per cent, as the most trusted influencer to communicate across 4 out of 5 topic categories including: engagement, integrity, products and services, and operations.

Prove value to your stakeholders, or your programme will be short-lived

If you are contemplating an employee advocacy programme, you will need to consider how you are going to measure, demonstrate value and deliver results. If you miss this critical step, the likelihood of your programme being short-lived is fairly high because you will not be able to secure the resources or investment you will need.

While ROI targets are typically financial, such as increasing revenue or decreasing costs, they may also be non-financial such as increasing productivity, improving operational efficiency or reducing time to market, which have financial implications. No matter which is right for your programme, you need to begin with establishing measurable ROI targets for the programme up front. It is not enough to set targets, you also have to determine how you will measure and report progress against them.

Another critical step is to consider what motivates stakeholders – depending which part of your company is sponsoring your programme they will likely have different motivations and attainment measures (the details on addressing stakeholder motivations is explained in my book, *The Most Powerful Brand on Earth*).

IBM is a leader in social business, committed to driving transformation, paving the way for open collaboration and employee engagement

My previous colleague, Colleen Burns, Manager of IBM's Influencer Engagement Team, shared IBM's belief that employees are one of the greatest sources of influence. Not just in IBM products, but in the entirety of the company. IBMers (as employees call themselves), play a critical role helping to set the agenda, as well as building and cultivating relationships.

The IBM Redbooks Thought Leaders Social Media Residency is a great example. The programme was designed to create a pipeline of thought leadership blogs and help motivate technical employees to establish their personal social eminence while sharing their technical knowledge and expertise while building engagement opportunities. Since its inception in 2011, programme participants have authored nearly 2,000 blogs across 11 business topics. In fact 800 posts published on IBM's Thoughts On Cloud blog have accrued 1.1 million visits and counting!

IBM's *Select* programme, designed to identify high-value experts to support social strategies aligned to go-to-market priorities, enabled SMEs to tag links and track inbound referrals from their personal blogs. This programme has quantifiably outperformed traditional marketing and paid media tactics, proving digitally engaged experts could achieve a 33 per cent conversion rate to a call to action.

IBM is also helping customers like Performance Bicycle achieve results by creating a community-based learning centre, which has become the go-to destination for cycling enthusiasts. Moderated by employees who are cycling experts, they have achieved a 300 per cent increase in traffic within the first four months while proving a 20 per cent higher conversion from the learning centre compared to other referral sources.

IBM's work with Illy, an Italian coffee and accessories retailer, resulted in a 40 per cent increase in traffic to the retailer's online shopping catalogue.

Amber Armstrong, Programme Director of IBM's Social Business team, launched a unique employee advocacy programme powered by Dynamic Signal with 200 initial subject-matter experts (SMEs). This elite group drove 146,000 shares to date, resulting in 188 million impressions and 603,000 clicks through to the call to action, with an estimated cost saving on media spend between US $300,000 and $1.2 million (Figure 9.2).

Figure 9.2   How employees drove 603,000 clicks to IBM web properties

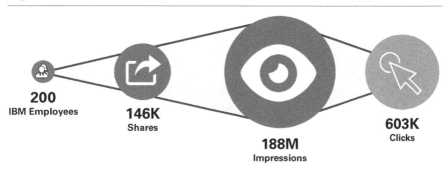

200
IBM Employees

146K
Shares

188M
Impressions

603K
Clicks

Bringing employee storytelling to life

10

Up until the point of launch, it may seem like the development of your employee advocacy programme has been an endless stream of research, observation, planning, more planning, deeper planning, surveying, and then planning again. And it has – to some degree, process creation will forever be an important element of growing and refining the programme. There will always be upcoming milestones to reach, numbers to hit and new content to share. Most crucially for the company at large, there will regularly be campaigns to support. Luckily for you, employee advocates are uniquely and ideally positioned to help sales and marketing efforts achieve major results.

Start off on the right foot by identifying where employee advocacy fits into your company's broader marketing initiatives. This is critical because you will want to ensure that the stories your employees are telling and sharing are closely aligned to the overall brand story. By doing so, you can surround-sound your customers with highly relevant content that will result in an action you want them to take – a click, a download, a phone call or even a sale.

But this is not easy. There is a surplus of content and media in the market today and it can be extremely difficult breaking through the noise to reach your distracted customers online. Not only are you competing with your direct competitors, but you must also consider every other company with a Facebook page and a budget.

Your customers can only ingest a finite amount of information at any given moment in time. It is the same reason for Twitter's 140-character limit or why the average Facebook user only has a few hundred friends. Most humans cannot manage their lives effectively with an excess of media sources competing for their attention. The abundance of content vying for their attention often outweighs what they can actually comprehend or believe. And because your customers have tunnel vision and only want to consume content that is relevant to their specific interests, it is critical that your stories are laser-focused, relevant and driven by audience intelligence.

Audience intelligence must be the foundation of all storytelling

The way to break through the clutter and tell a better story than your competitors is to get a firm understanding of your audience first. This will ensure that you take out as much guesswork as possible while also being more calculated when telling your story. Audience intelligence can help you determine which channels will be the most effective for engagement; inform your paid media strategy; and identify and activate your brand's stakeholders – influencers, customers and, of course, your employees.

As you might guess, the top of Figure 10.1 starts with audience intelligence. You will need to have access to a social listening platform, but the same methodology would apply regardless of which one you use. Platforms such as Crimson Hexagon and Netbase are two enterprise-level social listening technologies with capabilities that allow you to build, track and monitor the behaviour of very specific audiences.

An audience is really whatever you want it to be. It can include self-identified chief technology officers, data scientists or people interested in topics like Hadoop, machine learning or artificial intelligence, all of which are based on what is written in their online biographies. On the consumer side, it could be as basic as people who follow or mention your brand online, to more complex characteristics such as millennials in London who are interested in electronic dance music (EDM).

Before we dive into audience intelligence, we need first to define traditional social listening and explain the types of results you would get from a listening report. The definition is fairly straightforward: traditional social listening is a process of monitoring digital conversations to understand what the market is saying about a brand, industry or key topics online.

So imagine if you work for a company such as Adidas and you are a brand manager for their basketball shoe line. If you wanted to analyse the conversation surrounding your brand specific to basketball shoes, you would build a search query in a social listening platform that may look something like this:

Adidas AND (basketball OR shoes OR kicks OR high-tops OR sneakers OR 'James Harden' OR Harden OR 'Derrick Rose' OR Rose)

What we are doing here is telling the social listening platform to look for any mention of Adidas plus any of the keywords within the parentheses. This ensures that the results are relevant and specific to Adidas (eg the results would not include a mention of James Harden and not Adidas). And in case you didn't know – both James Harden and Derrick Rose are NBA

Figure 10.1 Audience-driven storytelling model

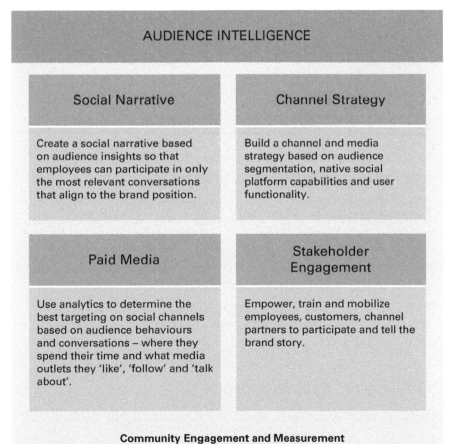

AUDIENCE INTELLIGENCE

Social Narrative

Create a social narrative based on audience insights so that employees can participate in only the most relevant conversations that align to the brand position.

Channel Strategy

Build a channel and media strategy based on audience segmentation, native social platform capabilities and user functionality.

Paid Media

Use analytics to determine the best targeting on social channels based on audience behaviours and conversations – where they spend their time and what media outlets they 'like', 'follow' and 'talk about'.

Stakeholder Engagement

Empower, train and mobilize employees, customers, channel partners to participate and tell the brand story.

Community Engagement and Measurement
Build a social governance model to ensure all content/ads are within brand/ FTC guidelines, listen and respond; monitor, track, report and escalate all conversations as needed.

Basketball players and have their own Adidas signature basketball shoe. The results will include a breakdown and volume of the specific conversations and where those conversations are happening online – social media, new articles, blogs and forums.

With audience intelligence, the process is a little different. With this approach, you build an audience first using the methodology mentioned above, and then you search within their conversations, media sharing habits and language either historically or in real-time. This will give you the most relevant insights into your audience. This method takes out the noise of the entire market so you can really begin to study your audience and learn a ton about their behaviours:

- What type of media publications is my audience sharing – *Forbes*, *Wall Street Journal*, *New York Times*?

- What kind of language and vernacular are my customers using when talking about my products?

- What keywords do my customers use in context with my brand, products or services?

- What hashtags do my customers use the most – and why?

- What are their interests and characteristics that make my customers unique from my competitors and everyone else?

- What channel(s) is my audience spending their time on the most? At what times are my customers frequently publishing content online?

- Other than my content, what are the other interests or passions of my customers? How do they vary by geography? How does that vary by lifecycle stage?

Finding the answers to these questions will take out the guesswork and result in more effective, data-driven marketing. If you're smart, you will start with identifying your core messages – your narrative; the stories that you want to tell that align to your brand promise, but also relevant to the discussions and passions of your audience.

Building your social narrative

In order to tell these relevant stories, you need to understand exactly what your audience cares about – and by using the intelligence mentioned above you can do this with precision. I have used the framework shown in Figure 10.2 for brand positioning workshops, but it also applies directly to an employee-driven content strategy too.

Figure 10.2 Audience-driven narrative development process

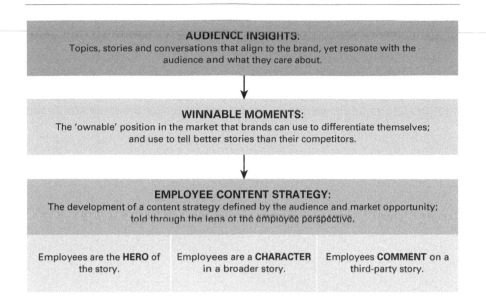

Again, audience data will give you the insights you need to find white-space in the market. Whitespace is that key nugget of information that no one else in the market owns. You can extract patterns of behaviour, conversation analysis and audience insights that will help deliver the core positioning of your employee-driven content.

The 'winnable moment' is that north star that makes your brand unique from everyone else and allows your brand (through your employees) to own a very specific piece of the conversation at large.

The employee content framework is one way to categorize your content and allows your employees to tell their stories through three different lenses, whereby:

- **Your employees are the hero of the story**: stories all about your employees, the value they bring to the market, products/services; sometimes can be perceived as narcissistic if not balanced with other types of stories.

- **Your employees are characters in a broader story**: stories about your customer, the value your customers receive from solving technology challenges or business problems in partnership with your employees; should not be self-serving and stories must show humility and lead with your customers first.

- **Your employees comment on a third-party story**: stories about your employees' point of view about a topic in the market, the market itself or a topic that resonates with an audience and also relevant to the brand; must add value to the market, educate and provide thought leadership.

Remember, employee advocacy programmes usually start with just sharing. The innovative and forward-thinking companies are taking it a step further and unleashing employees into the marketplace to tell amazing stories and share them all across the internet.

Even with the most remarkably advanced platforms and careful segmentation processes, getting your brand's message and assets in front of critical prospects is a bit of a gamble. Coupled with internet cookies and remarketing, algorithms can practically work magic when it comes to following your audience. But what those intricate, data-driven tools cannot replace is conversation, trust and the human connection. To reiterate, the formula for success here is simple:

1 Build your audience using the methodology from above.

2 Mine their conversations, weekly or monthly.

3 Extract key insights (media sharing, keyword and hashtag usage).

4 Feed that intelligence back to your employees.

5 Turn on the content engine.

We already know that people are 92 per cent more likely to trust recommendations from their peer networks than they are to trust a brand or advertiser (Morrison, 2016). We also know that the reason for this trust has a great deal to do with risk mitigation: if someone whose opinion and experiences you believe in tells you they have tried something and liked it, you are going to think there is a fairly decent chance you will like it, too. And if that same person says an article they read is terrible, you probably are not going to bother checking it out yourself. The same goes with restaurant recommendations and basketball shoes too.

The core component here is action; rather, getting someone to do something that you want them to do. That's the entire point of your advocacy programme: to inspire, encourage, motivate, push, drive – whatever you want to call it – people to take action. For employees, you want them to feel that they are an important part of the growth of the business, and to know that their roles are integral and valued. You want them to feel connected to the company, tell your brand's story, and share your content because they believe in its impact. Beyond your employees, you want prospects to take notice of your business and, ideally, buy your products. You want current customers to know that they have made a smart decision by choosing to engage with you and spend hard-earned budgets on your product and services. It is fitting, then, that the process of making a company recognizable and loved by consumers is known as brand activation.

To activate your brand with employee advocacy, the content and other assets that you develop or aggregate must align to those critical targets you are trying to reach, particularly the ones that might be missed without a human bridge between them and your company message. You want consumers to believe in your brand and what it stands for. This further encourages loyalty, which will bring prospects closer to purchase, and solidify existing customers' faith in the company. The key principles of brand activation make for a wonderful guide here as you categorize existing assets to be deployed, create new content for employee advocates to share or build your employee content framework. They are fairly simple:

1 In order to inspire demand for your products, brand message and content, you have to fully understand what your target audiences want or care about. You really are not ever going to be 'done' with research (sorry).

2 Creativity and strategy are equally important. Try very hard not to sacrifice one for the other.

3 Timing matters. Your content and message should always be relevant to world – or at least industry – issues.

4 Capitalizing on the need for person-to-person connection requires that you go beyond those things that can be digitally tracked. This means using in-person events such as conferences, meetups, panels and the like, to further cement the connection between your brand, employees and market.

Remember PESO? Here's how you can leverage each and every piece of your company's paid, earned, shared and owned media channels with employee advocacy – and provide the guidance your employees need to fully grasp how each type creates impact, supports the story of your brand and, most importantly, drives action.

Revisiting PESO: again, not the currency

From a content perspective, utilizing various types of digital assets – blog posts, video, infographics, slideshare presentations, webinars, etc – to cast a wider net for your message makes perfect strategic sense. But because not everyone understands how business content is created, how it is typically delivered or why it matters for different segments of your audience, it is critical to train your employees to be storytellers while also providing insight into the strategic function of various assets. To do this, you will need to develop an internal content plan for them that is a little more human.

While you work to humanize your content plan, be careful not to let the overarching business strategy fall by the wayside. Yes, employees need to understand what they are sharing and why, but that should not come at the expense of a game plan that makes sense for your company.

You get what you pay for

As mentioned in previous chapters, paid media is something you spend money on. This includes sponsored Facebook and LinkedIn updates, content syndication, promoted tweets and posts, display advertising, retargeting, search marketing – anything that gets amplified to a bigger audience because you paid for it. There are complicated algorithms and data in place to support paid content via all of the major social channels, so the old adage is absolutely true here: you get what you pay for. The reason it is so important to remember this is because, of all of the choices you make when developing content, what you put money behind should be selected or developed with the most focused, specific targets in mind. With paid media, failure to reach a desired audience is not just an unfortunate miss or a random mistake, it is a waste of effort and money that could have been better spent elsewhere.

For many businesses, mitigating that risk seems like too much work. Why spend money when you have to put so much energy into creating the right kind of content to support? Isn't it a fact that people don't trust advertisements nearly as much as they trust people, if at all? Why not just use alternative marketing tactics and employee advocacy to organically spread the content your company is already producing? Well, the answer here is clear: social channels need to make money and they are the gatekeepers to your audience. They have the power to override even the most amazing unpaid content with the stuff they have been paid to promote, and there is not a whole lot you can do about that.

Second, while it is completely fair (and smart!) to remember why trust matters and how it is earned when it comes to content, the critical mistake businesses make is assuming that 'more trustworthy' is the inverse of 'not trustworthy at all'. But it's not. People understand that businesses want to sell their products and services. In many cases, they are interested in learning about new offerings that reflect their taste, hobbies or lifestyle, and that they may not have known about if it were not for retargeting, promotions and other advertising. In this way, paid media works in tandem with both earned and owned media to help expand your business and customer base. Moreover, it is the only way to get your carefully tailored content in front of people who exactly match the demographic of your target customers and prospects. It doesn't hurt that it is easier to track than your organic content, either, since most social channels offer data tracking and analytics when you pay them to push your assets.

So the question here is simple. Why wouldn't you want to use paid media to surround-sound your customers with employee-driven content? Perhaps it is less of a question and more of a plea. It's smart marketing.

Earn your keep

Earned media is the kind of thing you might have paid for, but didn't have to because you did such an awesome job marketing and brand building. But make no mistake – earned media is not guaranteed and it is not intended to completely replace a paid media strategy. It can, however, complement paid media quite nicely. It is a useful tool for figuring out what kinds of content you should be spending money on, and even better? It can help you understand exactly how your employee advocacy programme is generating ROI.

Since we are talking about returns on investments, it is time to go back to the maths, so you can understand (and explain) how the value of earned media is measured. First, you will need a little bit of information from your existing paid campaigns:

- The average cost per engagement (CPE) that you spend on paid content via each social channel. An engagement is when someone interacts with your ad or content, such as clicking 'play' on a video.

- The average cost per 1,000 impressions (CPM) that you spend on paid content via each social channel (fun fact: the 'M' is in there because it is the Roman numeral for 1,000).

- The average cost per click (CPC) that you spend on paid content via each social channel. This means a click to read more, see your website and so on.

After you get an understanding of what you are spending, you can gauge the value of different interaction types. Let's say you spend an average of about $1.50 for every engagement that happens with your paid content via Twitter. Divide that number by engagement types (in this case, favourites, retweets and replies), and you end up with each type of engagement being worth $0.50. In this way, you can calculate the value of earned media engagement: 6 organic retweets are worth $3.00; 20 organic retweets are worth $10.00, and so on.

The reason you want to understand, and have your advocates understand, the value of earned media is so that everyone can: 1) realize the tangible value of your advocacy efforts; and 2) track the returns of the programme. If you spend $1,000 to get your advocacy programme up and running, and it results in 2,000 retweets in a couple of months, you have broken even. Anything after that can be considered profit, or at least savings (Malatesta, 2016). And that is a fairly good way to validate what you are doing.

Many view earned media as the result of traditional 'media relations'. You write a press release announcing a new product, pitch a few reporters and hope that one of them bites. Or, you write a byline on behalf of your CEO, pitch it to Entrepreneur or Forbes and then cross your fingers that it gets published. Of course, I am oversimplifying the public relations industry as a whole, but I think you get it.

But there is an additional opportunity here. As a data-driven marketer, you probably already have a pulse as to those 'earned media' conversations happening in the marketplace – on Twitter, LinkedIn or a blog somewhere. Imagine your employees – the content creators – being smack dab in the middle of those conversations, in a human, non-spammy sort of way. Maybe they are just participating, responding or even facilitating. In any of those cases, it is a win–win for everyone involved.

Make your stuff shareable

Yep, this is an obvious one and, basically, the backbone of your advocacy programme: shared media. It is almost exactly what it sounds like. But! Shared media is not all media; rather, it is the content you create that is specifically and actively designed to entice people to share it in social media. Sure, anything can technically end up being shared, and hopefully that happens a lot. But the most effective examples of this kind of media have the inherent shareability built right into the content itself.

So how do you even begin designing these types of assets? By leveraging your audience-driven social listening strategy. This will keep you continuously informed about trending topics in your industry, competitor tactics, content and events, and help you keep track of what your audience is saying and sharing. When you know this information, you can select existing content or develop new assets that align with your findings. Audience listening can do a lot more than help you shape content, too. With insights into your competitors, the industry at large and the needs of target customers, your business can start answering larger questions that may inform how your company operates as a whole.

These insights are important to your employee advocacy efforts, of course, because you can use them to point your advocates in a particular direction, keep an eye on certain dialogues, and watch out for trends and issues. But these insights can actually be even more valuable for the development of overarching business plans, product road maps, talent acquisition and growth strategies.

Own your story

Limiting your voice and content to brand-owned channels alone makes it difficult to break into important conversations and new markets, or to keep accurate tabs on the way your business is being perceived. A huge part of why employee advocacy matters is because it allows you to vastly extend the amount of control you have over your brand's message. This is where owned media comes in.

Owned media includes all content, assets and communication channels that your brand controls, such as company blog posts, executive byline articles, customer newsletters and, of course, your website, mobile website and product materials. Some of this content will not be immediately scalable to audiences outside of your customer base, but that is okay – it can still provide a foundation for long-term growth, merely by performing well (or not so well). That is because how people engage with your owned media tells you, more or less right away, if what you are doing is interesting and valuable.

The more owned media content you create, the better position you will be in to own as much real estate in the search engines as possible. Meaning, when a customer searches for a 'service that your company provides' in Google, your product pages, blog posts, webinars, white papers and any other long-form content will appear on the first page. The more real estate you own in Google the better, whether it is paid for or not.

Naturally, you want your owned media to demonstrate how amazing your company is and why everyone should buy your products, but that is not going to do much for your integrity as a business or for positioning your employees and executives as thought leaders. What will help in those areas is owned media that is not just about the stuff you are selling.

And that means giving away the most valuable content and assets you have to offer.

No, you don't have to offer your services for free or share any trade secrets. But you should not hold your most valuable insights and expertise hostage behind an online form, either. Webinars that allow you to showcase key influencers or unique concepts, educational resources that help other businesses to do better, and thought leadership pieces that demonstrate people's knowledge are all especially good for this. Regardless of the exact reason you create a piece of owned media, always be sure that it exhibits one or more of the following critical qualities:

- **It's useful**: it provides practical explanations, applications or other information that helps them do something more effectively.

- **It's educational**: it teaches people how to do something, why they should do something, and what tactics and tools they should use to get things done.

- **It's provocative**: it keeps people engaged and interested because it is creative, fun to consume and a little unexpected.

- **It opens doors**: it helps people expand their professional experiences, networks, contacts or markets because it encourages new connections and dialogue.

- **It makes people feel**: hopefully positive feelings, but at the very least it challenges commonly accepted best practices or sheds new light on the way things are done.

- **It provides hard-to-come-by insight**: people like to hear from other people who are close to stuff that is going on, whether it is something newsworthy or simply a story of personal experience. Find employees, industry influencers and customers that are able to provide anecdotes or data points that may not otherwise see the light of day.

- **It gives customers (or prospects) an exclusive perk**: this is the owned media you are probably used to creating, where it is all about the brand all the time. In addition to showing everyone how awesome your products are, use this to reinforce customer loyalty and entice prospects by providing deals, event tickets, discounted services and the like to people who already use your product – or those who need just a little extra push to sign up.

Now that you fully understand the media and content assets at your disposal, you can plug them into existing sales and marketing campaigns or develop new campaigns that will make the most of what you have.

Integrating employee-driven content into brand campaigns

Until now, content has undoubtedly been part of your core campaign strategy, and that is a really, really good thing – because 70 per cent of marketers around the world have realized exactly how valuable content is, and are ramping up to create and push far more branded assets than they did last year (Content Marketing Institute, 2017). But employee advocacy probably has not played as big a role in your marketing efforts (not the formal kind, anyway). Before we dive into how you can connect the moving parts of your marketing and sales campaigns to PESO content and advocacy tactics, it is worth revisiting the three types of employee-driven content that are most likely to do well with your employee's support.

Turn your employees into thought leaders and heroes of the story

Everyone is an expert on something, and when you are mining your company for thought leaders it is a good idea to start with what you know your employees know: their jobs. Seek out people who have already done some level of thought leadership activity, such as participating in a webinar or writing a guest blog about what they do. Offer opportunities for people to do this in relationship to your company, and see who expresses an interest. When you create content that is centred around the experience of someone who is part of the company, you solidify their position as a skilled, valuable member of the company and as a brand ambassador. People like to acknowledge when they are being recognized, and displaying confidence in your advocates will only make them more powerful for your brand. A lot of the time, this kind of content is a good candidate for the paid-media route.

Activate your employees to be characters in a bigger story

Expert or not, there are going to be influential people who just are not ready for the limelight, or willing to step into it. But that does not mean they cannot be part of larger stories that have to do with your industry or markets. Encourage these people to be interviewed if they are not interested in authoring a blog, or to be a part of analyst meetings so they can provide unique insight for industry reports. What is especially wonderful about positioning your employees this way is that they will typically be placed alongside other respected industry thought leaders. This not only strengthens your company's authority on relevant topics, issues and trends, but it also supports their individual credibility – and serves as an often-successful jumping off-point for earned media.

Encourage employees to share their knowledge with other industry experts

This is perhaps the easiest type of employee advocate 'content' that you can ask your employees to participate in: commenting. But we are not talking about just any old comment on any random internet post; these interactions from your employees must reflect company values and be made on external content that is in some way tied to your company, your industry or how your product sits in the broader marketplace. It is more commentary than it is commenting.

When employees participate in conversations that are relevant to the business, they are able to gather valuable intel that could prove highly useful for product iterations or marketing efforts. They are also zeroing in on passionate people who care about what is going on in your space, who they can then involve in meaningful conversations on behalf of your brand.

Making room for a new approach

There are many questions you will be asking yourself, and others, as you make the necessary shifts to involve employee advocacy with strategic sales and marketing plans. So, it is important that the process you use each time be vetted and repeatable, as well as flexible enough to be used for different types of campaigns, multiple verticals and with various types of assets. This is going to be one of the more challenging aspects of integrating employee advocacy into your larger marketing strategy, because there is a 100 per cent chance that the people who typically run these types of activation campaigns have a process in place that works for them.

How to connect amplification strategies to employee advocacy: 20 questions to ask

1   What actions do you want prospects to take as a result of this campaign? What information can your employees glean that may help you determine how likely (or unlikely) that will be?

2   Which unique element of your brand will be central to this campaign so that it stands out? What information can your employees provide to you so that you can capitalize on this part of your message (eg what is resonating in their networks)?

3   Who exactly is your target audience – including industry, role, seniority and other demographic information? Which of your employees most closely aligns with this persona? What level of interaction with the target are they willing or able to have?

4   How do you plan to create content and conversations that your targets will care about? How can you leverage employees to support these efforts?

5   What content will resonate with your target audience, and how evergreen will it be? What feedback will you solicit from employees about this content to support your choice?

6   What will you do to create a lasting impression that turns prospects from people who have heard of you into people who buy your products?

7   Is this campaign specific to a certain region or area? If so, which employees are most closely tied to that region, either because of the work they do or because of where they are located? What insight can they provide about regional customs or considerations?

8   How many targets is this campaign designed to reach? What percentage of that end goal is achievable with paid media, and what can be supported or better amplified through employee advocacy?

9   Is this activation campaign truly relevant to your message and core values? Is the connection between these elements transparent enough for employees to identify? If not, how can you make the necessary adjustments to achieve total alignment and earn the support of your employees?

10   What are your goals, and how can your employees help you reach them?

11   How do you plan to measure ROI, both in terms of monetary investment and in data capture? What additional measurements or perks will you put in place to entice employees to participate? What data will you share that may be beneficial to teams outside of the marketing and sales organizations?

12   What long-term benefits do you see this campaign resulting in for the company, and how can your employees help perpetuate or secure those returns?

13   What is the potential for this campaign to integrate with, or support, other marketing and sales activities going on within the rest of the company? How can your employees help bridge gaps, translate efforts across teams, and facilitate efficient communication and execution?

14   What elements of the campaign are flexible, in case you need to make changes so that the campaign will perform better over time? How can you tap into your employees to monitor campaign performance or, better yet, amplify it?

15   In what other ways will you use this campaign and its data to drive other promotional opportunities, such as digital advertising and PR? Which employees can help you best identify these opportunities?

16   How will this campaign generate new opportunities to target prospects or engage with customers? Who from your employee programme can take ownership of going after those new touchpoints?

17   How will you perpetuate the conversations and wins you generate, and how can employees help with that?

18   How will you use your findings to generate content that not only aligns with brand objectives and target needs, but that your employees support and identify with?

19   For this specific campaign, what will you offer advocates as goals to reach in order to earn perks and rewards?

20   How do you know that integrating employee advocacy is beneficial to your other marketing and sales strategies, and to the company as a whole?

Even more important than solidifying your integration blueprint will be proving that it works. Doing so involves figuring out how you extract data and insights from the analytics you collect, in order to inform additional strategic frameworks and social narratives. Those will help you shape the creation of future content and creative assets, as well as an editorial approach that categorizes content based on branding guidelines and emerging information that bubbles up as a result of your advocacy programme. But, at the root, you will need to have a formula in place that will allow you, after implementation, to answer one very, very crucial question:

How much money would you have to spend on paid media and advertising for a single campaign in order to generate the same results as you can using a laser-focused, content- and data-driven employee advocacy programme?

In other words, this is how you validate that your employee advocacy programme is worth the valiant efforts you have put into it. Like the previous example, you will need to know:

- Your average monthly cost per click (CPC) for each social network you spend money with.
- The total number of clicks generated solely from your employee advocacy programme via each of those networks each month.
- Finally, you will need to calculate any additional costs of running the programme that you incur on a monthly basis.

We will use Twitter, and its promoted tweets, as an example one more time – except this time we are going real-world with the numbers. Imagine that, when running a standard paid media campaign, you spend \$2.17 per click on Twitter. And let's say that your group of 175 employee advocates typically generates about 20,000 total clicks in one month organically.

There are three important formulas you need to solve, which in this example would read:

1 **20,000 clicks / 175 employees = Average goal of 114 social actions (clicks) per month.**

    This is the number you can use to set expectations for actions driven by individual employees.

2 **20,000 clicks × \$2.17 CPC = \$43,400 per month.**

    This is how you figure out the monthly cost of *not* using employee advocacy.

3 **\$43,400 per month / 175 employees = \$248 per advocate.**

    This is how much each individual advocate saves you in marketing spend each month.

Basically, this means that you would have to spend \$43,400 for a month's worth of the same actions you would get *for free* by activating 175 employees to actively create and share content. If you can demonstrate that kind of ROI, even if the numbers are not quite so large, you are in really good shape.

Maximize your content, media and digital assets

Many pages ago, we discussed the diversity of target audiences and how different people engage – differently – with some assets than they do with others. Assets, not concepts. So while it is true that one target may find infographics fascinating and another will think they are silly, this in no way means you have to sacrifice the chance to engage with either target. You just have to find ways to adapt your campaign ideas for different media, so you can flood an already impacted space with your own message.

Take, for example, a classic annual e-book that software companies like to produce: a collection of learnings from one year that helps their customers and prospects make decisions for the next year. Though commonly produced in a flat, PDF format that is rife with thoughtful text and (hopefully) beautiful design, an e-book is not going to resonate with everyone they want it to resonate with. It doesn't matter how amazingly written or aesthetically pleasing it is – some people just hate e-books. But rather than give up the ghost on your dreams of using this brilliant collection of data to convert prospects and secure customer faith, imagine how you can repackage and redeliver your findings in a variety of ways:

- **Infographics**: assuming your e-book is packed with data points, you can combine that data into a complete infographic. You can pitch it to reporters, as a byline or host it on a web page for others to embed, therefore increasing the number of inbound links to the page.

- **Infograms**: infograms are smaller, bite-sized and shareable graphics that take one data point from the larger infographic, coupled with a headline (post copy) that inspires action. Infograms can be shared across all social media platforms and link back to the full infographic.

- **Bylines**: ask executives or SMEs to write a byline summarizing the e-book; pitch the byline to relevant media publications.

- **Blog posts**: you can repurpose each section of the e-book to create a series of blog posts.

- **Slideshare**: even if the e-book itself is already hosted on Slideshare, you can break it up into various sections, highlight the data and use it more as a visual representation of the e-book without all the text.

- **Influencers**: as a part of the e-book production, you can invite influencers to comment on various topics that are relevant and sprinkle them throughout. Once the e-book is published, provide the influencers with the embed code to the Slideshare with some sample social media content.

- **Webinars:** host a series of webinars highlighting various topics of the e-book.
- **TweetChat:** ask an influencer to moderate a chat to discuss findings and insights from the e-book.

As with any kind of activity, you want the returns on your investments to significantly outweigh the investments themselves. This kind of multifaceted content strategy can dramatically tip the scales in your favour, and help you reach far more people than you would with just a single piece of content or one in-person event. Bonus? It will also give your employee advocacy efforts a boost because, after all, employees are people – and some of them hate e-books, too.

Activating the real-time, newsroom model to employee advocacy

Remember this model (Figure 10.3) from Chapter 8 when I talked about planning for all the roles and responsibilities needed to activate an employee advocacy programme? Let's dig in to see how this actually works. Remember, you are not going to launch this newsroom methodology on day one. It will take some time.

As usual, the model starts with research. To reiterate, you will want to build an audience using one of the methodologies mentioned earlier in this

Figure 10.3   Real-time listening and employee activation

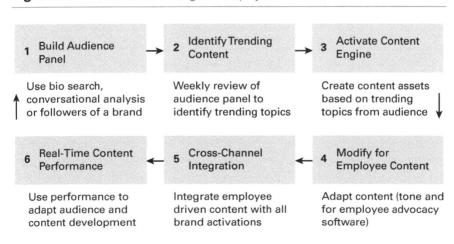

chapter – either using a bio search for job titles or keywords or performing a conversational analysis on key topics that are important to your business (branded or unbranded, industry keywords). Don't forget that you can also build your audience simply with your current social media followers, although I don't necessarily recommend this approach.

The second part of this process involves setting up an ongoing listening analysis. You can be proactive and manually search for terms to see what the audience is saying, sharing or just see what type of content is trending. You can manually search for your company name, products, executives and even your competitors. Trending content can include certain articles that are being shared or a technology conversation that is starting to pick up steam. If you have the resources, I would suggest mining through the data once or twice per week. You can pick up the pace and scale once the process is optimized and understood by everyone involved.

Once you can extract some trending content from the audience, you will have to turn on your content engine. Hopefully you will have a creative and content team on hand or maybe an agency to help develop assets. In some cases, you might just ask participating employees to write a blog post about the topic or put together a Slideshare presentation. And if you have planned accordingly, you would have already mapped all the existing content you have into a content library in case you need to repurpose some assets.

The key to this process is that it should take you less than 24 hours from the time you identify an opportunity from the audience panel to the time you distribute the content into the marketplace. I know, it seems impossible. But if newsrooms can do it, why can't you?

The next thing you will have to do is optimize the content specifically for the employee advocacy platform. Each platform is different so you will have to ensure that all the content is uploaded correctly and ready for distribution. This includes writing all the shareable post copy, hashtags and optimizing the correct pixel dimensions for any corresponding images.

Once the content is uploaded into the system and other employees are sharing it, you will want to determine if and how you will want to integrate it across all of your paid, earned, shared and owned media. If it is a blog post, perhaps you will throw some paid search behind it. Or, maybe you will amplify the content by using a promoted tweet or other sponsored updates. I would not suggest doing this with every piece of employee content, especially if you have hundreds of employees that are a part of the programme. Set some parameters, and then test to see what is working and what doesn't. This leads to the last step of the process: real-time insights.

You probably already have KPIs associated with your digital marketing programmes. Use these as benchmarks to see how well your employee's content is performing in the marketplace. Parameters staying the same, I would bet the employee-driven content outperforms branded content. The most important thing to remember about this last step of the process is to ensure that any findings are captured and used to improve your programme and, more importantly the content.

Here is an example of the newsroom model in action; let's assume you are Adidas again:

- You have built an audience panel of 30,000 millennials who play basketball in various leagues in the United States and you monitor that panel weekly for insights.

- On Monday, you notice that this audience is talking a lot about a current episode of *Game of Thrones*.

- On Tuesday, you produce a graphic of 'who would be your starting five on a basketball team if you had to choose from *Game of Thrones* characters'.

- You share it on Facebook and Twitter; and add $1,000 per channel for promotion.

- You add the content to your advocacy platform and broadcast it to all participating employees.

- You sit back and watch the clicks, shares and engagement grow.

Brand amplification does not happen without effort, and that effort can easily be wasted if you are unwilling or unprepared to leverage all the diverse resources at your disposal to integrate content and campaigns across your entire marketplace. Whether the assets you create are intended for paid media efforts, shareability, product endorsement or a combination of these, there is no doubt that the most efficient, cost-effective and impactful way to deliver them to your target audience is through your employee advocacy programme.

It doesn't take a maths whiz to figure out that the returns will wildly outweigh the investment necessary to turn your employees into true brand storytellers. And although finances are always a factor, it is the less quantifiable dividends that will prove to be the most valuable: customers who trust in your brand and products; employees who believe in your message and think it is worth talking about; and industry experts who are interested in your business's perspective and invested in your growth.

Any business can run a standard marketing activation campaign, but with the thoughtful, strategic execution of efforts backed by employee advocacy comes an authority and reputation in your given market that simply cannot be bought.

Follow these marketing leaders who exemplify employee advocacy

Of course, the most convincing examples of how things do or don't work are not based on theories and best practices. They are based on the trials and tribulations of real people working for real companies, who took the plunge after deciding the risk was totally worth it. Here are four impressive examples of employee advocacy integration with brand activation marketing, including why they did it, how they made it work, what they learnt and the results they ended up with.

Strategic-IC: catalysing brand awareness   Employee advocacy enables people to share company content they find valuable, which makes for an ideal method of amplifying brand awareness through an individual's networks, and backed by that person's own trustworthiness. This is important, of course, because people make things sound more human than brands do (go figure). But even so, the many algorithms put in place by social media channels are designed to keep branded content from taking over a person's news feed, focusing instead on showing them content that has been posted by their friends and family. Couple that with the fact that a social post's shelf life can be as short as 18 minutes, and it seems like brands are in trouble (Segal, 2015). That is, until they start using employee advocacy.

When it comes to social media, posts go 561 per cent further when shared by employees rather than a branded handle, and tend to generate about 24 times more shares (MSL Group, 2015). That is huge – and Strategic-IC, a UK-based digital B2B marketing agency, felt like the time was ripe to see what advocacy could do for them.

So, they used an incentive-based advocacy programme to encourage employees to share branded content – resulting in a 61 per cent click-through rate across all campaigns, and astounding engagement rate: 78 per cent of which is directly attributed to employee advocacy (Oktopost, 2015a).

Panaya: maximizing social selling   Of salespeople who engage in social selling 72.6 per cent regularly outperform their peers who do not utilize social media. They also exceed quota 23 per cent more often than non-social sellers (Fidelman, 2013). Employee advocacy, wherein people are provided with easy access to the content that they need when they need it, is a massive part of why social selling works. That was certainly the case at Panaya, a leading ERP software company focused on agile transitions.

Before implementing employee advocacy, the leadership team at Panaya was having issues dividing and developing content for their three global audiences. But by categorizing their content based on buyer personas and subjects, and encouraging employees to share what mattered to them, they were able to increase their low campaign conversion rate to 23 per cent (Oktopost, 2015b). This made the biggest impact for people on the sales team, who were able to use social media and targeted assets to better engage prospects and drive new sales opportunities.

Air Canada: deploying employee advocacy to build a more effective sales team Air Canada is the largest airline rooted in Canada, and the only one with the honour of bearing the national flag as their logo. They have been around for quite a while – since 1937 in fact – and help people and business to travel to 182 destinations across the globe. Even with their significant experience in internationality, they knew there was room for improvement in many areas of the organization. They wanted to convince customers to consistently make Air Canada their carrier of choice, help travellers make informed decisions during their trips, increase traffic to their website and other owned channels, and give Air Canada distinctly larger and more widespread impressions in new markets, in order to shape a more global presence.

To make this happen, they needed to communicate better across the board. They also wanted to make improvements to the narrative being told via sales pitches, create a more humanized voice and message for their customers and employees, and increase brand awareness across digital and social media. After launching their programme, they have now on-boarded 50 per cent of their entire sales team. They are also seeing some highly impressive results, including 32,000 shares across social media channels, 22,000 reactions, 17 million impressions and over 28,000 clicks on their branded content.

Hitachi Data Systems: the need for digital transformation Hitachi Data Systems (HDS) uses data to power the digital enterprise for better business outcomes. One of Thomson Reuters 'Top 100 Global Innovators', the company is reshaping how businesses work. HDS needed to embrace digital transformation, so what better way to do that than to start with employees.

HDS launched their employee advocacy programme with a core focus on social selling and overall employee engagement. While true digital transformation can take years to achieve, they also wanted to reach new audiences, enable the sales team and influence the influencers in the technology space. Their programme not only includes employees, but also external partners and industry influencers. They have a very robust programme – 15 different divisions tailoring to different interests and categories across five languages. The content is about 80 per cent Hitachi-focused, 10 per cent industry content and 10 per cent miscellaneous.

With over 500 employees participating in the programme, they have managed to garner 80,000 shares, 40,000 reactions, 41 million impressions and 180,000 clicks. The results sound more like they are coming from a paid media campaign.

Other than the stellar results that these four employee advocacy leaders have experienced, it is important to note that it doesn't matter how big, small, new or old your company is. Employee advocacy works for brand activation, social selling and campaign activation – the proof is in the numbers.

INSIGHT Content-marketing thought leader

Contribution from Michael Brenner, CEO at Marketing Insider Group

Every content marketer faces the challenge at some point of trying to figure out how to publish enough content to make a difference to your audience and your business.

But you only have a tiny budget. And you want to maintain a high level of quality. So how do you get the volume you need at a price you can afford?

Part of the answer comes down to building a volunteer army of contributors who will give you high-quality content, on the topics important to your business, for absolutely no money. That's right. You can get access to tons of articles, infographics and videos. And all you have to do is ask.

Let me explain.

How we built a media company with no employees

Back in 2010, Brian Rice and Dan Criel, two guys who worked for me at the time, as a personal favour helped me start B2B Marketing Insider. I started publishing my own rants and raves on content marketing, social media and marketing strategy right here.

Separately, Brian started a 'sister' site called B2C Marketing Insider (now Business2Community). This was based off some simple search engine optimization (SEO) analysis. And while I started writing my own posts twice a week, Brian eventually started reaching out to friends and family members who were already writing articles on social media and SEO and marketing strategy. They asked them if they wanted to contribute original guest posts.

The authors were all thrilled as the traffic and exposure they received were greater than what they could do on their own. This is the power of guest posting, which is now a common best practice for bloggers.

After months of publishing content from a small but growing group of authors, they submitted B2C Marketing Insider to Google for inclusion in their 'News' service. Google somehow accepted the site as a source of news and the traffic began to take off.

It was soon after this that the name was changed to Business2Community, and Dan and I joined as co-founders to try to help make this little side business take off. (I left the company over a year ago but continue to advise clients every day on the power of author curation and guest blogging.)

That site now has thousands of contributors who submit both original and syndicated content that allows them to publish hundreds of articles every day. The traffic on the site was once well over a couple of million page views per month!

Business2Community built an entire media company using an army of volunteer contributors.

SAP business innovation extends the model

While still at SAP, I took a similar approach to the company's Business Innovation site. I was given very little money to build the site and almost nothing to create original content.

I actually wrote the first 24 articles myself, summarizing white papers produced by our campaign team; six articles for each of the four categories we launched with.

But we wanted to publish one article every day for each of the four topics. So without any budget, how was I going to find authors and articles who would write for me for free?

The answer: I built an army of volunteer authors based on serving their own self-interest:

- **Step 1**: I identified all the internal employees who were already blogging on the topics I thought our audience was interested in. They had to already be writing high-quality content. Ideally, I also looked for those who had a built-in social audience. I found 12 great bloggers.

- **Step 2**: I approached them and pitched the dream I was chasing of building a world-class content-marketing hub. I tapped into their emotions and their own dreams of reaching new and bigger audiences. I asked them simply for permission to allow me to syndicate their existing blogs through an RSS feed. All 12 agreed and gave me permission to syndicate their content.

- **Step 3**: using the WordPress FeedWordpress plug-in, I added their existing RSS feeds and all their posts started coming in as new, full-length article drafts I could post on our site.

- **Step 4**: to make sure we were helping both our audience and the authors, we did a few things:

  - We generally waited a few days to post their articles so they could get all the benefit of their original posting.

  - We shared every story on our social channels.

  - We thanked our authors on Twitter.

  - We shared tips and tricks and created a sense of community with our authors.

  - We believed strongly in creating a sense of community with both our readers and our authors that went beyond just the traffic and exposure we were giving them.

- **Step 5**: using the amazing results from the traffic, engagement and conversion we started seeing, I requested and received budget for original content creation and, later, licensed content from NewsCred and a budget for paid distribution.

  We also started reaching out to external bloggers and thought leaders. At some point, we hit a tipping point and bloggers started coming to us and asking to become contributors for both original and syndicated content. We had reached what I love to call 'escape velocity', where growth becomes a virtuous cycle of publishing, sharing and engaging with more readers and contributors.

- **Step 6**: extending the community. My amazing former team sends out a weekly author newsletter that lists the 'top 10' posts of the week, recognizes an 'author of the week' and provides writing tips and examples of great content from others.

I am sharing these stories and tips and steps to building your own volunteer army of content contributors so that you can see the same kind of success that these sites, and now many more, are seeing.

Author curation

I call this approach 'author curation'. This combines some forms of social listening, influencer marketing, strategic content curation and content strategy.

All you need to do is align the interests of your audience with the topics you want to focus on, and the content written by influential authors, and you can make this work

Choosing the right employee advocacy technology 11

Remember all the planning, vetting, surveying, observing and researching you did to ensure that your employee advocacy programme would have the best chance for success? And remember how we inspired you to keep at it, even though it was time-consuming and challenging, because a solid plan is the most effective preventative medicine for failure? Of course you do. So it should come as no surprise, really, that you also need a technology platform that has been tried, tested and approved by leaders just like you in order to be successful.

After all, what is a plan worth if you have no way to execute it?

You have likely already mapped out and documented all of the requirements you need in a technology platform – integration capabilities with your existing content hub and social media accounts, advanced search functionality, gamification and leaderboard options to help motivate participation, in-depth analytics. All of these things are key, but it is especially necessary for you to provide a personalized, easy-to-understand experience for your employees in order to pique their interest and maintain their support. You want people to actively engage with your programme and its branded content – not because you are requiring them to, but because they believe in it. That takes work and strategy and listening, but it also takes an enablement platform that makes it simple (and fun) to contribute.

That's why your technology platform has to go beyond the obvious. You will need to define what matters most to you. Consider every crucial component of the programme and how you expect them to work together, and make note of how a platform can ideally help make that happen. It should facilitate not just your sharing efforts and data capture, but truly aid expansion and scalability, as well as collaboration between different teams and regions. It should be inviting for people at different stages of onboarding. It should reflect the way people work and support the tools and devices they use. It should meet your tracking requirements, in terms of segmenting content and different groups of employees, in addition to providing the insight you need into how different people and pieces are performing. Finally, it should be totally adaptable to your brand, your company and your culture.

Dynamic Signal is the solution. With current dedicated funding at US $43 million and growing, they have more investment backing than any other vendor in the employee advocacy category. The team at Dynamic Signal has several decades of experience exclusively focused on understanding, establishing, shaping, supporting and amplifying enterprise employee advocacy programmes. As a result, it is by far the most robust, comprehensive and well-equipped tool on the market to help you deploy, grow, measure and refine your employee advocacy initiatives. In a relatively short period of time, customers using Dynamic Signal have generated a collective 10 billion-plus impressions from external social sharing – which boils down to about 83 million impressions per month.

Clearly, the folks at Dynamic Signal know how to make a platform that drives what it promises. But even more importantly, their platform was specifically designed for employees. That matters, because even the most sophisticated, enterprise-grade technology cannot replace or truly mimic the behaviours, thought processes and power of people.

And advocacy means nothing – it has zero impact – without people.

Why Dynamic Signal is the leader in enterprise employee advocacy

Hundreds of leading brands use Dynamic Signal to further their employee advocacy programmes. Of the nation's top 10 social enterprises – companies that use commercial strategies to help people and the planet – seven are Dynamic Signal customers. Five of the top six PR agencies are, too (and they tell their customers it is awesome). Finally, 29 of the Fortune 500 (aka the 500 companies making the most money in the entire United States) are members of the Dynamic Signal roster. But why?

Frankly, it is because the platform is as appropriate and adaptable for enterprise organizations as it is for the people who drive them forward. Because they – the product and engineering teams who created Dynamic

Signal – are those people, too. They believe in long-term partnerships with companies that are collaborative and mutually beneficial when it comes to making employee advocacy more effective and efficient.

They understand that your platform, which is essentially your baseline support system, is much more than just a tool; it is a community that has a stake in the outcomes of your actions, and that can have massive impact on how those results unfold. They also understand how much trouble broken systems and processes can cause within a company, and how employee advocacy can help solve those issues in addition to amplifying brand awareness.

Of the many necessary things that can start to show wear and tear in an enterprise, communication is the one with the most power to make or break an organization. Part of the reason for this is because it is absolutely everywhere and part of literally everything. It has to happen between teams, leaders, customers, investors, vendors and prospects in order for anything at all to get done. With transparent and open communications amongst these many stakeholders comes increased efficiency, agility and an unmatched opportunity to catch hiccups before they become major issues.

Without it, the only thing that speeds up is the pace at which things start to disintegrate. In fact, Salesforce found that 86 per cent of corporate executives blame most workplace failures on ineffective communications (Business Wire, 2016). A lack of proper communication causes a ton of obvious problems such as multiple people doubling up on work, inconsistent processes that create frustrating bottlenecks, and employees who feel unheard and disengaged. None of these are as dangerous to a company's success and sustainability as lack of engagement, which can spread like wildfire when it goes unchecked.

You have probably heard that said many times before, and you may be wondering why it is such a big deal. Well, one of the primary reasons engagement matters so much is because without it your company is going to haemorrhage money. On average, a single disengaged worker costs a business approximately US $3,400 for every $10,000 in annual salary (Infosurv, 2017). So if that uninterested employee earns a base salary of $90,000 annually, you are going to end up losing another $30,600 on top of that. On the flipside, working to increase just one employee's engagement in the organization by a mere 10 per cent can increase profits by $2,400 per employee, per year. In this scenario, you would have to have approximately 12 engaged employees per each single disengaged employee just to break even. Ouch.

But what does engagement mean, exactly, and how can an advocacy programme help with it? Essentially, engagement means keeping an employee invested in the company, its growth, its success, and its performance internally and in the market. Believe it or not, multiple studies have shown that, while a fair salary is important, it is not by any means the only thing that drives a person's interest in where they work (The Fuller Life, 2016). Much more crucial to helping someone feel a sense of loyalty and belonging at their workplace are things like recognition, consistent feedback, new challenges and extracurricular activities, such as volunteer days and company-sponsored career development opportunities.

The stats prove it: 49 per cent of people confess that they would jump ship at a moment's notice for a company that clearly recognizes employee efforts and contributions. Over 43 per cent of highly engaged employees are used to (and welcome) weekly feedback, whereas employees who are not engaged rarely have conversations with their managers, and even then only because they are mandated. But constant feedback gives people clear direction and an understanding of their progress towards goals, all while increasing a sense of value and belonging at the company. The less tangible benefits of placing a premium on employee engagement include people who willingly and independently champion their employer, recommend new talent, are passionate about meeting company goals, are especially productive, and are satisfied with the balance they have achieved between work and their personal lives. Moreover, engagement drives innovation and ideation, improves safety and profits (by about 200 per cent, in fact), and reduces turnover (Inc, 2016). And you know what improves engagement? Advocacy!

That's right – employee advocacy programmes lead to an increase in engagement that simply cannot be matched with other efforts. That is because both engagement and employee advocacy are based, and developed, on the same fundamental characteristic: trust. In fact, 96 per cent of engaged employees trust company leaders, compared to the much smaller 46 per cent of actively *disengaged* employees (Fraden, 2014). Leveraging employee advocates is a superb way to build trust between the organization and its employees. Advocacy programmes give individual employees the authority and support to talk about the brand to their networks, showing them that they are vital and trusted, which in turn leads them to have greater respect for leadership and more confidence in their ability to steer the company well. That trust between the organization and its employees is a critical piece of solidifying and growing employee engagement efforts, and has a cyclical success effect on advocacy.

The team at Dynamic Signal understands the deep and mutually beneficial relationship between engagement and advocacy, which is why their platform is designed to be more than just a tool for getting people to share branded content. It also helps you nurture a community of employees that are significantly more invested in how well the company is performing, because they are an integral part of the process. It helps you equip them with the right content at the right time, in order to increase impact and relevancy. It will provide you with the features you need to really know your content, pay attention to the channels it is shared on, determine how well specific pieces are doing in those channels, and make the adjustments you need to make to drive performance forward.

From sophisticated divisions and permissions to global localization and security capabilities, Dynamic Signal is ideally constructed for enterprise companies – organizations that have been built on the premise that there is no growth cap, no singular end goal, no finish line, and therefore no limit on what they can achieve.

Distinctly dynamic: key features and differentiators

There are certain things you know you need your employee advocacy platform to do, and others that you may think are not as important (but would be nice to have, anyway). Thankfully, Dynamic Signal has a robust, comprehensive and unmatched set of features and capabilities that can help you take your employee advocacy programme from corporate pipedream to employee-driven sales pipeline.

Divisions and permissions

When it comes to making it easy for people to share your branded assets and messaging, it is important that you be able to easily segment various pieces of content, as well as communications, to get the appropriate content to the right employees at the most effective time. With Dynamic Signal, you are able to personalize the experience based on which team or region a person belongs to, and even customize messages for their language or interests. You can also assign advocacy managers globally, or to specific divisions, with configurable levels of platform permissions. For example, you can assign administrator permissions to different people in the programme, in order to give a specific level of control and access to different divisions and roles.

These include content curator, reporter, communications manager, global manager and division manager. This makes it easy to oversee global or division-specific roles – a critical component of being able to scale a programme across an organization (Figure 11.1). Otherwise, you might end

Figure 11.1   Build divisions based on language, country or region

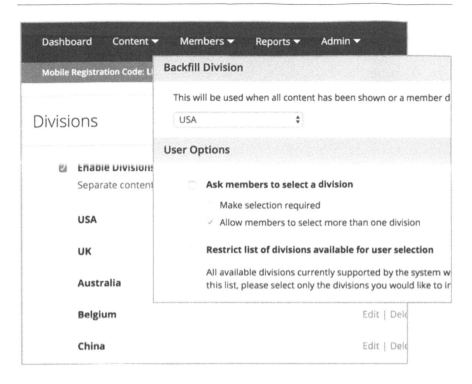

up with too many people overseeing and disseminating content that doesn't really pertain to them. Remember, a manager should only have access to the content and users they are directly responsible for. You can even re-create the structure of your organization within the platform, to better align admin permissions, communications and content segmentation based on roles or job functions – sales, HR, marketing, IT, engineering or product.

Employee segmentation and targeting

Long, long ago during the planning process for your advocacy programme, you spent some time getting to know your employees so you could understand their skills, interests, unexpected talents, and gain more insight into their experiences and perspectives. Dynamic Signal's employee segmentation and targeting functionality allows you to create divisions, groups and tags to ensure a personalized experience for everyone participating in the programme. You can categorize them by team, department, region, language, specific interests and more.

Figure 11.2   Segment employees based on job function, business unit or interest

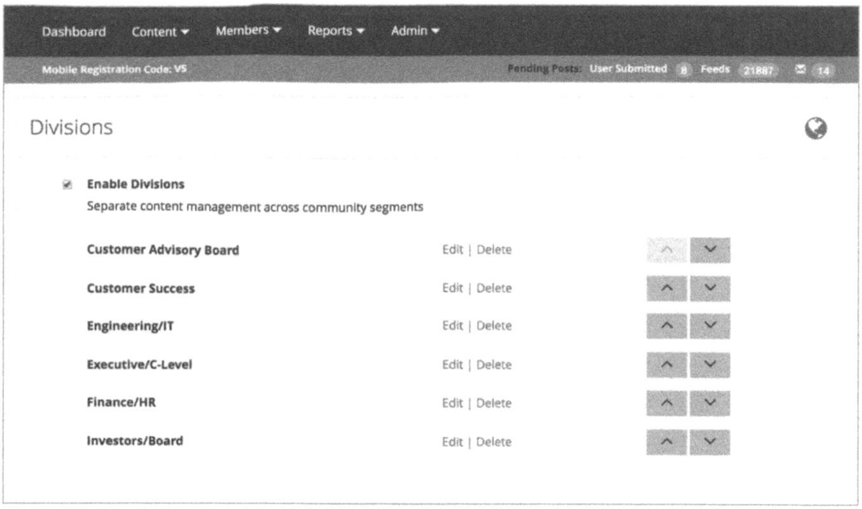

You may be curious as to why you would want to be able to do this. Primarily, it is because your organization is complex and unique, and the platform you use to support your employee advocacy programme needs to mirror the organization of your company in order to be truly effective. It will prove incredibly useful to create member groups so you can develop targeted communications and reports that are most relevant to them. When you find that you need separate content or communications strategies for different groups, you'll be able to completely segment those assets so they make sense for specific teams, departments and regions, making it incredibly simple for your global teams to get acquainted with the programme and become an integral part of the entire advocacy process (Figure 11.2).

Global capabilities

Though employee advocacy is a worthwhile endeavour regardless of the size of your company or its stage of growth, global capabilities are paramount for businesses that plan to spread and scale.

Dynamic Signal is the only technology solution that is truly ready for company-wide initiatives for globally distributed enterprises. That is because it has built-in international localization, targeting available in 13 major languages, international social network integrations, and options for regional targeting and admin permissions.

You will need this if you have disparate networks operating in various countries or within different business units, and it will prove especially valuable when hiring, prospecting and selling internationally. You have the option to add social listening feeds, buttons, navigation tools, mobile applications, and more in several different languages, which allows your programme to be truly global (Figure 11.3).

Plus, this inclusivity is an amazing way to demonstrate that *all* of your employees are important to the success of your organization – not just the ones who happen to work at headquarters.

Figure 11.3 Employees can engage with the platform in their local language

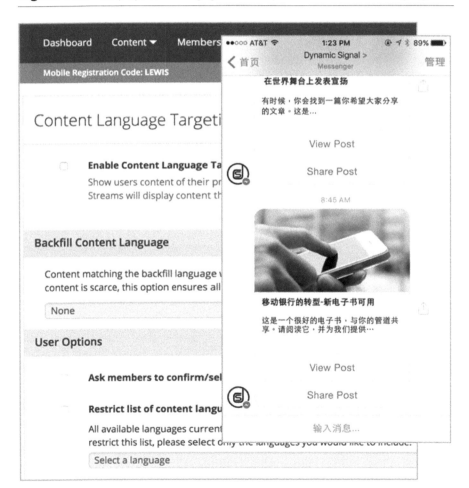

Security compliance plus SSO

If there is one thing that enterprise companies have to be sure of, it is that their proprietary data will stay safe and secure when they start sharing it with a new platform. Dynamic Signal has an enterprise-vetted data and security protocol, as well as built-in tools to ensure maximum security and compliance while maintaining the integrity of your content and messaging.

Tools like automated disclosures to ensure FTC compliance and verify that people are properly disclosing their relationship with your brand as an employee. This is a critical feature that will help you keep from misleading social media audiences, who – without a clear disclosure – may not realize that the person they are interacting with is an employee who is advocating for the brand.

You will also have the ability to blacklist certain keywords and phrases, as well as prevent sharing of content or messages that may include them. While your training efforts and company guidelines are often enough for you to be confident that no one employee will compromise your efforts, these compliance tools add guardrails to how employees share and discuss branded materials on social media. Employees are able to access the platform using single sign-on (SAML 2.0 SSO), so that employees can log in using existing company credentials (Figure 11.4).

Figure 11.4   SSO allows employees to login to Dynamic Signal with their existing credentials

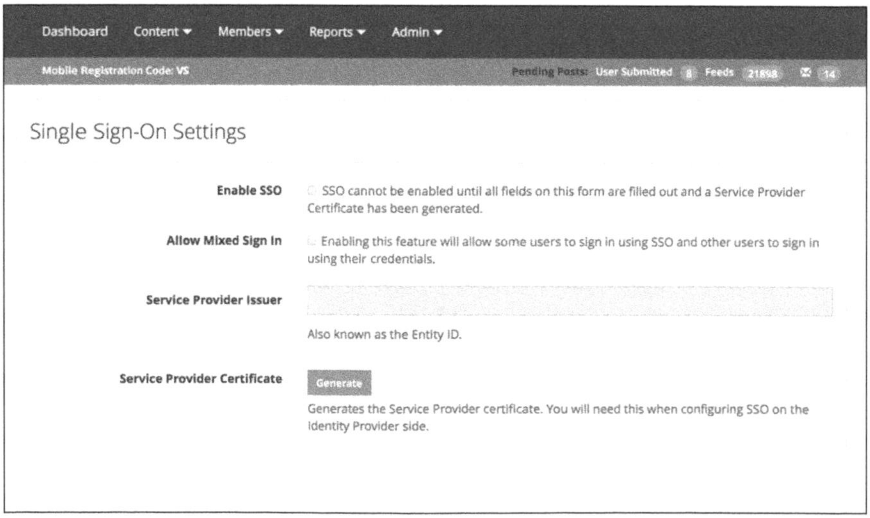

You can also easily host and refine training materials, require regular acceptance of updated social media guidelines, add automated sharing disclosures for sensitive content and, most importantly, rest assured that all of your information will remain protected under a very strong proverbial lock and key. Your IT department will be pleased.

Integration capabilities and mobility

Whatever your company's primary mission, there is no doubt that you have several tools in place to help execute it. So, the ability to seamlessly integrate Dynamic Signal with your current enterprise platforms is an absolute must. In addition to the aforementioned SAML SSO, Dynamic Signal also syncs up with Salesforce, Chatter, Adobe Marketing Cloud, Facebook Messenger, Google Analytics, Slack, Yammer, IBM Connections, Jive, SAP Jam, and many more industry standard platforms. This will help you to easily encourage participation across the organization and promote expansion of the programme.

Mobility is another crucial feature of Dynamic Signal that makes it a step above other offerings on the market. As a culture, we live on our devices and expect to be able to take our digital world with us wherever we go – and that includes the things we do for work. Dynamic Signal offers internally branded and fully customized mobile applications, mobile-responsive design, push notifications, and many other native mobile features for both iOS and Android.

In this age of digital transformation, people interact with their personal and professional social media networks on a near-constant basis (in fact, the average person checks their phone about 150 times per day). Dynamic Signal's mobile feature will not only increase adoption rates within your company, but will also drive increased web traffic and conversion rates. In addition to accessibility and the flexibility to share posts on the go, your advocates will get the freedom of one-click sharing and notifications that indicate when posts are published or recommended. You also get access to in-app analytics, content sharing and scheduling functions, and even the various leaderboards that are paramount for healthy competition and advocate recognition (Figure 11.5).

Automated programme management

Anyone who has ever managed a project knows that even the simplest, shortest jobs take some organization and planning. But the larger the initiative, the more intense and time-consuming that process becomes. Dynamic

Figure 11.5   Mobile application increased adoption and usage of the platform

Signal's automated programme management system will help you scale programme-wide rollouts for practices or campaigns – massive amounts of broad, widespread content can be analysed quickly, tagged, recommended and loaded into the content hub by both administrators and participants (instead of manually copied and pasted) (Figure 11.6). The burden that is usually placed on an administrator to manually input and distribute the content is removed, and that manager can instead focus on productivity and strategy, as well as overseeing and approving high-impact content and announcements.

Figure 11.6   Connect branded social channels to import content dynamically

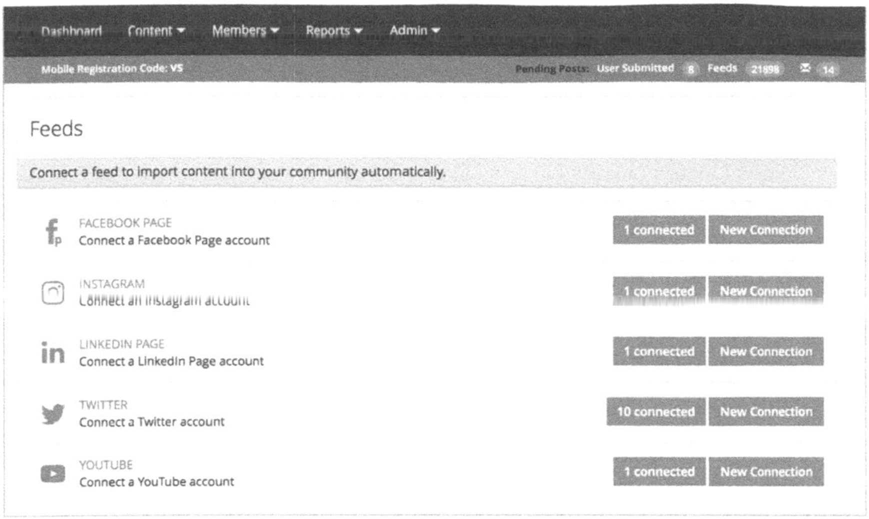

Content categorization, messaging and sharing

As you are well aware, content curation, messaging and sharing is the absolute most important piece of your employee advocacy programme – second only to the people who bring it to life. With Dynamic Signal, you can curate and deliver relevant brand and industry news to employees in real time, on any device, and even track who views what. You can also submit, send or share video – a major win, because video has completely taken over the way we as consumers interact with content. It has proven to be the most effective way to communicate a message, so being able to take full advantage of video in order to connect with employees, especially on mobile, is revolutionary.

In Dynamic Signal, content categorization (much like employee segmentation) can be easily tagged and distributed to users based on their roles, teams, departments, regions, interests, language and other individual elements. This diversification of content is far more effective in advocacy than a blanket approach that asks everyone to share the same things all the time. This is because you not only want to increase the likelihood that people will share this content with their networks (which they won't do if it is irrelevant to them), but delivering a customized experience for your employees will help them to remain engaged and supportive of the content (Figure 11.7).

No single employee is exactly the same, even if they work in similar roles or share common interests. The experience they have when logged into your employee advocacy app or hub should always reflect who they are, where

Figure 11.7 Employee profile

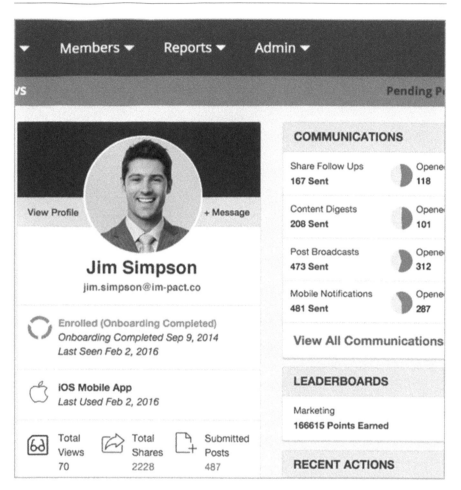

they work and what they do. To facilitate this, programme managers can provide multiple options for the messages or posts that accompany each piece of content, as well as the social channel that content is intended for. This is especially great for employees who are willing to participate but who don't want to think about it too much. And, for those advocates who have something personal to say about what they are sharing, those messages are completely customizable.

How employees are able to share content is nearly as important as what they are sharing, and Dynamic Signal makes that easy, too. Users can share content and posts natively via any application on their mobile device or computer: via text, chat, e-mail, Facebook Messenger, Slack, WeChat, What'sApp, and more. Participants can schedule those posts to be shared for specific times in the future or set up an automatic posting schedule so that things stay consistent. Communication also gets major support from this leading platform. Manager-to-member messaging allows administrators to deliver important announcements, messages, company information, alerts and more to employees in real time, via any device, and track who sees or engages with what. Member-to-member messaging lets members send one-to-one messages or start group chats. Employees can also comment on content, upload interesting assets they think are worth sharing with the community, and send content directly to one another to start discussions and further advocacy efforts.

Communications and gamification

Being able to communicate within the advocacy hub is key, but that is not the only place you want to be able to discuss advocacy initiatives and news – nor is it the only place that important company or industry updates will happen. Dynamic Signal has a full, integrative communications suite that provides member-to-member messaging, customizable templates, automated 'drip' e-mails, and integration with the other communications platforms that are used throughout your organization, which will make it easier to expand the reach of the programme and utilize a cohesive communications strategy across all of your internal channels and platforms (Figure 11.8).

Gamification is yet another component of the Dynamic Signal platform that makes it so ideal for enterprise advocacy programmes and scalability. Rewarding and recognizing your employee ambassadors is crucial to your programme's success, because it is directly tied to a person's emotional state, morale and engagement in the company.

Leaderboards can be configured for specific groups of employees as well as time frames, so you can set goals for various segments of people or associate them with specific campaigns, events or other initiatives (Figure 11.9). Actions like sharing a specific piece of content or particular post, sharing to a certain channel, submitting relevant content, meeting a daily share goal, or X can be assigned point values based on overarching programme objectives. You can even create in-hub surveys and polls for targeted groups, to periodically gather feedback from your advocates, refine process and advance your programme further.

Platform and participant analytics

Finally, analytics. The data you need to know, without a doubt, which tells you how your employee advocacy efforts are going. The information will tell you what is working and what isn't, so you can stay squarely on the

Figure 11.8 Member-to-member messaging and communication

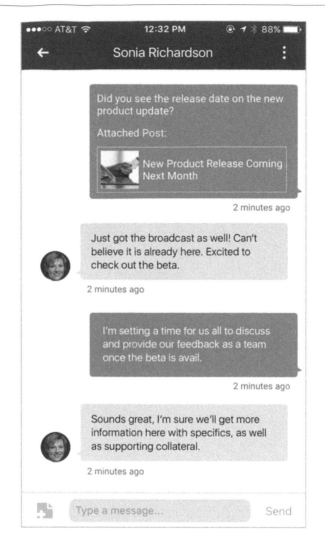

path of continuous improvement and exponential returns. With Dynamic Signal's proprietary platform analytics capabilities, you can quite literally track everything that happens within the platform, externally, and measure successes and struggles in adoption, participation, shares, clicks, social reactions, impressions, reach, traffic, leads, and even how those various actions turn into tangible sales. In this way, you will never not know which teams and individuals are directly impacting the performance of your brand (Figure 11.10).

Figure 11.9   Company leaderboard (mobile view)

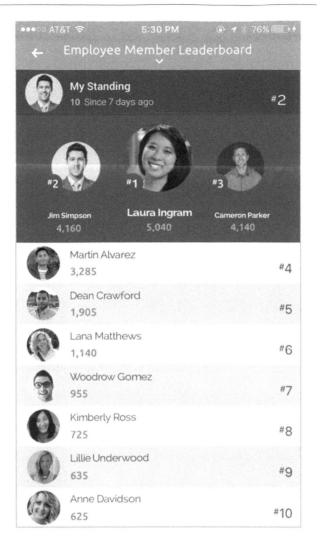

With member analytics, you can deep-dive into the activity of users and groups, from specific user engagements like logins, post views and submissions, to how frequently they read admin communications. And of course, you can easily keep tabs on their sharing habits and how each of their shares creates an impact.

An employee advocacy programme is an ever-growing project – its progress is tied gravitationally to its participants. Of the multitudes of components necessary to create a programme that is impactful, efficient,

Figure 11.10 Track reach, impressions, engagement at the company and employee level

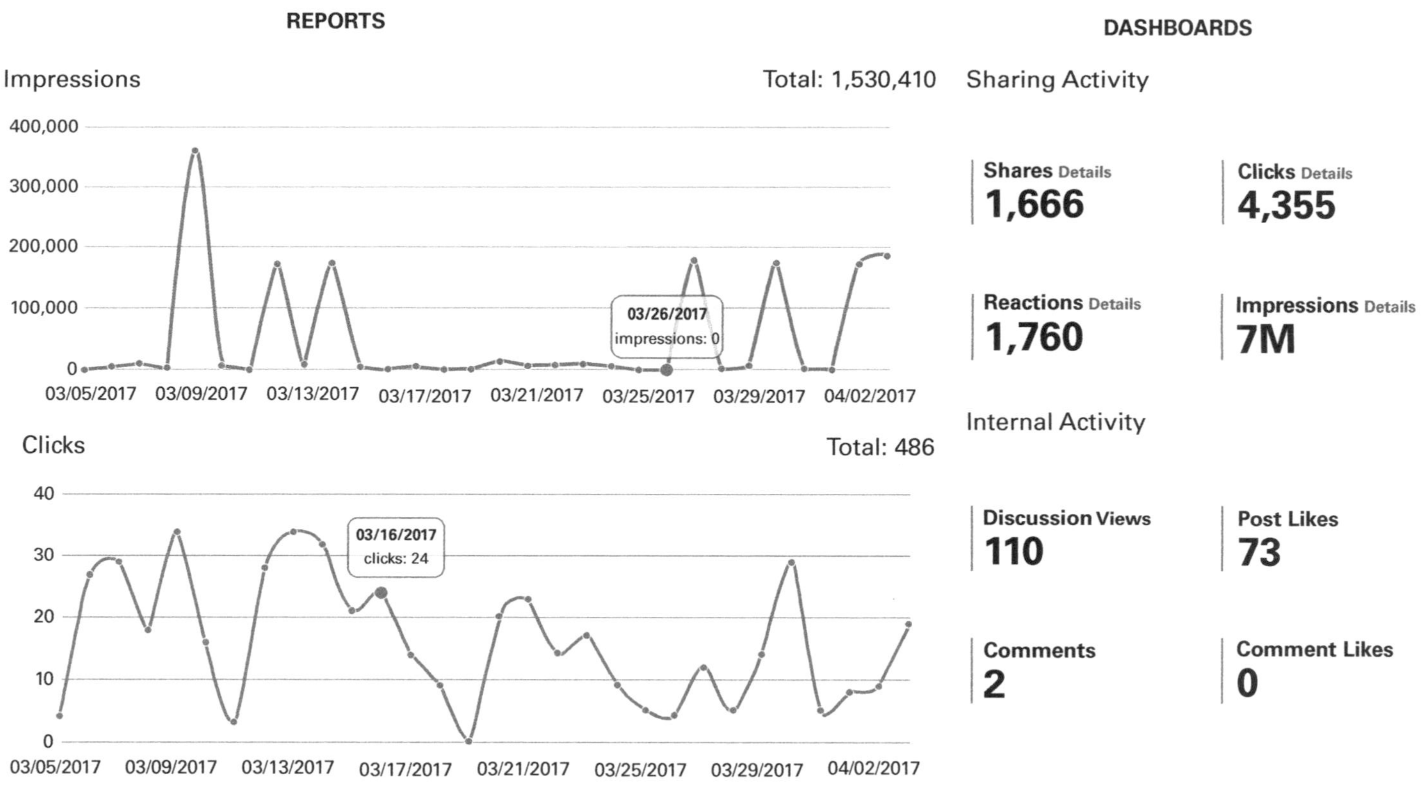

REPORTS

DASHBOARDS

Sharing Activity   Total: 1,530,410

Shares Details
1,666

Clicks Details
4,355

Reactions Details
1,760

Impressions Details
7M

Internal Activity   Total: 486

Discussion Views
110

Post Likes
73

Comments
2

Comment Likes
0

Impressions

400,000

300,000

200,000

100,000

0

03/26/2017
impressions: 0

03/05/2017   03/09/2017   03/13/2017   03/17/2017   03/21/2017   03/25/2017   03/29/2017   04/02/2017

Clicks

40

30

20

10

0

03/16/2017
clicks: 24

03/05/2017   03/09/2017   03/13/2017   03/17/2017   03/21/2017   03/25/2017   03/29/2017   04/02/2017

scalable, adaptable and powerful, not one of them will remain untouched by the unique ways in which your organization operates. Not one will go unaffected by your internal culture, core values, or the emphasis you place on strengthening connections with your people. Because of this, how you launch and grow your employee advocacy programme will always be completely unique to your business. By understanding what truly matters to your company, and how every component of your advocacy programme – its content and its people – will help you get there, you can experience the massive success that so many other enterprise organizations have seen. You will get out of your advocacy programme what you put in.

You will achieve the results you make possible through your own strategy, as well as the strength of the foundation you provide for the programme. Yes, your enablement platform should mirror the way your people work. It should make it possible for you to share your unique and wonderful story with the world, and open the avenues to new markets and opportunities. It should be a reflection of the goals, values and milestones that have made your brand what it is today. But finally, it should take you further than you ever thought you had the possibility to go, and have the functionality, capacity and intelligent capabilities to bring your brand – and your people – into tomorrow.

INSIGHT *New York Times* bestseller and thought leader

Contribution from Jay Baer, President at Convince & Convert

For content marketers, the good times are over.

Businesses of all shapes, sizes and descriptions understand that traditional, interruption marketing is now less efficient than ever. This awakening has powered the shift to inbound and content marketing, and the accompanying belief that 'content is king'.

But here's the problem: if no one can find the king, and most people distrust the king, are you still king?

For a while, the first movers in content marketing had an advantage. In truth, one of the reasons my blog – Convince & Convert – is so popular is because Google ranks it very high for key terms, and that is driven by consistency and longevity (among other factors).

But being first is a short-term advantage. Once it became clear that content marketing could actually work, *everyone* started doing it. As my friend Mark

Schaefer predicted, this created content shock – a glut of mediocre content that overwhelms and confuses many prospective customers, and makes the average results for each piece of content spiral downwards continuously.

Due to the increase in competition and technology changes, reach and engagement are more and more difficult to garner. First, Google, among others, killed RSS feeds (more or less). Back in the old days, people consumed blogs the way they consumed music albums: as a whole. We subscribed to our favourite 10, 20, 30 or 40 blogs, and read just about every post on those publications. It was a cosy and familiar routine. We knew the authors. We knew the commenters.

Now, however, traffic to blogs and other content comes less from consistent fans that read the publication daily, and more from casual observers who see a link in social media or search results and pop by based on a specific post or piece of content.

In short, the content business has gone from the album era to the singles era on approximately the same time horizon. Today, like most blogs, approximately 90 per cent of my traffic comes from 10 per cent of what we publish. That is the impact of the move towards hits.

But now, the technology has changed again. Using social media to drive content consumption has become exceedingly difficult. The near-death of organic reach on Facebook, combined with Twitter's own algorithm changes, has made free traffic from social media very difficult for all but the most spectacular content executions. As if that is not a high-enough bar to clear, business in general is trusted less today than at any other time in the recent past.

Your employees can power your content marketing success

But there is a way around these obstacles. A way for you to get your content read, watched, downloaded and shared. This method is not only right under your nose, it is also not being done very well by most other businesses. So you still have that lucrative, first-mover advantage. The secret is simple: use your employees.

Why would you do this? Why would you try to rely – at least in part – on your employees to create awareness? Because they can, and because it works.

Fundamentally, there are three reasons why employees are so effective at getting content seen and shared:

1 Because they are 'real people' who are trusted and believed much more than the brand itself.

2 Individuals do not have the same technology disadvantages that brands do, especially in social media (eg posts on a personal Facebook page often outperform the same post on a business Facebook page).

3 They have more (and more varied) connections than the brand does, potentially exposing the content to a broader audience.

Because the present difficulty faced by content marketers in trying to get attention is acute and existential, many companies are exploring the power of employee advocates. Research from Prophet (admittedly, a small sample size) found that approximately 90 per cent of businesses are, in some way, working on employee advocacy initiatives (Prophet, 2016).

Unfortunately, however, these programmes – even the runaway successes – almost always rely on the same construct. The software package may vary, but invariably these employee advocacy thrusts revolve around asking team members to share content on their personal social media channels (most commonly Twitter, Facebook and LinkedIn).

Don't get me wrong, I like social media employee advocacy. So much so, in fact, that I invested in a company that provides software to run those programmes. But the reality is that if you and your company are relying on social media to power the entirety of your employee advocacy efforts, you are not maximizing your opportunities to use employees' connections and trust advantage to get your content consumed.

Here's why:

- **Not everyone is on social**: social media – especially Facebook – is, of course, incredibly pervasive. But not every employee is on social media. When you rely solely upon social media to power employee advocacy, you are running a programme that is of interest to only a particular segment of your team members.

- **It mixes business and personal**: most of the time, your employees will want to share company happenings and great content with their friends and neighbours. After all, as I wrote in my first book, *The NOW Revolution* (2011), if your employees are not your greatest advocates, you have a much bigger problem than social media. This becomes even more true when company communicators, desperate to get more clicks, start asking employees to share items that really are not interesting to people who are not prospective customers. That is not only ineffective, but starts to chip away at the employees' credibility among their friends, which is the whole basis for their success as advocates.

- **Requires employees to take action**: while some employee advocacy software is quite intuitive and easy to use, every one of these platforms requires that each employee takes some form of action to distribute messages to their networks. This requires time, even if it only takes a few minutes.

- **Potential for miscommunication**: most employee advocacy programmes let team members modify content before sharing. (Some do not, however.) I prefer this option, as my personal reasons for sharing a piece of content with my friends may be completely different than my co-workers' motives. Plus, I like being able to add some context, commentary and rationale. But, this capability also creates risk, as employees can (and do) share content with accompanying messaging that is not controllable by the brand. And that message may be less than ideal in style and tone.

Overall, I'm a big fan of employee advocacy in social media. In fact, I don't see a circumstance in which a company would not want to do it. BUT, the reality is that these programmes are leaving opportunities on the table.

Where? How? With e-mail. Each of your employees is sending e-mail. A lot of it. Estimates say each employee sends over 10,000 work-related e-mails per year. Your results may vary, as I send at least 30,000. Either way, that is a lot of e-mail sent from the employees of your company.

Historically, those e-mails have been flooded with a mediocre signature block that is too often a mixture of fax numbers, comic sans font and quasi-inspirational quotes. This hodge-podge of e-mail signatures does less than nothing for brand consistency, but it has the potential to do the exact opposite, and a lot more.

Employee e-mail signatures are the secret weapon of employee advocacy and content marketers. It is a resource that is almost entirely untapped. If you have 500 employees and each of them sends the average 10,000 work e-mails yearly, you have 5 million unique, mostly targeted opportunities to promote your content.

Here are five reasons why e-mail signatures should be included in every employee advocacy programme, augmenting social media initiatives:

1 **Visual content promotion**: many social media employee advocacy platforms are driven primarily by text. With e-mail signature employee advocacy (like Sigstr) the promotion is entirely visual and is created by the marketing/ communications team.

2 **Controllable**: as mentioned above, with social media employee advocacy, the employees themselves are often able to add their own 'spin' on the message, creating inconsistency and risk. With e-mail employee advocacy, the content marketing promotions are controllable entirely by the marketing and communications teams, and are appended to e-mails as a signature file. No risk. No worry. No freelancing.

3 **Testable**: content marketing promotions are not universally effective. Maybe one has a better graphic. The other has a better headline. The third has a

stronger call-to-action. With social media employee advocacy, you get one bite at the apple: the marketing team writes the 'recommended' post, and employees send it, or modify it. With e-mail, marketing can create multiple versions of the same promotion (a forthcoming Webinar, for example) and can test the efficacy of each version in a controlled, scientific fashion. Maths rules!

4 **Automatic**: one of the challenges of employee advocacy is that employees have to click at least some buttons to share content. With e-mail advocacy (like Sigstr) that is not an issue, because the relevant promotions show up dynamically every time an employee sends an e-mail. Plus, the creative can be modified by department, region or other condition. A salesperson in Iowa will automatically have one piece of content marketing promotion show up as part of his or her e-mail signature, whereas a HR worker in Tennessee will have a completely different promotion in his or her e-mail signature. You just set up your segments, and it works.

5 **Flexible**: certainly, e-mail-based employee advocacy is terrific for promoting content marketing. But there is so much more you can do with it. Imagine asking employees to take a survey on where they would like the annual retreat to be located. What about a notice that health insurance sign-ups are around the corner?

With technology like Sigstr, the employee e-mail signature becomes not only an untapped promotional tool, but also a robust internal communications channel.

REFERENCES

Introduction

Altimeter Group (2015) The 2015 State of Social Business: Priorities Shift from Scaling to Integrating [Online] http://go.pardot.com/l/69102/2015-07-16/sgj4w [accessed 1 March 2017]

Employee Brand Storytelling (2016) Lessons from Brand Marketers on Building an Employee Advocacy Program [Online] http://www.employeebrandstorytelling. com [accessed 2 June 2016]

Hinge Marketing (2015) Understanding Employee Advocacy on Social Media [Online] https://hingemarketing.com/library/article/understanding-employee-advocacy-on-social-media [accessed 1 January 2017]

Mckinsey (2012) The Social Economy: Unlocking Value and Productivity Through Social Technologies [Online] http://www.mckinsey.com/industries/high-tech/our-insights/the-social-economy [accessed 1 December 2016]

Nielsen (2015) Recommendations from Friends Remain the Most Credible Form of Advertising [Online] http://www.nielsen.com/us/en/press-room/2015/recommendations-from-friends-remain-most-credible-form-of-advertising. html [accessed 1 March 2017]

Chapter 1

Altimeter Group (2015) The 2015 State of Social Business: Priorities Shift from Scaling to Integrating [Online] http://go.pardot.com/l/69102/2015-07-16/sgj4w [accessed 1 January 2017]

Consumer Executive Board (2015) The Digital Evolution in B2B Marketing [Online] https://www.cebglobal.com/marketing-communications/digital-evolution.html [accessed 12 December 2016]

Edelman Public Relations (2017) 2017 Edelman Trust Barometer [Online] http://www.edelman.com/trust2017 [accessed 8 March 2017]

Kahn, W A (1990) Psychological conditions of personal engagement and disengagement at work, *Academy of Management Journal*, 33, 692–724

Roth, D (2015) Why Vocal Employees are a Company's Best PR [Blog] *Adweek*, 25 March [Online] https://www.fastcompany.com/3044156/hit-the-ground-running/why-vocal-employees-are-a-companys-best-pr [accessed 1 December 2016]

Social Business Journal (2015) *Social Business Journal*, vol. 3, Digital Transformation [Online] http://socialbusinessengine.com/socialselling/dell.pdf [accessed 3 October 2016]

Chapter 2

Altimeter Group (2016) The 2016 State of Digital Transformation [Online] http://www2.prophet.com/The-2016-State-of-Digital-Transformation [accessed 1 February 2017]

BI Worldwide (2016) A Look Ahead: Employee Engagement Trends for 2016 [Online] https://www.biworldwide.com/globalassets/us-en/research-landing/thought-leadership/2015/engagement-trends-2016/employee-engagement-trends-2016.pdf [accessed 18 December 2016]

Corporate Executive Board (2013) Connect Customers to Your Brand [Online] https://www.cebglobal.com/marketing-communications/b2b-emotion.html [accessed 1 December 2016]

Fahrenbacher, K (2015) 5 Ways to Make Big Companies More Innovative, *Fortune*, 11 March [Online]

Gallup (2014) Majority of US Employees Not Engaged Despite Gains in 2014 [Online] http://www.gallup.com/opinion/gallup/182432/organizations-lead-world-employee-engagement.aspx [accessed 1 February 2017]

Gallup (2015) Employee Engagement in US Stagnant in 2015 [Online] http://www.gallup.com/poll/188144/employee-engagement-stagnant-2015.aspx [accessed 3 February 2017]

Gallup (2016) What Millennials Want From Work and Life [Online] http://www.gallup.com/businessjournal/191435/millennials-work-life.aspx [accessed 1 November 2016]

Kramer, B (2014) *There is No B2B or B2C: It's human to human, #H2H*, PureMatter, San Jose

Ries, E (2011) *The Lean Startup: How today's entrepreneurs use continuous innovation to create radically successful businesses*, Crown Business, New York

SiriusDecisions (2013) Summit 2013 Highlights: Inciting a B-to-B Content Revolution [Online] https://www.siriusdecisions.com/Blog/2013/May/Summit-2013-Highlights-Inciting-a-BtoB-Content-Revolution [accessed 4 September 2016]

SiriusDecisions (2014) It's Not Content – It's a Lack of Buyer Insights That's the Problem [Online] https://www.siriusdecisions.com/Blog/2014/Jan/Its-Not-Content--Its-a-Lack-of-Buyer-Insights-Thats-the-Problem.aspx [accessed 1 December 2016]

University of Arizona (2016) Lack of Feedback and Communication [Online] https://executive.eller.arizona.edu/2016/11/14/small-business-employees-say-lack-of-feedback-and-communication-leaves-them-unfulfilled [accessed 6 November 2016]

Chapter 3

Arruda, W (2016) Why Social Savvy Employees Hold the Keys to Business Success, *Forbes*, 8 November [Online] https://www.forbes.com/sites/williamarruda/2016/11/08/why-social-savvy-employees-hold-the-keys-to-business-success/#8407ab254912 [accessed 1 January 2017]

Arthur, C (2006) What is the 1% Rule?, *The Guardian*, 20 July [Online] https://www.theguardian.com/technology/2006/jul/20/guardianweeklytechnologysection2 [accessed 1 January 2017]

Elite Daily (2015) Millennial Consumer Trends 2015 [Online] http://elitedaily.com/millennial-consumer-trends-2015 [accessed 15 August 2016]

Kapadia, A (2016) 8 Statistics that Will Change the Way You Think About Referral Marketing [Blog] *Ambassador*, 15 February [Online] www.getambassador.com [accessed 15 January 2017]

Prophet (2016) Tapping Into the Power of an Engaged Social Workforce [Online] https://www.prophet.com/thinking/2016/03/social-media-employee-advocacy-tapping-into-the-power of an engaged social workforce [accessed 9 February 2017]

Chapter 4

Carnegie (2016) Employee Engagement Best Practices for Smaller Businesses [Online] http://www.dalecarnegie.com/white-papers/employee-engagement-best-practices [accessed 22 November 2016]

Glassdoor (2016) Glassdoor's 5 Job Trends to Watch in 2016 [Online] https://www.glassdoor.com/blog/glassdoors-5-job-trends-watch-2016 [accessed 8 December 2016]

GloboForce (2014) Adapting to the Realities of our Changing Workforce [Online] http://go.globoforce.com/rs/globoforce/images/Spring2014MoodTrackerGloboforce.pdf [accessed 12 May 2016]

International Labor Organization (2017) World Employment and Social Outlook [Online] http://www.ilo.org/global/research/global-reports/weso/2016/lang--en/index.htm [accessed 22 March 2016]

Scancapture (2015) How Maslow's Hierarchy of Needs Influences Employee Engagement [Online] http://www.scancapture.co.uk/how-maslows-hierarchy-of-needs-influences-employee-engagement [accessed 1 January 2017]

Stahl, A (2016) Here's Why Employers Should Adopt Amazon's 30-Hour Workweek, *Forbes*, 26 September [Online] https://www.forbes.com/sites/ashleystahl/2016/09/26/heres-why-employers-should-adopt-amazons-30-hour-workweek [accessed 22 August 2016]

Thompson, A (2015) The Intangible Things Employees Want From Employers, *Harvard Business Review*, 3 December [Online] https://hbr.org/2015/12/the-intangible-things-employees-want-from-employers [accessed 1 November 2016]

TINYpulse (2015) The Best Time To Act For Employee Feedback [Online] https://www.tinypulse.com/blog/employee-engagement-survey-the-best-time-to-ask-for-feedback [accessed 1 January 2017]

TINYpulse (2017) Is Employee Recognition the Key to Satisfaction in Your Workplace? [Online] https://www.tinypulse.com/sem-whitepaper-v2-recognition-report [accessed 1 December 2016]

Chapter 5

ASG Consulting (2016) Social Media and Sales Quota Report [Online] http://info. asalesguyconsulting.com/social-media-and-sales-quota-attainment [accessed 1 June 2016]

Boland, B (2014) Organic Reach on Facebook: Your Questions Answered, *Facebook*, 5 June [Online] https://www.facebook.com/business/news/Organic-Reach-on-Facebook [accessed 2 March 2016]

Content Marketing Institute (2016) 2016 Benchmarks, Budgets and Trends [Online] http://contentmarketinginstitute.com/wp-content/uploads/2015/09/2016_B2B_Report_Final.pdf [accessed 1 February 2017]

Hawley, D (2014) What Can Social Media Marketers and Brand Managers Gain From Employee Advocacy? *Wired*, 27 October [Online] http://insights.wired.com/profiles/blogs/what-can-social-media-marketers-and-brand-managers-stand-to-gain [accessed 1 June 2016]

Kusinitz, S (2014) The Definition of Social Selling in Under 100 Words, *Hubspot*, 7 June [Online] https://blog.hubspot.com/marketing/social-selling-definition-under-100-words [accessed 1 June 2016]

PEW Research (2014) 6 New Facts About Facebook [Online] http://www.pewresearch.org/fact-tank/2014/02/03/6-new-facts-about-facebook [accessed 11 March 2017]

Chapter 6

CNN (2016) Americans Devote More Than 10 Hours A Day to Screen Time, and Growing [Online] http://www.cnn.com/2016/06/30/health/americans-screen-time-nielsen [accessed 1 January 2017]

Deloitte (2016) Winning Over the Next Generation of Leaders [Online] https://www2.deloitte.com/content/dam/Deloitte/global/Documents/About-Deloitte/gx-millenial-survey-2016-exec-summary.pdf [accessed 15 March 2017]

Dynamic Signal (2016) How Pitney Bowes has Transformed Brand Perception Through Employee Advocacy [Online] http://resources.dynamicsignal.com/h/i/282828216-how-pitney-bowes-has-transformed-brand-perception-through-employee-advocacy [accessed 9 February 2017]

Nielsen (2013) Under the Influence: Customer Trust in Advertising [Online] http://www.nielsen.com/us/en/insights/news/2013/under-the-influence-consumer-trust-in-advertising.html [accessed 19 November 2016]

Salesforce (2016) Top 5 Use Cases For Employee Advocacy [Online] https://www.salesforce.com/blog/2016/10/top-5-use-cases-for-employee-advocacy.html [accessed 1 February 2017]

Social Media Today (2015) Making the Case For Employee Advocacy at Your Firm [Online] http://www.slideshare.net/smtoday/making-the-case-for-employee-advocacy-at-your-firm [accessed 7 January 2017]

Chapter 7

Accenture (2014) CMOs: Time for Digital Transformation [Online] https://www.accenture.com/us-en/-/media/Accenture/Conversion-Assets/DotCom/Documents/Global/PDF/Industries_14/Accenture-CMO-Insights-Web.pdf [accessed 8 February 2017]

Everson, R (2015) 6 HR Facts Business Owners Should Never Forget, *CBS Pulse*, 21 September [Online] http://cbspulse.com/2015/09/21/6-hr-facts-never-forget [accessed 9 January 2017]

Link Humans (2016) How Employee Engagement Drives Employee Advocacy, with Dave Hawley of SocialChorus [Podcast] 3 June [Online] http://linkhumans.com/podcast/employee-engagement-dave-hawley [accessed 1 March 2016]

Winfrey, G (2014) 10 Ways To Build a Strong Team (infographic), *Inc*, 14 November [Online] http://www.inc.com/graham-winfrey/10-ways-to-improve-internal-communication.html [accessed 8 February 2017]

Chapter 8

Academia (2013) A Study on Training Importance for Employees of Their Successful Performance in the Organization [Online] http://www.academia.edu/5320155/A_Study_on_Training_Importance_for_Employees_of_their_Successful_Performance_in_the_Organization [accessed 22 November 2016]

Edelman Public Relations (2017) 2017 Edelman Trust Barometer [Online] http://www.edelman.com/trust2017 [accessed 1 January 2017]

PEW Research (2016) News Use Across Social Media Platforms 2016 [Online] http://www.journalism.org/2016/05/26/news-use-across-social-media-platforms-2016 [accessed 6 March 2017]

Weber Shandwick (2014) Employees Rising: Seizing the Opportunity in Employee Activism [Online] https://www.webershandwick.com/uploads/news/files/employees-rising-seizing-the-opportunity-in-employee-activism.pdf [accessed 17 January 2017]

Yahoo (2017) US Newspapers Cut More Than Half Their Jobs Since 2001 [Online] https://www.yahoo.com/tech/us-newspapers-cut-more-half-jobs-since-2001-213704882.html [accessed 27 April 2017]

Chapter 9

Edelman Public Relations (2017) 2017 Edelman Trust Barometer [Online] http://www.edelman.com/trust2017 [accessed 1 January 2017]

Emerick, Susan (2014) How IBM Drives ROI Through Employee Advocacy [Blog] 21 September [Online] http://susanemerick.com/ibm-drives-roi-employee-advocacy [accessed 12 December 2016]

Ferriman, J (2013) 7 Major Learning Styles – Which One Are You?, *Learndash*, 8 November [Online] https://www.learndash.com/7-major-learning-styles-which-one-is-you [accessed 21 February 2017]

Gallup (2013) How Employee Engagement Drives Growth [Online] http://www.gallup.com/businessjournal/163130/employee-engagement-drives-growth.aspx [accessed 11 February 2017]

Visual Learner (2015) What Is My Learning Style, 'Visual' [Online] http://www.whatismylearningstyle.com/visual-learner.html [accessed 1 June 2016]

Weber Shandwick (2015) Socializing Your CEO III: From Marginal to Mainstream [Online] http://www.webershandwick.com/uploads/news/files/socializing-your-ceo-iii-exec-summary.pdf [accessed 29 March 2017]

Chapter 10

Content Marketing Institute (2017) 2017 Benchmarks, Budgets, and Trends [Online] http://contentmarketinginstitute.com/wp-content/uploads/2016/09/2017_B2B_Research_FINAL.pdf [accessed 2 February 2017]

Fidelman, M (2013) Study: 78% of Salespeople Using Social Media Outsell Their Peers, *Forbes*, 19 February [Online] https://www.forbes.com/sites/markfidelman/2013/05/19/study-78-of-salespeople-using-social-media-outsell-their-peers [accessed 19 January 2017]

Malatesta, Stephanie (2016) How to Measure Earned Media Value in an Employee Advocacy Program [Blog] *LinkedIn*, 26 May [Online] https://www.linkedin.com/pulse/how-measure-earned-media-value-employee-advocacy-stephanie-malatesta [accessed 13 December 2016]

Morrison, K (2016) Why Influencer Marketing is the New Content King, *Adweek*, 3 April [Online] http://www.adweek.com/digital/why-influencer-marketing-is-the-new-content-king-infographic [accessed 20 November 2016]

MSL Group (2015) Social Employee Advocacy [Infographic] [Online] https://www.scribd.com/doc/249863818/Infographic-Social-Employee-Advocacy [accessed 11 March 2017]

Oktopost (2015a) Strategic-IC Average 61% Click-Through Rate Across All Campaigns [Online] https://cdn-www.oktopost.com/assets/docs/case-studies/Oktopost+Strategic-IC+Case+Study.pdf [accessed 12 April 2017]

Oktopost (2015b) Panaya Generates A 23% Conversion Rate Using Oktopost [Online] www.oktopost.com/assets/docs/case-studies/Oktopost+Panaya+Case+tudy.pdf [accessed 1 January 2017]

Segal, Sapir (2015) How To Measure Long-Term Social Media ROI [Blog] *Oktopost* [Online] http://www.oktopost.com/blog/how-to-measure-long-term-social-media-roi [accessed 23 November 2016]

Chapter 11

Business Wire (2016) Dynamic Signal Raises $25 Million to Help Organizations Increase Employee Productivity, Engagement, and Advocacy Across the Globe [Online] http://resources.dynamicsignal.com/h/i/310639329-dynamic-signal-raises-25-million-to-help-organizations-increase-employee-productivity-engagement-and-advocacy-across-the-globe [accessed 3 December 2016]

Fraden, R (2014) The Link Between Employee Engagement and Employee Advocacy, *ClickZ*, 25 April [Online] https://www.clickz.com/the-link-between-employee-engagement-and-employee-advocacy/31805 [accessed 11 October 2016]

Inc (2016) Infographic: Why Employee Engagement Matters [Online] http://www.inc.com/comcast-business/why-employee-engagement-matters.html [accessed 22 February 2017]

Infosurv (2017) Want To Make More Money? Engage Employees [Online] http://www.infosurv.com/want-to-make-more-money-engage-employees [accessed 16 March 2017]

Prophet (2016) Tapping into the Power of an Engaged Social Workforce [Online] https://www.prophet.com/thinking/2016/03/social-media-employee-advocacy-tapping-into-the-power-of-an-engaged-social-workforce [accessed 9 February 2017]

The Fuller Life (2016) 10 Reasons Why Employee Engagement Matters [Online] http://www.thefullerlife.com/blog/?p=25 [accessed 21 February 2017]

INDEX

Note: bold page numbers indicate figures; italic numbers indicate tables.